FOOTBALL IN THE AMERICAS:

FÚTBOL, FUTEBOL, SOCCER

Football in the Americas

Fútbol, Futebol, Soccer

Edited by
Rory M. Miller and Liz Crolley

British Library Cataloguing-in-Publication Data
A catalogue record for this book is available
from the British Library

ISBN (paperback) 978-1-900039-80-2
ISBN (hardback) 978-1-900039-86-4

INSTITUTE FOR THE STUDY OF THE
A M E R I C A S
UNIVERSITY OF LONDON · SCHOOL OF ADVANCED STUDY

Institute for the Study of the Americas
31 Tavistock Square
London
WC1H 9HA

Telephone: 020 7862 8870
Fax: 020 7862 8886

Email: americas@sas.ac.uk
Web: www.americas.sas.ac.uk

CONTENTS

TABLES AND FIGURES

Tables

Figures

PREFACE AND ACKNOWLEDGEMENTS

The papers in this volume arose from the conference on 'Fútbol, Futebol, Soccer: Football in the Americas' hosted by the Institute of Latin American Studies (ILAS) (now the Institute for the Study of the Americas, or ISA) at the University of London in October 2003. The conference was the first large-scale academic gathering in the United Kingdom to assess the state of research on the role of sport in society in Latin America and the sports business in the hemisphere, and it attracted an attendance of over 200 academics, postgraduate students and journalists. It would not have been possible without the support of three institutions and their directors: the Institute of Latin American Studies in London and Professor James Dunkerley, who supported this project wholeheartedly from the point at which it was first suggested to him; the Centre for Brazilian Studies in Oxford and Professor Leslie Bethell, who financed the attendance of the Brazilian scholars who have contributed to this volume; and the University of Liverpool Management School and Professor Denis Smith, its founding Director. Olga Jiménez and Karen Perkins of ILAS undertook the local arrangements for the conference in London with their customary efficiency. We are extremely grateful to all of them.

Alongside the papers printed here, a number of other papers and talks were presented at the conference — by Alex Bellos, Jimmy Burns, Matthew Hayes, Eduardo Salazar, Alan Tomlinson, Fernando de Tomaso and Alexandre Rocha Loures. The latter two, in particular — as representatives respectively of Racing Club of Avellaneda and Atlético Paranaense of Curitiba — contributed significantly to our understanding of the possibilities and constraints facing those who are attempting to modernise the management of the football business in Latin America. Thanks are due also to the authors in this volume for their patience with the editors when their other duties intervened to stall its completion, and for their swift responses to our inquiries. Finally, we wish to thank our families for their interest in seeing us complete this project, and for their support of our long-standing predilections for Arsenal FC and Liverpool FC respectively, as well as our appreciation of South American football and footballers.

Rory Miller
Liz Crolley
Liverpool, January 2007

NOTES ON CONTRIBUTORS

Antonio Aidar is a Professor at the Fundação Getúlio Vargas (FGV) in São Paulo, one of the top-ranked Latin American business schools. He also is the Director of FGVProjetos, the consultancy branch of the university. He has been working on the transformation of football management in Brazil for the last ten years, providing consultancies to several clubs. He has published on Brazilian football in Brazil and in England, and has been in charge of courses in the professional management of football at FGV. Aidar is currently involved in an international project investing in player development. He has supported the 2005 World Club Champions, São Paulo Futebol Clube, for over 50 years.

Pablo Alabarces has a PhD from the University of Brighton. He is Professor at the Faculty of Social Sciences of the University of Buenos Aires (UBA) and a researcher at the National Council for Scientific Research (CONICET). In Buenos Aires, he created and coordinated the Popular Cultures Study Group at UBA and the Sport and Society Workgroup at CLACSO (Consejo Latinoamericano de Ciencias Sociales). He has been a Visiting Professor in Brazil, Mexico, Chile, Uruguay and England. His recent books are *Fútbol y Patria* (Prometeo, 2002), *Futbologías* (CLACSO, 2003), *Crónicas del aguante* (Capital Intelectual, 2004) and *Hinchadas* (Prometeo, 2005).

Liz Crolley is a member of the Football Industry Group at the University of Liverpool Management School. Her research draws on her background as a linguist, and examines the social, political, historical and business aspects of football culture. She has published widely in these fields, focusing on the structures, organisation and media coverage of football in Europe and Argentina. Her publications include several co-authored books: *Football, Nationality, and the State* (Longman, 1996, with Vic Duke), *Football, Europe and the Press* (Frank Cass, 2002, with David Hand), and *Football and European Identity* (Routledge, 2006, also with David Hand).

Vic Duke is a political sociologist who spent most of his career at the University of Salford. His main research work in the 1980s involved a longitudinal project to analyse the economic, social, and political effects of Thatcherism, culminating in *A Measure of Thatcherism* (HarperCollins, 1991, with Stephen Edgell). In the 1990s, his research interest switched to the political sociology of football, leading to the publication of *Football, Nationality and the State* (Longman, 1996, with Liz Crolley). He then spent six years as Senior Research Fellow at the University of Liverpool. Now retired, he retains an active interest in the politics of football in Argentina, Belgium and the Czech Republic.

Alan Gilbert is Professor of Geography at University College, London. He graduated in social sciences from the University of Birmingham, and obtained his doctorate from the London School of Economics, as well as being awarded a DLit by the University of London. He is also an elected member of the Academy of Learned Societies for the Social Sciences. He has published extensively on housing, poverty, employment and urban problems in developing countries, particularly those in Latin America. He has authored or co-authored nine books, edited four others, and written more than a hundred academic articles on these topics. He has lived and/or worked in Colombia, Mexico, Chile and Peru.

Richard Giulianotti is Professor of Sociology at the University of Durham. He is author of *Football: A Sociology of the Global Game* (Polity, 1999), translated into Portuguese as *Sociologia do Futebol* (Nova Alexandria, 2002); and *Sport: A Critical Sociology* (Polity, 2005). He has recently co-authored, with Adrian Walsh, *Ethics, Money & Sport* (Routledge, 2006). He is editor or co-editor of nine books on sport, most recently *Football in Africa* (2004, with Gary Armstrong), *Sport and Modern Social Theorists* (2005), and *Sport, Civil Liberties and Human Rights* (2006, with David McArdle).

Katharine Jones is Associate Professor of Sociology at Philadelphia University. She has a BA from Oxford University in Politics, Philosophy and Economics, and an MA and PhD from Rutgers University in Sociology. Her areas of specialisation include identity, culture, and gender, race and class. Her first book was *Accent on Privilege: English Identities and Anglophilia in the US* (Temple University Press, 2001). She is currently working on a second book investigating the identities of English football fans. She has written and presented papers on the ways fans use authenticity to place themselves into hierarchies, female fans' responses to sexism at football, and attitudes towards anti-racist policies among football fans. Although originally from the United Kingdom, she has lived in the United States for 16 years.

Elena Landau has been a Senior Consultant to Sergio Bermudes Solicitors Ltd since 2002. Prior to joining this law firm, she ran her own advisory company, working extensively as a consultant to companies in the energy sector and on restructuring projects for football clubs. Her previous positions also include periods as Managing Director of Bear Stearns of Brazil (1996–97), as a Board Member of BNDES, the Brazilian National Development Bank (1993–95), and as Advisor to the President of the Social Democratic Party, the PSDB (1991–93). She also developed an academic career as a Professor of Economics at the Catholic University in Rio de Janeiro (1981–2002). She holds Bachelor's and Master's degrees in Economics and a BA in Law awarded by the Catholic University of Rio de Janeiro.

José Sergio Leite Lopes is Professor of Social Anthropology at the Federal University of Rio de Janeiro. He has been investigating working-class cultures in Brazil for more than 20 years. He also works on subjects such as environment and social control; sport and the working classes; and the history of the social sciences in Brazil. He is the author of *O Vapor do Diabo: O Trabalho dos Operários do Açúcar* (The Steam of the Devil: The Labour of Sugar Workers) (Paz e Terra, 1976); *A Tecelagem dos Conflitos de Classe na Cidade das Chaminés* (The Weaving of Class-Conflicts in the City of the Chimneys) (Marco Zero, 1988) and *A Ambientalização dos Conflitos Sociais: Participação e Controle Público da Poluição Industrial* (The Environmentalisation of Social Conflicts, Participation and Public Control of Industrial Pollution) (Relume Dumará, 2004). He has published a number of articles about the social history of football in Brazil in international journals and books.

Roger Magazine is Professor and researcher in the Graduate Programme in Social Anthropology at the Universidad Iberoamericana in Mexico City. He received his PhD in anthropology from Johns Hopkins University in 2000 for research on street children and soccer fans in Mexico City and is the author of a number of scholarly articles and book chapters. These have appeared in the *Journal of Latin American Anthropology* and in *Fear and Loathing in World Football* (ed. by Gary Armstrong and Richard Giulianotti, Berg, 2001). His forthcoming book on football fans in Mexico will be published by the University of Arizona Press. Currently, he is conducting research on the effects of and reactions to urban expansion in a village outside the Mexican capital.

Luiz Martins do Melo is Professor of Economics at the Federal University of Rio de Janeiro. He has particular interests in innovation, investment and intellectual property rights in developing economies, and has held the post of Secretary of the Fundação Universitária José Bonifácio.

Rory Miller completed his MA and PhD in History at Cambridge University, and has taught at the University of Liverpool since 1973. By training, he is a business historian, with particular interests in the activities of foreign multinationals in Latin America, although his earlier research concentrated on the socio-economic history of nineteenth- and twentieth-century Peru. He is the author of *Britain and Latin America in the Nineteenth and Twentieth Centuries* (Longman, 1993) and articles in several journals, including *Business History Review*, *Journal of Latin American Studies* and *World Development*. He is currently one of the joint editors of the *Journal of Latin American Studies*. An Arsenal fan since the 1950s, his academic interest in football arises from his appointment as the inaugural director of Liverpool's MBA (Football Industries) programme in 1997.

Aldo Panfichi has a PhD in Sociology from the New School for Social Research in New York. He is currently Professor and researcher in the Department of Social Science and director of the Master's programme in Political Science at the Universidad Católica del Perú. His fields of research are civil society and democracy in Latin America, the sociology of sport, and new forms of social and political leadership in local communities. He has also been active in promoting educational and sport programmes with young people. His most recent publication is *A Disputa pela Construção Democrática na América Latina* (Unicamp/Paz e Terra, 2006, with Evelina Dagnino and Alberto Olvera).

Gideon Rachman is Chief Foreign Affairs Columnist for the *Financial Times*. He joined the paper in 2006 after a 15-year career at *The Economist*, including stints as a foreign correspondent in Brussels, Washington and Bangkok. Prior to the 2002 World Cup in Japan/South Korea, he researched and wrote *The Economist*'s survey of the world football business.

Rogan Taylor was a founding member of the Football Supporters' Association that emerged in Liverpool after the Heysel Stadium tragedy in 1985. He soon became a well-recognised spokesperson for organised fans in England. In 1989 he was invited to conduct research on the social history of supporters' organisations at the Centre for Football Research at Leicester University. Two years later, he published the first of his five books about football, *Football and Its Fans: Supporters and Their Relations with the Game, 1885–1985* (Leicester University Press, 1991). He is currently the Director of the Football Industry Group at the University of Liverpool Management School.

Jorge Thieroldt is a sociologist from the Pontificia Universidad Católica del Perú. He is currently Professor of Sociology there and at the Universidad de Lima. His main areas of interest include the sociology of youth, urban violence and popular culture.

David Wood is Senior Lecturer in Hispanic Studies at the University of Sheffield, where he teaches on Latin American history, society and culture. He has a special interest in Peru and Cuba, as well as in questions of popular culture and the interface between sporting practices and texts. These latter areas have been the focus of much of his recent research, resulting in the book, *De sabor nacional: el impacto de la cultura popular en el Perú* (Instituto de Estudios Peruanos, 2005) and co-editorship of a special issue of the *International Journal of the History of Sport* devoted to 'Sporting Cultures: Hispanic Perspectives on Sport, Text and the Body'. He is a lifelong Arsenal supporter.

PART I:

INTRODUCTION

1

Introduction:
Studying Football in the Americas

Rory Miller

At the end of June 1970, Carlos Alberto, the captain of the Brazilian national team, lifted the World Cup after a stunning 4–1 victory over Italy, watched by millions across the world on colour television. With this, its third victory in four World Cups, Brazil won the Jules Rimet Trophy outright. The 1970 selection became known as the 'Beautiful Team', such was the quality of the football it played.[1] On the road to the final, Brazil defeated two other leading South American teams, Peru and Uruguay, as well as England — the World Cup holders and the country most associated with the introduction of football to Rio de Janeiro and São Paulo at the end of the nineteenth century. The entire squad of 22 players played their club football in Brazil, most in the São Paulo or Rio leagues. Four years later, in the elections for the presidency of the Fédération Internationale de Football Association, or FIFA — international football's governing body — Dr João Havelange, head of the Confederação Brasileira de Desportos (CBD), ousted Sir Stanley Rous, who had been the dominant administrator in the English game and was very much a representative of the gentlemanly amateur traditions of the (English) Football Association. The New World of football, it might be said, had finally defeated the Old, especially as Havelange expanded the World Cup and launched the rapid commercialisation of international football (Sugden & Tomlinson 1998).

Since then, and despite four more World Cup triumphs — two for Argentina (1978 and 1986) and two for Brazil (1994 and 2002) — football in South America, in the eyes of many observers, has descended into chaos. Most professional clubs flirt persistently with insolvency, staving it off by delaying the payment of taxes to the state, and salaries and bonuses to their players, or by transferring their young stars to clubs overseas; matches at many grounds are marked by violence among the fans, deterring families from attending; and allegations of corruption, on and off the pitch, frequently hit the news. The best, and particularly the most creative, footballers have reacted by emigrating to Western Europe or, in the case of lesser players, to Eastern Europe and Asia. At the 2006 World Cup finals, only three members of the Argentine squad — two of them goalkeepers — still played in their domestic league, while just two of the Brazilian players were still playing their club football in their own country (World Soccer 2006). When Brazil and Argentina played a friendly match two months later, it was indicative of the changing balance of power in the global football business that they did so at Arsenal's new Emirates Stadium in London, partly so that the European-based players in their teams did not have to take long overnight flights, but also for purely commercial reasons.

In many South American countries, fans now rarely see the stars of the national team play in the flesh, other than in World Cup and Copa América qualifiers. However, this is not the case throughout the Americas. The Mexican World Cup squad of 2006, which reached the last 16 before losing a tight match to Argentina, had only two members playing their club football elsewhere. Organisationally distinct from football in most South American countries, in that clubs are for the most part *de facto* subsidiaries of large domestic firms rather than independent social entities, Mexican football retains most of its stars. In the case of the United States, the national squad in the 2006 World Cup was roughly split between those still playing in Major League Soccer (MLS), the US professional competition established after the 1994 World Cup and the first such league to succeed in North America, and those registered with clubs overseas. And, while football in South America remains primarily a male sport — both in terms of the players and the spectators at matches — women's soccer has made enormous headway in the United States, particularly at international level where the US team was successful in the Women's World Cup in 1991 and 1999 and the Olympic Games in 2004.

The chapters in this book derive from papers originally presented at a conference in October 2003, and explore aspects of the contemporary state of football in the Americas. They do not claim to offer a comprehensive overview, and important aspects of what would constitute such a volume have unfortunately had to be omitted here — there is nothing, for example, on the role of key individuals from the two regional federations, CONMEBOL and CONCACAF, in the governance of world football, and nothing on the often murky internal politics of the federations or national associations themselves. Some key countries in the history of South American football, in particular Uruguay and Colombia, are also under-represented.[2] Instead, the chapters focus on two sets of issues, one of which develops themes already established in the academic literature, while the other concentrates on an area where there is little academic research. The first, more established, theme is the meaning of football to people living in the Americas — in other words, its relationship with the construction and re-creation of national, ethnic, class and gender identities, and the role that the game plays within society. The more poorly researched theme is the contemporary business of football. Given the importance of Argentina and Brazil in the world game, several papers pay attention to these two countries, but alongside these there are other contributions on Peru, Mexico and the United States, as well as three essays that range more widely.

Football in South America: A Century of Evolution

While debate continues about the extent to which indigenous societies in the Americas may have played a form of football, there is general agreement that British sailors and immigrants introduced the modern game to South America in the final quarter of the nineteenth century — although, in the case of Brazil especially, Germans such as Hans Nobiling played a significant role. The standard histories of football in the region highlight the role played by pioneers such as Charles Miller, an employee of the English railway company in São Paulo, Alexander Watson Hutton, a schoolteacher in Buenos Aires, and Oscar Cox, an Anglo-Brazilian businessman who became the first president of the Fluminense club in Rio de Janeiro (Mason 1995; Santa Cruz 1996; Pereira 2000). Initially based in British clubs and schools, football quickly became organised: the first Argentine league was founded in 1893 by Watson Hutton; in Chile in the same year, representative teams from Santiago and Valparaiso played each other twice. The Uruguayan league was founded in 1900, and the São Paulo league the following year. These developments were exactly contemporary with the spread of football in southern Europe: Juventus was founded in 1897, Barcelona in 1899 and Real Madrid in 1902 (Walvin 1975, pp. 93–97).

This early history has to be seen in the context of developments in both British sport and Anglo-Latin American relations. Like many modern sports, the rules of (association) football had been codified by English sporting gentlemen in the middle of the nineteenth century, and the Football Association (the FA) was formed in 1863. National competitions were established soon afterwards, the FA Cup in 1871–72 and the Football League in 1888–89. Significantly, though, participation in organised sport was regarded in Victorian Britain as one of the essential elements of the education of the 'Christian gentleman', and football spread widely in independent schools while also attracting the attention of workers in the rapidly expanding industrial cities, who found it an easy and cheap sport to play in streets and parks, and on waste ground. Many graduates of the independent schools and ancient universities, in their role as clergymen, encouraged young working-class men to play sport in preference to more sinful pursuits, but elsewhere in Britain football emerged autonomously in workplaces and neighbourhoods. At precisely this time — from the late 1860s onwards — British trade and investment in Latin America were growing rapidly, in particular in Brazil and the countries of the southern cone (Argentina, Uruguay and Chile) (Miller 1993). As a consequence, thousands of young British men emigrated to South American cities to take up employment opportunities in the new railway and tramway companies and banks, the British communities grew in size and influence, and the newcomers founded their own networks of schools, clubs and other institutions. Moreover, in the view of South American elites, while the French might symbolise European culture, the British epitomised modern business attitudes, and they were subject to admiration and imitation for that reason.

Football thus spread quickly in the South American countries most subject to British economic and cultural influence; by the second decade of the twentieth century, the infrastructure of the modern game was in place, despite frequent conflicts within national associations. Regular international matches commenced, initially between Argentina and Uruguay, and CONMEBOL, the Confederación Sudamericana de Fútbol, was founded in 1916. By then the administration of football had escaped from the hands of the British who had introduced it. The game had been 'creolised' — taken over by the respectable classes of South America — and then popularised as working-class men participated in their thousands, both as players and as spectators.

The clubs that comprised the local leagues had a range of origins. First, just as many of the early British football clubs in South America began in schools and colleges, local students also formed their own teams. The most obvious example is the eponymous Estudiantes de La Plata in Argentina, founded in 1905; Nacional, which became one of the two dominant teams in twentieth-century Uruguay, had been founded by students in Montevideo six years earlier. Second, elite members of social clubs that participated in other sports began to organise football teams. While many of these amateur clubs remained exclusive, others formed teams that played at the highest level: Flamengo, now the most popular club in Brazil, was born when a group of rebel players from Fluminense joined the Clube de Regatas do Flamengo, or rowing club, in 1911 (Leite Lopes 1997, pp. 55–57). Third, workplace teams were formed, either at the owners' initiative or through the self-organisation of the firm's employees. Peñarol, Nacional's leading rival in Montevideo, was based initially in the workshops of the Central Uruguayan Railway, but it was not just railway companies — Ferrocarril Oeste and Rosario Central in Argentina are other examples — that provided workers with opportunities to join in sporting activities. One of the earliest teams in Rio was Bangu, belonging to an English-owned textile mill. As workplace-based teams developed, the owners — interested in the prestige they could bring as well as the potential of football as a means of controlling workers — might offer valuable employment opportunities to talented players. Fourth, clubs represented particular ethnicities or political groups, such as Alianza Lima (the black community of La Victoria in Lima) or Vasco da Gama (the

Portuguese community in Rio).[3] In Chile, a club named Chile Obrero FC was formed as early as 1897; in Argentina, as Eduardo Galeano points out, both Argentinos Juniors (founded as Mártires de Chicago in 1904) and Chacarita (1906) had their origins in anarchist celebrations of 1 May (Galeano 1996, p. 37). Finally, clubs represented towns or particular *barrios* or neighbourhoods in cities — a factor that might overlap, as in the case of Alianza, with ethnicity. With the formation of clubs came the development of local rivalries and the *clásicos* or 'local derby' matches that frequently attracted thousands of partisan spectators: Flamengo-Fluminense in Rio de Janeiro, Boca Juniors-River Plate in Buenos Aires, Independiente-Racing in Avellaneda, São Paulo-Corinthians in São Paulo, Alianza-Universitario in Lima and, later, ColoColo-Universidad de Chile in Santiago.

Urban history, as Pierre Lanfranchi (1994, p. 29) comments with regard to Europe, is 'a fundamental element for an understanding of the mechanisms of the spread of the game and the playing of the game', and this is just as true of Latin America. The late nineteenth and early twentieth centuries saw a rapid expansion of Latin American cities as thousands of immigrants poured in, from Europe and from the interior, to service the commercial economy. While many were able to obtain formal employment in the railways, commercial firms and banks, urban utilities and docks, in particular, others remained informal casual workers, lacking roots and identity. Football provided a sport that was easy and cheap for young working men to play, a game with simple and adaptable rules that could take place on any piece of open ground, and an arena in which migrants could form friendships and collective identities. The improvement in rail communications allowed teams to travel for matches (between Rio and São Paulo, for example, or Santiago and Valparaiso), while urban tramways and suburban railways allowed spectators to watch their teams in local games.[4] As attendances at top matches increased, the press began to print reports that reached the literate portion of the public, although it was not until the 1930s that the advent of radio really allowed football commentary to reach illiterate fans. By then, however, literacy rates in countries like Argentina and Uruguay had improved markedly, thanks to universal primary education, and specialist sports journals had begun to appear, such as *El Gráfico* in Buenos Aires.

For people in such an environment, playing for and supporting a football club provided a significant sense of identity and belonging and, for the very talented players, real possibilities for public recognition. Above all, football was an egalitarian sport, requiring little in the way of expensive equipment but rather physical skills, endurance, and a 'football brain'. In what was probably a unique piece of oral history, scholars in Lima in the 1980s interviewed former players from 60 years before to ascertain why they had enjoyed the game, and found a remarkable coincidence in the responses. In the words of one informant, apart from their 'love of the [team's] shirt', they gained 'the appreciation and respect of the *barrio* and of friends. That was the satisfaction a footballer had: to attract friends, to show off to girls, and to party.' Another added that simply winning medals was an enormous source of pride to someone from a poor background (Deustua et al. 1986, pp. 137–38). But the egalitarian potential of football was also a source of conflict, as 'respectable' elites struggled to maintain control of the sport. Many of the *clásicos* were centred on issues of class and race: white students and members of the middle class versus ordinary people of colour in the case of Universitario-Alianza in Lima or Fluminense-Flamengo in Rio. Race, and the fact that many of the most gifted footballers in countries like Peru or Brazil were mulatto or black, initially provided a source of tension rather than one of national pride. Indeed, in the first South American championship of 1916, the Chileans are said to have demanded the annulment of Uruguay's 4–0 victory on the grounds that the winning team had included two blacks (Galeano 1996, p. 42). In Brazil, Vasco da Gama's triumph in the Rio championship in 1923, using mulatto and black players, provoked a split in the organising body and the introduction of literacy requirements to try to exclude players from the lowest social ranks (Leite Lopes 1997, pp. 62–67). The continuing racial conflicts in Brazilian football were evident also in the way in which Barbosa, the national team's black goalkeeper, was blamed for the tragic defeat suffered at the hands of Uruguay in the 1950 World Cup Final in the Maracanã.[5]

If one of the attractions of football was that the poor could compete with the rich and win, this was also true at the international level. South American teams dominated the Olympic Games in 1924 and 1928, with Uruguay winning on both occasions, enjoying victories over Switzerland and Argentina respectively. Uruguay defeated Argentina again in 1930 in the inaugural World Cup in Montevideo. Tactically, as well as in terms of individual skills, the South American countries had advanced faster than the Europeans, and the style of football they played also helped to form a national identity, as Eduardo Archetti (1994a, 1995a) has explained in the case of Argentina. From the time Boca Juniors successfully toured Europe in 1925, Argentine journalists contrasted their skilful, individual style with the muscularity of the English teams and the brutality of the Uruguayan *charrúas*. English football, *El Gráfico* wrote in 1928, resembled a rather monotonous — if powerful — machine, while in the River Plate footballers 'made use of dribbling, and brave individual effort, in defence as well as attack, which resulted in a style of football that was more agile and attractive' (Archetti 1995a, p. 429).[6] Brazilians, slightly later, came to regard their football as the sporting expression of other key elements of Brazilian popular culture, samba and capoeira, developing a style of football that was not only world-beating but also entrancing for spectators to watch (Archetti 1998a, pp. 94–96; Gordon and Helal 2001, p. 146).[7]

The peak of South American football probably came in the period 1930–1970, between the first World Cup won by Uruguay and Brazil's third triumph (between them, Uruguay and Brazil won five out of nine World Cups in this period).[8] In the 1930s and 1940s, full professionalisation replaced the 'shamateurism' of the preceding era in Argentina, Uruguay and Brazil: new, modern stadiums were built in the major cities; domestic football was played at a high level of skill and competitiveness; and most players stayed at home, although those who did venture to Europe — such as Alfredo di Stéfano (Real Madrid) and Omar Sivori (Juventus) in the 1950s — could only enhance the reputation of South American football for producing skilful individual players. Brazil's first World Cup victory in 1958, with players such as Garrincha, Didi and Pelé, offered further evidence.

In the last third of the twentieth century, however, some of the inherent problems of football in South America became all too evident. Again, the economic and political context within which football was being played was important. Although the individual trajectory of each differed, the countries where football had developed most became marked by unstable populist regimes, military coups and, increasingly in the 1960s and 1970s, authoritarian governments and political repression. Economically, policies of import substitution industrialisation — which also involved a rapid expansion of the public sector — resulted in bouts of ever-worsening inflation, sharp recessions as governments attempted to curb it by limiting fiscal deficits and consumption, and business instability, from which football clubs were not immune. With the partial exception of Chile, political corruption became widespread, helped by the growth of the public sector.

The domestic football of the major South American countries thus became marked by a number of characteristics which together forced it into a spiral of decline. First, the role of politicians in football — whether civilians or military — changed from that of being an ordinary spectator or honoured guest to active intervention and interference. This did have its positive aspects in terms of public funding of major stadiums — for example, the completion of the Monumental (home of River Plate) in 1938 and La Bombonera (Boca Juniors) in 1940, followed by the construction of three more stadiums for clubs in Greater Buenos Aires under the first presidency of Perón (Mason 1995, pp. 62–66; Duke & Crolley, 1996a, p. 105).[9] The Brazilian military government of the 1960s and 1970s financed the construction of several large stadiums across the country. However, the increasing bitterness of politics brought national football associations into close contact with government and restricted their autonomy. World Cups, in particular, became a focus for authoritarian regimes anxious both to appease the public and to fly the nationalist flag. The best-known examples are probably the military's propaganda use of Brazil's 1970 World Cup victory and the Argentine military's investment in using the 1978 World Cup, which FIFA had awarded to the country before the military coup of 1976, to restore its international image after three years in which its savage repression of the left had attracted worldwide criticism. Domestic football could also be used as a means of social control; it is said that one reason for the frequency of televised games in Argentina in the late 1960s was to keep potential demonstrators indoors. For civilian politicians, identification with a football club was a means of increasing their public profile and support, helped by the fact that, since most clubs in South America were formed as mutual clubs with periodic elections for the *socios* (members) to choose their new directors, they gained valuable campaigning experience as well as media exposure and sources of patronage. Instances of civilian politicians being closely involved with the management of football clubs abound: the best current example is probably Mauricio Macri, the president of Boca Juniors since 1995 and a potential candidate to become Mayor of Buenos Aires in 2007. However, football could also be used in attempts to subvert politicians and political regimes. Under authoritarian governments in particular, football stadiums were frequently the only venues where large crowds could legally gather on a regular basis. Anonymity provided the opportunities for verbal attacks on the forces of order, and for political slogans — for example, the Brazilian fans' chanting of '*direitas já*' at matches in 1983, as Brazil moved towards civilian rule (Humphrey & Tomlinson 1986, p. 104).[10] In a few cases, too, the legitimacy conferred by fame provided professional footballers with the opportunity to intervene in politics against the established order, most noticeably in Sócrates' support of free elections and democracy in the same Brazilian transition (Shirts 1988).

A second problem was the growth of crowd violence, initially in Argentina in the 1950s and 1960s but spreading to Brazil, Peru and Chile in the final decades of the century. This has been linked directly to the status of football clubs as social organisations with periodic elections, which led candidates to make links with organised fan groups who could intimidate opponents (Duke & Crolley 1996b). In return for the support of the *barras bravas*, as the Argentine fan groups became known, the directors of clubs began to distribute tickets, merchandise and facilities for travel to away matches.[11] They could also use them to intimidate players (for example, those on the point of signing a new contract), coaches and match officials, as well as in political demonstrations. This symbiotic relationship between elected club officials and the leaders of the *barras*, however, was not one that the former could necessarily control; patronage could easily turn into extortion. Violence spread within and outside stadiums, not only as the *barras* of different clubs came into conflict, but also as rival *barras* of the same club fought for access to spoils. For example, *Clarín* reported in March 2005 on violent internal conflicts within the *barras* of Estudiantes, Argentinos Juniors, Racing, Newell's, and Rosario Central, quoting the head of security for Argentine football as stating: 'They're not interested in football but simply in sharing out the cake. To lead a *barra* represents the ability to manage tickets, travel, and profits.' (*Clarín*, 1 March 2005) Partly because they could seek the protection of the powerful, and partly because of the frequent failings of the police and criminal justice in Latin America, most members of the *barras* — with the occasional exception of leaders who overstepped the boundaries — operated with impunity. The consequence for football, however, was to deter other sectors of the population from attending matches. Most South American domestic football has seen a steady decline in attendances over the past 30 years.[12]

Corruption in the management of clubs, and occasionally in the fixing of matches, also became evident. In one scandal that broke out in Brazil in 1996, the head of the refereeing committee of the Confederação Brasileira do Futebol (CBF) was taped negotiating with club officials for payments to fix matches. He later claimed that he wished to accumulate funds to finance a political career (Taylor 1998, pp. 102–04). A further refereeing scandal erupted in 2005 when São Paulo's organised crime unit accused one of Brazil's elite FIFA referees, Edilson, of agreeing to throw more than 20 domestic matches in return for payments of between R$10,000 and R$15,000 a time (Veja, 28 September 2005).[13] Serious problems have also arisen from the fact that in most countries social clubs were not obliged to produce audited accounts. This meant that their financial dealings were far from transparent. Again, Brazil is probably the country where scandals have been most frequent, with accusations about the destination of the money that the CBF, under the presidency of Ricardo Teixeira, Havelange's son-in-law, received from its 1996 contract with Nike, followed by the disappearance of the substantial foreign investments made in Brazilian clubs between 1997 and 1999, and accusations that the coach of the national team was taking 'bungs' from agents and clubs who wished to increase the transfer value of the players they owned. These allegations resulted in two congressional inquiries into corruption in Brazilian football.[14]

Like football clubs in many parts of the world, therefore, those in South America have always been near to insolvency. In many cases, they have relied on influential politicians to guarantee their survival. There are several examples of governments — unwilling to suffer the unpopularity that would result from a failure to act — ensuring that teams avoided bankruptcy. One of the best-known cases is the legal change that allowed Racing Club to survive in Argentina at the end of the 1990s.[15] For much the same reason, clubs have acquired impunity for missed payments to the tax authorities: the well-known Rio club of Botafogo, for example, was said in September 2006 to owe the state US$55 million and the total debt of football clubs to the Brazilian state apparently exceeded US$500 million (*Soccer Investor Daily*, 7 September 2006). Another frequent device employed by clubs facing cash flow problems has been to leave players unpaid, precipitating strikes and delays to the start of seasons. Poor attendances and difficulties in generating other sources of income have therefore left clubs dependent on television revenues, together with the proceeds of player transfers, for much of their income. In the case of Brazil in 2004, broadcasting revenues and transfers each accounted for approximately 30 per cent of the US$400 million income of the top 20 clubs (Casual Auditores Independentes, 2006a). In Argentina, the proceeds from transfers reached 50 per cent of the clubs' total income in 2006 (*Clarín*, 19 December 2006). While recognising that clubs in Latin America have faced problems that those in Western Europe do not — for example, the impact of inflation and sudden economic crisis, the relative lack of disposable income among fans, the lack of legal protection for trade marks and the piracy of merchandise — the quality of business management in South American football has generally been poor.[16] However, this has become more acute with the commercial revolution that has taken place in Western European football which, together with the Bosman Judgment of 1995 abolishing quotas on 'foreign' players in European competition, has stimulated the migration of players to Europe and elsewhere.

Player migration to the European leagues has a long history in South America: many talented footballers have been descendants of the immigrants of the late nineteenth century who could claim dual nationality and had the right to European passports. The migration of the best players to Italian clubs following the 1930 World Cup was indeed the principal catalyst for the formal adoption of professional football in Argentina, Uruguay and Brazil between 1931 and 1933 (Mason 1995, pp. 47–53). There was also considerable movement within Latin America — most notably when, on the back of booming coffee revenues in the late 1940s, several Colombian clubs recruited Argentines following a players' strike there. However, for a long period the real outflow was to Southern Europe, and the most desired players were the most creative ones, the attacking midfielders and the strikers. Even before the Bosman Judgment, between 1980 and 1993 over 2,000 Argentine professionals are said to have moved overseas, including every season's leading goal-scorer (Mason 1995, p. 137). Since the 1998 World Cup, three years after the Bosman Judgment, over 500 Brazilians have moved abroad every season.[17] Their migration thus further devalued football as a spectacle in South America, as the opportunities to watch stars of the national team in action became fewer. In addition, of course, such transfers further increased the opportunities for corruption.

It could therefore be argued that, over the final third of the twentieth century, football in the South American countries where it had been introduced most successfully a century earlier entered into the vicious circle depicted in Figure 1.1.

Figure 1.1: The Vicious Circle of South American Football

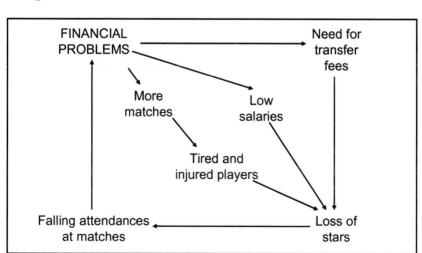

Short-termism is prevalent in the management of football clubs throughout the world, but in South America the combination of external political and economic factors, poor internal management, and low standards of governance and behaviour has made the problems more acute. One commentator has described football as exhibiting all the features of political *caudillismo*, including the clientelistic ties between the *patrón* and his followers, together with the endemic violence for which Latin America is notorious in the European imagination (Ghersi 2003, p. 41). The careers of Julio Grondona, president of the Argentine Football Association since 1979, and Ricardo Teixeira, president of the CBF since 1989 despite repeated allegations of corruption, would certainly also fit with the characterisation of South American football as being dominated by *caudillos*.[18] Both are senior members of FIFA, and prominent in the international administration of the game. Another example would be Eurico Miranda of Vasco da Gama, who used his congressional role to protect his personal interests and forestall reform (Bellos 2002, Ch. 13). The football authorities of the region have generally been unable to control the crime and corruption inherent in the game, and indeed have frequently been implicated in it themselves. These comments provide some clues as to who makes money from football in South America, even in a climate where the live domestic game is in a state of decay.

The beneficiaries of the contemporary football industry in South America might be categorised into five groups. There are two sets of business actors who are much more aware of international realities than most football clubs, and thus able to take advantage of their greater access to information *vis-à-vis* the amateurs who run most clubs and national associations. These are, first, the media companies — particularly the broadcasters — and, second, the marketing firms — most notoriously Nike. As long as football has fans — especially on television — it provides a vehicle for clever marketing by firms that want to reach its demographic profile.[19] Third, star players and agents have opportunities to accumulate enormous personal wealth, relatively little of which flows back into South America. International agents such as Juan Figer (a Uruguayan) or Pini Zahavi (an Israeli) have the highest profile and attract the most adverse publicity, but at a lower level there are thousands of intermediaries trying to benefit from negotiating transfers and contracts on behalf of poorly educated footballers from socially deprived backgrounds.[20] They are helped by a system, common in South America, where frequently a player's registration is not owned in its entirety by his club, as it generally is in Europe, but shared between the club and private individuals. The agents' assets lie in their address books and contacts, making them indispensable to Latin American clubs short of money. The fourth group benefiting from the sport, but frequently taking large amounts of money out of it, comprises corrupt club and association officials. The problems are best documented in Brazil, thanks to two parliamentary inquiries; however, similar accusations of malversion of funds — albeit on a smaller scale — have been made elsewhere (Bellos 2002, Ch. 14).[21] Finally, at a much lower level, the leaders of the *barras bravas* frequently make profits on the resale of tickets and the gifts that they have received or extorted from their clubs.

Football Elsewhere in the Americas: Arrival on the World Stage

Thus far this chapter has concentrated on the South American countries that became the heartlands of football in the Americas in the early twentieth century. While others have their particular histories — that of Colombia, for example, is dominated by its break with FIFA which allowed it to sign foreign players and enjoy a golden age in the early 1950s, and then by the impact of wealthy cocaine dealers on the football business — most share many of the features described here. Clubs originated in similar backgrounds, although other Latin American countries lacked the numerous southern European immigrants who arrived in the River Plate and Brazil. In most countries, however, there were small British communities associated with commerce and investments who played a significant role in introducing the sport.[22] Once the final stages of the World Cup were expanded from 16 to 32 teams under the presidency of Havelange, other countries were able to qualify for this lucrative festival of football, creating conditions for the construction and development of national identities linked to football similar to those that had occurred elsewhere earlier in the century.[23] Other footballing countries in South America have faced similar financial problems to clubs in Argentina, Uruguay and Brazil: inadequate income streams; an increasing dependence on television; and the increasing devaluation of the domestic game as the best players have moved towards wealthier countries.[24] However, two exceptional cases in the Americas require some further explanation.

The first of these is Mexico. As in South America, football appears to have been introduced by British immigrants — in this case, miners — but it took longer to take off than it did further south and, due to the competition from other popular sports — in particular, boxing, wrestling and baseball — it never obtained the dominance that it did in the Plate. Nonetheless, a specialised magazine called *Fútbol* was in circulation by the 1930s (Brewster 2005). The Mexican national squad qualified frequently for the World Cup finals as the representative of CONCACAF, the North and Central American and Caribbean federation, but achieved little. The growth of Mexican football really took off, however, with the advent of commercial television and the staging of the World Cup of 1970. Two organisational features of Mexican football stand out which differentiate it from South America. First, multiple ownership of clubs is permitted, as in the United States; in most leagues, this is prohibited because of the danger that owners will manipulate the competition or transfer players between clubs as needed. Second, the majority of clubs have been operated by companies or social organisations, most obviously the two major television companies, Televisa and TV Azteca, but also by manufacturing firms, financial institutions and universities. Commercially successful, the Mexican league has historically imported footballers from elsewhere in Latin America rather than exporting them to Europe.

In the United States association football — or soccer — has never been significant in the sporting imagination since the invention of the classic US sports — baseball, gridiron football and basketball — at the same time as football was spreading in Europe and South America at the end of the nineteenth century. In different ways, these sports epitomised late nineteenth-century values in the United States much more closely than football did — baseball because of its speed and requirements for ingenuity and individual initiative, and gridiron because of its organisation, routine and obsession with statistics (a sporting form of Taylorism). In keeping with US attitudes at the time, their popular adoption also reflected a rejection of Europe and the Old World. The crucial point, at the time that inter-collegiate sport was developing in the 1870s, was Harvard's refusal to join Rutgers and Princeton in playing a soccer-like game, opting instead for a version of rugby that its students had learned from McGill University in Montreal (Markovits 1990). While large numbers of schoolboys in Boston continued to play a form of football that more closely resembled the English game, and football was played widely by immigrant workers in the northern United States in the 1880s and 1890s — indeed, until World War I — no successful professional league was ever formed at this time, in contrast to baseball (Abrams 1995).[25]

These characteristics of football in the United States — the disjuncture between mass childhood participation (at least until the mid-teens) and an almost complete lack of interest in watching the professional game regularly, and the identification of football with immigrant communities rather than 'true Americans' — have remained to the present day. The attempt to form a professional league, the North American Soccer League (NASL), in the 1970s failed to capture the popular imagination despite, or perhaps because of, the dominance of the teams by ageing stars from overseas. Major League Soccer, inaugurated following the 1994 World Cup, has survived despite its failure to capture a mass television audience, in part because of the refusal to allow the league to become dominated by foreign players, but also because the major entertainment groups which own teams have been able to cross-subsidise losses. The comment made by the first MLS commissioner — '40 per cent of our audience is ethnic first- or second-generation American, and most Latinos' — is in many respects symbolic of continued weaknesses (Delgado 1999, p. 50). Even though the US national men's team rose as high as fourth in the world rankings in April 2006, before an unsuccessful World Cup campaign pulled it down, professional soccer still falls outside the consciousness of most male working-class sports fans in the United States, and is routinely attacked by mainstream sports journalists who have a profound nationalistic belief in the superiority of US sports (Collins 2006).

Thus, whereas football became a source of identity formation in South American countries, dislike of soccer became a marker of identity for men of all classes once assimilated into the United States. Playing and watching football was part of the 'melting pot' in the River Plate; it was not in the United States, precisely because of its identification with immigrants and its European origins. However, there are also contrasts between the United States and South America in terms of gender. In part because the US women's soccer team has been more successful internationally than the men's, but also because of the differing relative importance of men's and women's soccer in US college sports, soccer in the United States has also become viewed as a women's sport, whereas in South America in the early twentieth century it helped to define the essence of masculinity.[26] Even so, attempts to establish a professional women's soccer league in the United States foundered in 2003.[27] In South America, in contrast to the United States, women's football has made little headway — except, perhaps, in Brazil, the beaten finalists in the 2004 Olympics.

Academic Research on Football

For a long time, football was the object of academic disdain rather than research, despite its popularity in so many countries. At the time that a few social scientists and historians in the developed world were beginning to develop an interest in sport in the 1970s, social science activity in much of South America was disrupted by political repression and exile. In such circumstances, Latin American social scientists had more important subjects to study than football, and many in fact treated it as a means of social control rather than an area of autonomous popular expression.[28] Moreover, researchers in the key disciplines where academic interest in football was growing in the developed world — history, economics, sociology and anthropology — were preoccupied with topics that either seemed irrelevant to Latin America or relied on data that was impossible to collect there. It was only with the growth of interest in nationalism and identity, stimulated by writers such as Benedict Anderson (1983), that research themes began to appear which had clear resonance in Latin America. Yet even as late as 1998, Argentine scholar Eduardo Archetti could lament that Latin American anthropologists, despite their concern with ritual and the construction of identity, still showed little interest in sport. When they did, it was viewed as a means by which elites imposed hegemonic values on the young and the poor, rather than as an arena in which participants and consumers might exercise some autonomy, and indeed challenge the hegemony of elite values (Archetti 1998a, p. 91).[29] In such circumstances, the earliest serious work on football in Latin America tended to come not from academics but from journalists like Mário Filho in Brazil, Pablo Ramírez in Argentina and Abelardo Sánchez León in Peru. The tradition of serious journalism was continued by the Uruguayan Eduardo Galeano, who published his enormously influential collection of essays, *El fútbol a sol y sombra* (*Football in Sun and Shadow*) in 1996, as well as by foreign writers fascinated by Latin American football such as Jimmy Burns (1996), Chris Taylor (1998) and Alex Bellos (2002).[30]

Against this background, some of the earliest academic interest in football in Latin America, especially Brazil, came from overseas (Rachum 1978; Levine 1980). These early historical articles were followed by the attempt of a US sociologist, Janet Lever, to uncover the role that football played in Brazilian society (Lever 1983). Lever's innovative study relied heavily on the methodologies of sociology, in the form of questionnaires and interviews conducted during an extensive period of fieldwork in Rio de Janeiro, to argue that football both ritualised conflicts within Brazilian society, through the identification of football clubs with particular social groups, but also transcended them by integrating fans in support of the national team. She noted also that football was much more segregated, in terms of gender, than comparable sports in the United States.[31] At much the same time, a well-known Brazilian anthropologist, Roberto da Matta, edited a collection of academic essays which, by emphasising the ritualistic role of football in Brazilian society, made it for the first time in Brazil a subject worthy of academic attention (da Matta 1982). Yet, while these works brought the study of Brazilian football into a position of acceptance within the social sciences, elsewhere the process was much slower. It was only in the 1990s that Eduardo Archetti, an Argentine anthropologist exiled in Norway, began to produce a series of articles exploring the role that football had played in the formation both of Argentine national identity and of Argentine masculinity — a trajectory that culminated in the publication of *Masculinities: Football, Polo and the Tango in Argentina* (Archetti 1999). Elsewhere, with the exception of work on the connections between football and politics, academic studies of football were rare until the 1990s, one exception being the work of oral history in Peru undertaken in the course of a much wider project on the popular classes of Lima (Deustua et al. 1986). Since then, research by historians and social scientists has become more common although, in contrast to North America and Europe, work on the economics and business side of football remains extremely rare.[32]

Janet Lever's book on Brazilian football coincided with the last years of the military dictatorship, and both there and in neighbouring Argentina the relationship between football and contemporary politics became a primary area of concern, especially for foreign scholars. In both cases, World Cup successes became a particular focus of attention. In Brazil, Janet Lever notes, the military regime introduced a national sports lottery to finance welfare programmes and encouraged the CBD to introduce a national championship for the first time as a means of promoting integration. Lottery funds were used to prepare the national football team for the 1970 World Cup, and its success in Mexico resulted in a unprecedented welcome for the players in the presidential palace in Brasilia as President Médici attempted to identify the military government with the success of the 'Beautiful Team'. Several scholars commented on how the close connection between the military regime and football success was epitomised in Admiral Heleno Nunes' dual role as president of the CBD, after the departure of Havelange for FIFA, and head of the military's stooge party, ARENA, in Rio de Janeiro (Levine 1980, pp. 246–47; Lever 1988, pp. 91–93). The 1978 World Cup in Argentina has also been recognised as a prime example of a repressive military regime using football for its own political purposes, as well as providing extensive opportunities for its adherents to benefit from graft and corruption. Later research has shown how the regime coerced the domestic media into praise of its organisation of the World Cup, though commentators have noted the difficulties the junta faced in preventing the foreign press from observing the poverty resulting from Argentina's economic recession and questioning the regime's human rights record (Arbena 1990; Kuper

1996, pp. 174–77; Smith 2002). Yet football could also offer a vehicle for protest. Matthew Shirts, as already noted, has highlighted Sócrates' use of his position in football to promote democracy in Brazil, and César Luís Menotti, the left-wing coach of the Argentine national team in 1978, has claimed that he ordered the players to pay respects to the popular stands rather than the expensive seats occupied by members of the regime (Archetti 1995b, pp. 213–14).[33] Certainly, the interconnections between football and politics in Latin America became one of the main areas for comment by foreign scholars in the mid-1990s, Tony Mason devoting an entire chapter of his historical survey to the subject (Mason 1995; see also Duke & Crolley 1996b).

For sociologists and anthropologists, other themes came to dominate the study of football. Issues such as national integration, social division and violence had clear political implications, but were also studied in their own right. The work of writers such as Archetti on the construction of nationality and masculinity in Argentina through the medium of football, of José Sergio Leite Lopes on race in Brazilian football, and of Vic Duke and others on the growth of the *barras bravas* in Argentina has already been noted. A further important theme in the study of football in Latin America, contributing to the construction of identity, has been the importance of iconic figures to football fans in Latin America, in particular those stars who represent the triumph of men from a poor background over the wealthy and powerful. Eduardo Santa Cruz comments that the football icon, in the eyes of South American fans, becomes 'the champion who will defend our honour, our history, and our collective pride, and/or the man who has arrived where we would all like to be'. The world-class footballer from a poor background thus becomes a representation of popular feelings and achievements in the face of a world that is often distant and threatening (Santa Cruz 1996, p. 85). Perhaps the classic examples are Diego Maradona, a *pibe* from one of the poorest areas of Buenos Aires, whose individual genius overcame the rigidly organised European teams of the 1980s, and Garrincha, the *mulato* from a poor town outside Rio who embodied the spirit of the *malandro*, and whose funeral in 1983 attracted thousands of ordinary people to mourn someone who, like them, had suffered injustice and prejudice throughout his career and died in poverty (Archetti 1997; Leite Lopes 1997, p. 72; Archetti 1999, pp. 97–99).[34] The social and cultural differences between football in South America and Western Europe — the interconnection with politics, the relationship between football and national and social identities, the cult of the star, and patterns of violence — thus finally gave an impetus to research on football in South America itself in the second half of the 1990s, balancing the early efforts of foreign scholars on the history of the game. It also gave research on football in the Americas a distinct agenda.[35] One important outcome, reflecting this surge of interest, was the publication of two volumes of collected essays by an international group of scholars coordinated by Pablo Alabarces, together with Alabarces' own book on football and the imagining of the nation in Argentina (Alabarces 2000, 2002, 2003).

Football, Identity and Society: The Contribution of This Book

David Wood's paper in this volume commences with a quotation from Aldo Panfichi, another contributor, to the effect that football is 'a central instrument in the imaginary construction of socio-cultural identities' at both local and national level, and this has been a consistent theme of studies of football in Latin America for the past 20 years. Football, in Archetti's words, created 'imagined Argentine qualities' around players, teams and victories (Archetti 1994a, p. 231). Other writers have emphasised how qualification for the final stages of the World Cup provides opportunities for the self-affirmation of small nations such as Costa Rica in 1990 or Bolivia in 1994 (Bar-On 1997, Section 2.3).[36] But a deeper question is perhaps how defeat is interpreted, especially in those countries with high expectations of success. As Archetti has pointed out, Argentina did not defeat the English national team until 1964 and, given the British pre-eminence in the country in the early twentieth century and the nationalist reaction to it, this was a crucial point of self-affirmation, especially after the humiliation Argentina suffered in the 1958 World Cup finals (Archetti 1995a, p. 429). However, this overwhelming desire for victory over England meant that defeat in 1966, with Rattín, the captain, sent off early in the match, could only be explained in terms of a European conspiracy.[37] For Brazil, as Leite Lopes explains in his chapter here, defeat to Uruguay in the Maracanã in 1950 raised questions for many Brazilians about the country's ethnic hybridity, while debate over the loss of the final to France in 1998 became much more focused on the commercial demands of sponsors and the corruption inherent in the game in an era of globalisation. At a national level, therefore, the soul-searching that follows defeat can provoke a range of reactions that may vary over time, from anger at the continued 'conspiracies' of the developed world against Latin American countries to examination of deep-rooted internal characteristics that appear to epitomise the failings of a national culture.

If football can focus internal debate about national cultures or the relationships of particular countries with the outside world, it can also provide a window on to society in other ways. As Gary Whannel has commented: 'Sport functions as a cultural site wherein competing visions of democracy, equality, and capitalism, among other concepts, are articulated and contested.' (cited in Delgado 1999, p. 41) Historically, football has offered an arena where ethnic or other social groups can affirm identity, but where they can also integrate themselves — and not just on the elite's terms — into the nation. Delgado, for the contemporary United States, makes the point that television executives and the businessmen who own MLS franchises have deliberately sought out the Latino audience. At the same time, Latino audiences have resisted the conglomeration of their individual national identities by the white Americans who control the league, the teams and the media (Delgado 1999). The chapters here on fans in Mexico and Peru emphasise the self-affirmation of fan groups and their questioning of contemporary structures of business and politics — for example, in the Pumas' fans' rejection of Nike's association with their team or their demands for genuine democracy rather than a form of *caciquismo*.[38] Football can be particularly important because, at least in terms of active participation in attending games, it attracts a demographic profile — young, single men who are frequently disaffected members of the society in which they live — which social scientists may find it otherwise difficult to reach. It thus provides a window on to wider aspects of male youth culture, as Pablo Alabarces's chapter on Argentina indicates, as well as on what middle-aged and middle-class members of society would regard as the principal threats arising from this particular section of the population, violence and crime.

There are two other important features of youth culture that are particularly evident in the studies here. The first is the rapidity of change as older members leave the group and younger members adhere. This is evident in debate over styles of support, the governance of fan groups, and the wording of the particular chants and songs employed at matches. The second is the self-labelling of subgroups in opposition to others, here seen in Panfichi and Thieroldt's discussion of the *barras* of Alianza Lima and Universitario in Peru. Most work of this kind is undertaken by anthropologists using ethnographic methods. Aidar and Taylor, in Part IV of the book, also provide insights into the self-image of fans through conventional market research methods in discovering that the fans of Internacional in Porto Alegre regard themselves as 'monkeys' — originally an insult thrown at them by rival Grêmio supporters, but appropriated by the Internacional fans because of its connotations of belonging to the popular classes of the city. Like earlier authors, Aidar and Taylor also touch on one of the most significant aspects of Latin American fan culture: the emphasis that the fans of one club put on their own masculinity and their questioning of that of the opposition (Archetti 1992, p. 225).

The Business of Football: The Contribution of this Book

Football clubs in Latin America know very little about their fans, whether those who attend matches or those who watch on television. This is an indication both of the lack of sophisticated management in the industry and also the relative shortage of research on the business aspects of football, in contrast to historical, sociological and anthropological approaches.[39] The chapters in the fourth part of this book thus offer important insights into the state of the South American football business, but also a counterpoint — the failure of the professional women's soccer league in the United States which, in terms of the management and marketing abilities available in the US sports industry, ought not to have fallen into the traps that it did. The overall view that emerges from Gideon Rachman's chapter, supported by the case studies of Argentina and Brazil that follow by Liz Crolley and Vic Duke, Luiz Martins do Melo, and Elena Landau, is that, although football clubs in South America certainly suffer from an adverse economic environment, exacerbated by the globalisation of the football industry and the commercial success of European clubs, there are also clear failings in the transparency and quality of management. Most Latin American clubs do not publish audited accounts, and there have been continual suspicions of corruption and rake-offs on the part of club and federation officials.[40] The management of clubs has also tended to lag far behind that of clubs in Western Europe, although there are beacons of good practice: Elena Landau's chapter outlines that of Atlético Paranaense in Brazil. However, most clubs in South America have failed to recognise the symbiosis apparent in Western Europe between good results on the pitch and good management off it; for the most part, the demands of fans for quick results at any cost have predominated, and governments and tax authorities — to whom a considerable proportion of their debt is often owed — have been complicit in being unwilling to pursue clubs to the point of declaring them insolvent. Few clubs have taken the step towards either outsourcing management to specialist companies or altering their legal status so that they become limited companies accountable to shareholders and perhaps more financially responsible.[41] Especially in the light of Latin American countries' experiences with privatisation, there are real popular fears if private companies take over the management of clubs, and past attempts to do this — as Elena Landau shows for Brazil and Liz Crolley and Vic Duke for Argentina — have been fraught with problems.[42]

The football business in South America is fragile. Even the most famous clubs operate at a much lower level of income than their European counterparts, many of them carry large historic debts, and their ability to remain solvent is handicapped by the difficulties of generating revenue streams of the same type and on the same scale as the major clubs in Europe. One of the two leading Argentine clubs, River Plate, epitomises many of these problems. Reported in mid-2006 to have an outstanding debt of US$20–25 million and an annual operating deficit of US$10 million, the club survives only by selling players overseas or offering shares in their contracts to individuals who wish to speculate on their eventual transfer value. Moreover, the club's president, José María Aguilar, was indicted on charges of evading taxes in order to keep River afloat during the Argentine financial crisis of 2001–03 (*Soccer Investor Daily*, 28 July 2006, 24 August 2006, 3 November 2006, 24 November 2006). In Europe, broadcasting contracts, sponsorship and, in the case of England especially, stadium reconstruction and high ticket prices have brought about a rapid increase in the income of clubs. In South America, in contrast, football remains dependent on television contracts negotiated from a position of weakness *vis-à-vis* media companies like Torneos y Competencias in Argentina or TV Globo in Brazil; sponsorship income which, although rising, falls far short of the leading European clubs; the income from exhibition matches in the United States and East Asia; and player transfers. Ticket prices cannot be raised far without excluding large numbers of fans, and merchandising has little potential in countries with major inequalities of income and little legal protection for brand owners against piracy.

The exceptions to this general picture of business gloom in the Americas are Mexico and the United States. In Mexico, the combination of high attendances, good broadcasting contracts with Televisa and TV Azteca, and the management practices introduced by the companies and entrepreneurs that own many Mexican clubs has created a thriving business that has retained its players and begun to expand into the United States (Kramer 2006). In the United States itself, Major League Soccer was structured on the lines of most professional sports in the country, with a single-entity structure where clubs took the form of franchises, salary caps were imposed, and the management developed long-term plans to lay a firm base for professional soccer before expansion could take place. Since the turn of the century several new soccer-specific stadiums have been constructed, and the league has twice announced plans to expand the number of teams participating. However, MLS is still assumed to have made significant losses in its first decade, and such a structure does not guarantee success if management makes mistakes and audiences diminish, as Katharine Jones shows in her study of WUSA, the women's professional league, in this volume.

While South American football clubs are mired in debt, however, many of the star players exported to Europe are not, and it is this promise of future wealth that encourages the constant flow of talent from poor homes in Latin American cities. The attraction of professional football for much of its audience depends ultimately on skilled players and coaches, yet very few have studied the impact of the increasing flow of footballers from South America to Europe and East Asia. Historically, South American footballers have tended to migrate to the leading footballing nations of Southern Europe — Italy, Spain, and Portugal — where the problems of adaptation to language, culture and climate have not been so great. However, since the 1995 Bosman Judgment that opened Western European clubs to an influx of talent from elsewhere in the world, more players have gone to Northern Europe, where the problems of acclimatisation are that much greater and a poor decision, often at the behest of an agent earning commission on the deal, can wreck a player's career. For this reason, Marcela Mora y Araujo's chapter in this book is all the more important, as she explores — largely on the basis of interviews with the players — the problems that they face and the shortcomings of the English clubs that have recruited them.

The consequences of poor management and the emigration of the best players mean that most clubs depend upon journeymen footballers who never quite achieve the move to the riches of Europe. In terms of the quality of the football on offer, watching South American players in televised matches in the major European leagues makes much more sense than going to matches locally. Alan Gilbert, at the end of his chapter on competitive balance, laments the decline of football in cities such as Montevideo that historically were its cradle. The combination of globalisation and the problematic socio-economic environment of South America have meant that the domestic game has become extremely unattractive to many fans, even if a closely fought championship, historic rivalries or the final stages of the Copa Libertadores can still arouse passions.

Future Directions

This book provides a step along the path to a greater understanding of the rapidly changing nature of football in the Americas, but research in the field is young. The contents, the balance and the omissions of the book all indicate possible future directions for research. There is space here only for a handful of suggestions.

In terms of the geographical and chronological balance of research on football in the Americas, it is clear that the two most important and successful footballing nations in South America — Argentina and Brazil — have both attracted and generated the largest volume of research, and that the history of football elsewhere is much less known. To some extent, this is less serious a problem than a decade ago, thanks to the work of the research network sponsored by CLACSO and coordinated by Pablo Alabarces (Alabarces 2000, 2003). Nonetheless, the serious bibliography on countries like Peru, Chile, Colombia and Mexico is still very sparse, and in most countries there are just one or two pioneering historians and social scientists. Moreover, even for Argentina and Brazil, more is known about the early pre-professional stages of the game than the mid-twentieth century. Few have followed the route pioneered by José Deustua and Susan Stokes in the case of Lima and used oral history techniques to recapture and re-analyse the past. Such methodologies might also contribute to another gap in historical analysis: the development of football tactics, the evolution of distinctive club and national styles of football, and the impact of South American teams and players on the world game. Along with Central Europe (Austria, Hungary and Czechoslovakia), Argentina, Uruguay and Brazil were probably the most innovative countries tactically in the middle third of the twentieth century, a fact that deserves much more exploration than it has received. In the 1950s, at international level, Brazil — along with Hungary — played the most innovative and imaginative football, and with its World Cup victory in 1958, Brazil introduced the world both to a new style of organisation on the pitch and to the benefits of proper scientific preparation of athletes. A further aspect of tactics, touched upon in academic work both on Brazil and Argentina, is the eternal conflict in South American football — more marked, perhaps, than elsewhere — between the desire for flair, artistry and imagination on the one hand and the functionalist requirements of winning matches and tournaments on the other (Archetti 1995b, pp. 202, 213–16).

This brings us back to questions of identities, and the way in which football has fed in to the construction and contestation of identity and culture in the Americas. While work on ethnicity in football has tended to concentrate on Brazil in particular, trends towards globalisation are opening up new questions. The leading international clubs now routinely market themselves to a global fan base which they can reach through television and the internet. In the case of Latin American clubs, the massive emigration of the past two decades to North America and Europe opens new possibilities, but also introduces new threats. The growing importance of exhibition games in the United States, which normally attract large attendances with a high Latino content, has already been mentioned, but other developments may also prove to be significant. One of the most interesting — corresponding to the deliberate marketing of the MLS to Latino communities — has been the entry of Chivas USA (owned by the Guadalajara club of the same name) to play in the MLS. At an international level, CONMEBOL has incorporated Mexican clubs into its flagship club competition, the Copa Libertadores, and extended invitations to CONCACAF countries to compete in the Copa América. Yet there are also threats. In the United States, clubs from Latin America are competing with European clubs to capture this potential international market. Since the turn of the twenty-first century, Barcelona and Real Madrid have made enormous strides in international marketing, targeting South American markets as well as the United States and East Asia. They can build on the Latin American stars in their teams, the reputation of the Spanish league, linguistic and cultural affinities, and the extensive coverage of European leagues on cable television. All these changes have profound implications for the business of football in the Americas.

These trends also raise questions about the consumption and commodification of football. In Britain, particularly, clubs have come under attack for both the profit-taking of private individuals and the increasing alienation that many traditional working-class fans feel as the game becomes increasingly commercialised (Conn 1997, 2004). Is the sport escaping from its roots in the poorer sections of society? Some work on the growth of soccer in the United States has linked it not so much to the Latino immigrant communities as to its appeal to suburban middle-class parents who were searching for a sport for children that was non-violent, safe and multicultural (Andrews et al. 1997; Markovits & Hellerman 2003). In the case of

Brazil, Sérgio Leite Lopes has also drawn attention to the increasing proportion of top footballers in Brazil coming from middle-class backgrounds, arguing that this, together with pride in the national team's achievements on the world stage, has created an inversion of traditional hierarchies in the sense that working-class activities have helped to define the identity and aspirations of the middle classes (Leite Lopes 1997, pp. 76–79). However, assessing the changing social basis of both professional footballers and fans, and hence the consumption of football in Latin America, demands the development of much more ethnographic and longitudinal research, especially amongst key middle-class groups such as the student communities which historically have been closely linked with the development of professional football in South America.[43]

A final question worth noting is the issue of gender and football. Janet Lever (1983) highlighted the exclusion of women from most football activity in Brazil; indeed, one reviewer asked sharply how she could argue that football integrated Brazil when her evidence indicated that half the population was marginalised by it (Corsino 1984). Women were forbidden by law to play football in Brazil until 1979, and their participation had hardly progressed at the time that Lever published (Votre & Mourão 2003). Yet the recent growth of women's football there, despite male prejudice against it, has been remarkable, undermining the notion that women's football succeeds only where men's football has not become hegemonic.[44] The contrast between the picture painted by Lever on the basis of research conducted in the late 1970s and the role of women's football a generation later thus raises new questions about changing gender relations and sport in Brazil. The growth of football on television and the increasing commercialisation of the game are also clearly having an impact on women's interest in men's football. While relatively few women attend matches in Latin America, in part because of the threat of violence and the undercurrent of macho sexuality discussed by Roger Magazine in his chapter here, the evidence of marketing surveys and the pitch of television advertisements suggest that consumer goods firms and broadcasters detect a substantial female audience for football. Recent work on Argentina has suggested that women's attendance at matches began to grow in the 1990s, challenging male representations of the sport (Rodríguez 2005). In the United States, the female interest in football, and the success of the national women's team, was sufficient to stimulate the attempt to found a professional women's league, even though it quickly failed. The relationship between gender and football in the Americas is thus one of potentially significant change, and also one which is beginning to attract some interesting academic research.

Notes

1 For a journalist's rediscovery of what had happened to the 'Beautiful Team', see Jenkins (1998).

2 On the rise and decline of Uruguayan football, see Giulianotti (1999a).

3 For more on the origins of Alianza Lima and its ethnic/*barrio* background, see the chapter by Panfichi and Thieroldt in this volume.

4 On an early Peruvian rivalry, between Alianza Lima and Atlético Chalaco, which always involved large numbers of travelling supporters coming from the nearby port of Callao, see Deustua et al. (1986, pp. 144–45).

5 See the chapter in this volume by José Sergio Leite Lopes. On the continued suffering of Barbosa, see Bellos (2002, pp. 56–57).

6 On Argentines' pride in the development of an attractive and effective style of football, see also Karush (2003).

7 A popular chant at English football grounds in the 1990s, especially when a lower-division team was playing unexpectedly well, was 'Brazil… It's just like watching Brazil' to the tune of *Blue Moon*.

8 Gordon and Helal (2001, p. 142) see Brazilian football's Golden Age as lasting from the onset of professionalisation in 1933 to the World Cup victory of 1970.

9 The president of Boca Juniors at the time that La Bombonera was constructed was the son-in-law of President Justo.

10 The cry was for direct elections when Brazil returned to democracy, rather than the indirect, more easily controllable system that the military favoured.

11 Increasing spectator violence in Brazil has been associated with the growth of the similar *torcidas organizadas*: see Gordon and Helal (2001, p. 149).

12 Attendance figures for matches in Latin America are often problematic because frequently the *socios* of the club are not counted in the gate. On the decline of attendances at Brazilian football matches, see Gordon & Helal (2001, pp. 149 and 153).

13   At current exchange rates, this was worth between US$4,000 and US$6,000 a match.

14   On the relationship between the CBF and Nike and the inquiry conducted by the Chamber of Deputies, see Rebelo & Torres (2001). For a British journalist's discussion of corruption in Brazilian football, see Bellos (2002, Chs 14–15). On the foreign investments of 1997–99, see Elena Landau's chapter in this volume.

15   On the case of Racing, see the chapter by Liz Crolley and Vic Duke in this volume. On earlier cases, see Mason (1995, p. 75).

16   On the contemporary business problems of football clubs in Argentina and Brazil, see the chapter by Gideon Rachman in this volume.

17   I am grateful to Oliver Seitz for this information.

18   For a brief biography of Grondona, see <www.conmebol.com/comunicados_ver.jsp?id=2607&slangab=S>; on Teixeira, see Bellos (2002, pp. 342–56).

19   One survey in 1998 estimated that 71 per cent of the Latin American population watched football regularly on television, with a high of 85 per cent in Brazil. There was little distinction in terms of class, age or gender, although there were substantial differences between countries. See 'Watching Soccer on Television in Latin America', <www.zonalatina.com/Zldata117.htm>.

20   On Juan Figer, see Goos (2006). On Pini Zahavi and his interests in South America, see Jackson (2006).

21   On the Brazilian case, see Elena Landau's chapter in this volume.

22   In contrast, in Central America, the Hispanic Caribbean and Venezuela, baseball became the dominant sport due to the more substantial US presence at the turn of the century.

23   For an insightful discussion of the linkages between football and the construction of national and masculine identities in Costa Rica before and during the 2002 World Cup, see Sandoval-García (2005).

24   Note, however, that the leading Buenos Aires clubs have often offered a staging post for players from elsewhere in South America: examples are Nolberto Solano from Peru, Marcelo Salas from Chile and Diego Forlán from Uruguay. Transfers of players to Argentina did not normally bring much reward to the clubs in other countries that had trained them.

25   On some of the problems of forming professional leagues in a country as geographically extensive as the United States, in contrast to the ease with which this could be done in England, see Cain & Haddock (2005).

26 It has been argued that it was precisely because it was not seen as a male sport that women's soccer in the United States has been so successful: see Markovits & Hellerman (2003, pp. 14–16, 27–29).

27 On the failure of WUSA, see the chapter by Katherine Jones in this volume.

28 On the assumption of many radicals that sport is the modern-day 'opiate of the people', see the chapter by Richard Giulianotti in this volume. Ironically, Antonio Gramsci and Che Guevara, two of the icons of the Latin American left in the 1970s, both loved football.

29 For further discussion of the ways in which social scientists have viewed football, see Alabarces 2004, and Richard Giulianotti's chapter in this volume.

30 On Mário Filho, see Gordon and Halal (2001, pp. 144–45). Ramírez published a series of articles in the Argentine historical magazine *Todo es Historia*. Sánchez León published a series of articles in the Peruvian journal *Debate*.

31 Interestingly, Lever's book was criticised much more heavily in reviews by scholars based in England, who had a much closer acquaintance with the sport and sociological work on it, than by her colleagues in the United States: see Cashmore (1984) and Humphrey & Tomlinson (1986).

32 The main exception to this generalisation is Aidar et al. (2000).

33 Menotti incurred considerable criticism from the left for his tacit endorsement of the military government; he had been appointed coach of the national team after the 1974 World Cup but remained in post despite the coup.

34 A *pibe*, in Buenos Aires, is a small boy from the shanty towns who has no sense of responsibility and confronts authority through cunning and improvisation; a *malandro* in Brazil was originally a slave trickster, and has also come to mean someone who achieves his ends through cunning.

35 One distinct advantage of the unpopularity of soccer in the United States is that researchers in this field have not suffered from the attempts of the US academy, especially some of its more radical members, to impose their own agenda on Latin American studies. In this respect, the study of football contrasts with many other areas of history and the social sciences.

36 The expansion in the number of national teams participating in the final stages has created more opportunities for surprising success in the CONCACAF and CONMEBOL qualifiers. Other examples, which have not yet attracted academic research, would include Jamaica

in 1998, or Ecuador and Trinidad/Tobago in 2006. On a later Costa Rican example, see Sandoval-García (2005).

37 The referee who sent off Rattín was German. The FIFA official in charge of allocating referees to matches was Ken Aston, an Englishman. Argentina's continuing economic problems have frequently been explained by populist politicians in terms of conspiracy by bankers and governments in the developed world.

38 On the Pumas fans, see Roger Magazine's chapter in this volume.

39 Given the general sophistication of the sports industry in the United States, one can assume that the commercial managers of MLS clubs know rather more, though this remains to be investigated.

40 Since 2004, Brazilian clubs playing in the national championship have been forced by law to publish their accounts, enabling Casual Auditores to publish an annual report on Brazilian club finances along the lines of Deloitte & Touche's valuable reports on European football (Casual Auditores 2006a, 2006b).

41 An exception is ColoColo in Chile, which was rescued from bankruptcy in 2005 by a restructuring that put it under the control of a limited company, Blanco y Negro SA. Blanco y Negro subsequently raised US$32 million through a public offer of shares. In Argentina, Racing Club was similarly restructured and its management put under the control of Blanquiceleste SA.

42 Since these chapters were written, further questions have arisen concerning the investment made by a shadowy London company, Media Sports Investments (MSI), in Corinthians of São Paulo. In August 2006, MSI transferred two Corinthians players whose registrations they owned, the Argentine internationals Javier Mascherano and Carlos Tévez, to West Ham United. Shortly afterwards it was reported that the Brazilian authorities were investigating accusations of money-laundering by MSI (*Soccer Investor Daily Report*, 24 October 2006). See also *The Times*, 1 September 2006.

43 On students as fans, see the chapters by Roger Magazine and Aldo Panfichi and Jorge Thieroldt in this volume. For an interesting historical discussion of university rivalries in professional football in Chile, see Obregón (1981).

44 For this argument, see Markovits & Hellerman (2003).

PART II:

A CENTURY OF FOOTBALL IN THE AMERICAS

2

Football, South America and Globalisation: Conceptual Paths

Richard Giulianotti

South America was one of the earliest recipients of — and certainly had the most spectacular success in — the early globalisation of football. The British helped spark South American football interest in three specific ways. The first was through education: British-run schools adopted the game, led notably by Alexander Watson Hutton in Buenos Aires, while expatriates like the Brazilian Charles Miller returned from British schooling with an evangelical passion for football (Mason 1995). The second channel of influence was through investment and trade connections: British railway workers in cities like Montevideo, or British seafarers in South American ports, demonstrated some early football skills to local peoples. Third, the game was promoted through tours: teams like The Corinthians or Southampton landed in South America to tackle local opponents and promote football further. While those early inspirations were certainly significant, the intensive cultural receptivity of South American peoples towards football has been at least of equal importance, so that the game quickly became by far the dominant sporting form in the region.

South American football is now heavily engaged within global football culture. According to the Swedish anthropologist Ulf Hannerz, globalisation is marked by the emergence of a global ecumene, where ecumene is defined as a 'region of persistent cultural interaction and exchange' (Hannerz 1989, p. 66). We might suggest that we inhabit, more precisely, a 'global football ecumene', with South America as a crucial element of such cultural interaction and exchange.

Globalisation registers an intensified 'cosmopolitanism' among football followers, as they become more knowledgeable and appreciative of football in other societies, in aesthetic, institutional, historical and economic terms. In part, this rising cosmopolitanism can be one of the cultural weapons with which struggles for 'distinction' are fought, in Pierre Bourdieu's sense, as football followers seek to claim greater cultural capital over their friends and rivals through a claim to broader factual knowledge and critical understanding of the global game (Bourdieu 1984). Thus the levels of knowledge and understanding of football in other societies, such as those in South America and Africa, can become referents for judging the degrees of cosmopolitanism among followers of the game.

Moreover, as the work of Arjun Appadurai (1996) indicates, through mass media and mass migration, fantasy and imagination have gained central ground within our global age. Football — and in particular Latin American football — has contributed much to the global football imagination, to soccer-centric 'world memories' (cf. Smith 1999). Televised images of international football events fill the imaginations and memories of diverse peoples. Football is also an important cultural medium through which diasporic populations across the world can reimagine their cultural and national identities — for example, with regard to culturally 'frozen' conceptions of their 'home' nation, or with reference to the hybrid emergent cultures within their new environs.

This chapter is generally theoretical, suggesting how we might read South American football through the critical optic of globalisation theory. It draws heavily upon sociological and anthropological perspectives on globalisation to argue for a balanced account that integrates more 'structural' and 'socio-cultural' frameworks into readings of the South American game. It begins with a brief discussion of the historical aspects of globalisation relative to South American football before turning to consider these more structural and socio-cultural perspectives in turn.

Football and Historical Globalisation: South American Dimensions

Turning to what we mean by globalisation, three basic points can be derived from the work of Roland Robertson (1992). First, by way of succinct definition, globalisation possesses subjective and objective elements. Subjectively, we increasingly imagine the world as a single place. Objectively, globalisation is marked by the increased compression of time and space — most obviously through the communication of symbols and information via global media networks. In that sense, Europeans imagine South American football as having greater proximity, as being part of an increasingly apparent 'football world', as reflected through mundane everyday media coverage of the main issues, controversies and rumours surrounding Latin American celebrities, teams and competitions.

Second, terms such as 'the global' or 'the universal' are often set out in direct opposition or contradistinction towards terms denoting specificities, such as 'the local' or 'particularities' or 'singularities'. However, these binary oppositions overlook the interdependencies between the global *and* the local. In many ways, globalisation processes help to give stronger definition to conceptions of the 'local', to intensify the 'relativisation' of identities. Indeed, senses of locality and particularity have been globalised as cultural expectations. International football events, for example, provide continental or global platforms for the advanced expression of forms of national identification among different supporter groups, through the display of flags and team shirts, anthems and songs, group association and particular body techniques. Thus European football tourists arrive at the World Cup finals with great anticipation of their likely encounters with the colourful, sensual and different fan cultures from South American nations.

Third, globalisation has undergone various historical phases since the fifteenth century. The first two phases, arising prior to the 1870s, do not impact directly upon football history. The shape of the next three phases is heavily influenced by the interplay of four 'reference points': individuals, the nation, international society and 'humankind'. It may be useful to look at these historical phases in a little more detail.

The third phase of globalisation, the 'take-off phase', runs from the 1870s to the 1920s. During this period, football 'took off' as an organised sport, undergoing massive international diffusion. British 'mini-globalisation' ensured that trade, development and educational connections spread football in South America, notably in the growing urban centres, the national and regional capitals such as Buenos Aires, Montevideo and São Paulo (Mason 1995).

Football enabled *individuals* (males) to explore and advance their corporeal capabilities, and to engage in alternative competitive relations with others. At this time, *national* identities were constructed through the invention of national traditions. Football became part of that process through establishing favoured national styles, constructing derby oppositions and building national symbolism through international fixtures. As Eduardo Archetti (2003) has demonstrated, South American sports styles are closely connected to national dances: Argentina to the Tango, Brazil to the Samba, Cuba to the *Danzón*, and so on. National distinctiveness was also asserted through 'vernacularisation', in particular the translation of football terms and the names of football associations from English into the dominant national language.[1] For example, the Argentine football association switched to a Spanish title in 1912, and became the Asociación Argentina de Football. International society took off with the founding of the South American football governing body, the Confederación Sudamericana de Fútbol (CONMEBOL), in 1916, and the growth of international fixtures and tournaments. Ideas of cross-cultural *humankind* were explored through struggles to advance the social inclusion of marginalised groups — particularly the lower classes and non-whites. In Peru, for example, the multi-ethnic, lower-class club of Alianza Lima struggled to establish itself against elite clubs, notably Universitario de Deportes (Benavides 2000; Millones et al. 2002).

The fourth phase of globalisation, the 'struggle for hegemony', runs from the 1920s to the late 1960s. In general, this period witnessed global warfare, the Cold War, new systems of global governance (notably the United Nations), nationalism, civil rights struggles and the rise of the Third World. During this period, football became increasingly important to the establishing of the nation via international competition. Uruguay, for example, was moulded as a nation to a significant degree by its World Cup successes in 1930 and 1950. Football became a nationalist ideological tool of authoritarian populists (notably Perón, and then the military juntas in Argentina and elsewhere) (Scher 1996, pp. 153–201). But it also opened up dilemmas in South America as to whether the 'European' or 'modern' way was appropriate in this part of the world, whether in football culture or in the wider society more generally (Alabarces et al. 2001). The cross-cultural inclusion of non-whites became central to football struggles, notably in Brazil. Subsequently, Latin American football teams have come to project a spectacular football style that is central to the emerging global aesthetic within the game.

The fifth phase of globalisation, the 'uncertainty' phase, runs from the late 1960s through to the current period. Through this time, we have witnessed the end of the Cold War, the rise of alternative politics, multiculturalism, ideas of world citizenship, new kinds of global institution and more expansive media systems. Through this period in football, we have witnessed the massive migration of Latin American players into 'core' societies, notably in Europe but also in wealthier emerging football markets in North America and Japan. Typically, nations like Argentina and Uruguay have over 400 players plying their trade abroad (Crolley & Duke 2001; Giulianotti 1999b). We have witnessed also the qualitative transformation of football-centred imaginations through the mass media, notably since the 1970 World Cup finals became the first major international tournament to be televised in colour. Since then, the techniques and player formations of South American teams have become more familiar to world audiences, heavily influencing the practical sports reasoning of players and the mental images of spectators at the everyday level across the globe. South America also remains the major destiny for European coaches and spectators embarking on a cosmopolitan quest for cultural diversity, for technical exoticism, within international football. Yet South America has also contributed crucially to the contemporary *Realpolitik* of world football. Through the rise of João Havelange, Ricardo Teixeira and Julio Grondona in particular, international football's governing bodies have become increasingly commercial in orientation and murky in their financial transparency (Sugden & Tomlinson 1998). Football's world system has become more fluid through the intensified international flows of labour, capital, images and information. South American football officials, financiers, media correspondents, agents, marketers and players all play significant roles within this maelstrom of movements. Yet, reflecting football's connections with humanitarianism, South American players like Ronaldo have become global symbolic referents for transcultural dialogue by endorsing the work of international non-governmental organisations.

Against this historical backdrop, we can begin to analyse the globalisation of football in more critical, theoretical terms. In general, there tend to be two philosophically opposed approaches towards this problem. On one hand, there is the more structuralist approach that adopts a comparatively deterministic reading of globalisation with a more abstracted notion of power relations. On the other hand, there is the more socio-cultural approach which accords greater freedom to the critical agency of social actors.

Theorising Football's Globalisation: Structuralist Approaches

There are three strands to structural approaches to the problem, which need to be analysed in turn.

Critiques of Development

This line of analysis generally attacks inequities in the world system, arguing that South America and other 'peripheral' nations are squeezed economically and culturally by 'core' or 'First World' nations. These arguments are understandably critical of the older 'modernisation theories' which assumed that poorer nations could quickly modernise, democratise and raise all their citizens' living standards dramatically if they followed the historical paths already mapped out by European and North American nations. There are different strands to arguments of this kind.

First, the *anti-development thesis* of social scientists like Serge Latouche (1996, pp. 129–30) and Arturo Escobar (1994) posit that development has inescapably nefarious, root consequences within non-Western cultures. Development and modernisation are seen as part of a Western 'techno-economic machine' which systematically destroys indigenous cultures.

Football has inevitably been part of this 'anti-culture', contributing to the obliteration of indigenous peoples and their pre-colonial cultures. Football and sport generally reflect the hegemony of Western values, such as strong competition, the need to break records and the 'win at all costs' mentality. If this approach turns to look at politics *within* the world football system, it is likely to argue that South American football culture should resist the modernisation path taken by

European football nations. This latter, 'developed' path leads to excessive seriousness and sterility, and will not succeed for Latin Americans in the way that it has for Europeans.

This position is analytically impractical in wishing that Westernisation had never happened. While globalisation can lead to the global *dis*connection of the most impoverished societies, the shift of non-Western societies into a kind of transnational closed economy would surely be even more harmful to their citizens. The thesis also underplays the extent to which the everyday activities of South Americans are *practically* orientated and so combine both local and Western forms of cultural knowledge.

Second, the *under-development* thesis is most obviously associated with André Gunder Frank (1971). This thesis posits that South American societies have only modernised through the creation of a dependency relationship with northern, 'core' economies. As a process, under-development has meant that post-1945 global inequalities have intensified. In football terms, this thesis would mean that the South American game (notably at club level) has declined in terms of its technical standards, competitive capability and financial health, as the whole region has become increasingly dependent on the rich Northern Hemisphere, particularly the purchase of southern players by European clubs. Moreover, it could be argued that European football clubs benefit from South America's under-development: if football is seen as one of the few ways that poor South Americans can escape from poverty, then these clubs will have a constantly replenished reservoir of young, eager and cheap talent to exploit. More broadly, this thesis would seek confirmation in the deteriorating South American football infrastructure (especially the stadiums), compared with the refurbished grounds of Europe. However, the under-development thesis underplays the extent to which economic growth and foreign direct investment have been possible within the South American 'periphery' (Halliday 2002, p. 83). Similarly, it pays inadequate attention to cross-cultural flows between South America and 'core' nations, notably European ones.

Football and Endo/Neo-colonialism

Here, the term 'endo-colonialism' denotes how elites within specific South American nations establish and reproduce oppressive relations with the majority of their fellow citizens. The term 'neo-colonialism' refers to the arrangement by which the Bretton Woods institutions (the International Monetary Fund and the World Bank), transnational corporations and northern states still manage to control the economies — and thus social policies and cultural life — within 'independent' South American states. There are different strands to this argument.

The first approach might be termed *False Needs 1* or *Authoritarian Populism*. This argument would posit that sport and other popular cultural domains tend to be relatively straightforward, ideological media through which ruling elites are able to harness the masses' political energies and thereby maintain oppressive social relations. For example, South American military regimes and Peronist-style political leaders have arguably patronised sport in order to promote the 'national-popular' and thereby germinate support for the ruling elites.

This thesis assumes too readily that football followers are cultural dopes who can be manipulated ideologically. There is much evidence that the South American masses expressed dissent within football towards military juntas. More generally, while a diversity of political forces have sought to organise and 'normalise' their peoples according to specific ideologies, the results are typically unsuccessful, notably among male football followers (see, for example, Rosemblatt 2000).

A different argument, which might be termed *False Needs 2* or the *Culture-ideology of Consumerism* emerges from the work of Leslie Sklair (1995), and argues that the 'culture-ideology of consumerism' is promoted through South American sports. A key role is played by the 'transnational capitalist class', which includes key decision-makers in major corporations, bourgeois consumers, and political leaders, who all promote Western consumer norms that benefit Western transnational corporations.

While Sklair's sociological analysis of the transnational capitalist class and transnational corporations is strong, he resorts to a 'false needs' argument, associated with Herbert Marcuse (1964), to explain the relationship of popular culture to capitalism. The emphasis is therefore again on how sport, as an element of popular culture under capitalism, appears as a political diversion, a form of mass cultural sedation. Sklair's analysis would be enhanced by amendment through exploring, first, the relationships of particular cultural practices and traditions to specific social classes, and then, second, the impact of commodification upon those cultural activities.

A number of arguments arise from critiques of contemporary neo-liberalism, the first of which might be termed *neo-colonialism*. According to this position, South America's elite athletes are treated like its natural resources — such as coffee or bananas — by powerful Western sports corporations and their rich markets. The best South American athletes are a 'raw material' that is mined, refined and exported to the wealthiest markets overseas; the inferior residue, rejected by exporters, is left for domestic consumption.

Certainly, there is no doubt that the overseas migration of thousands of South American players has damaged the standard of domestic football. However, while world football player markets are heavily skewed in favour of 'core' nations, the richest clubs are not so systematic in expropriating the finest South American football resources. A few 'partnerships' do exist between South American clubs and wealthy ones in Europe and Japan. Nevertheless, many European coaches favour recruitment only of those players already proven in South America, or suspect that South American talents are 'opaque products' only suited to the South American game (cf. Clark & O'Connor 1997).

A second critique of neo-liberalism might be termed the *Brazilianisation* argument. This is suggested by Beck (2000), and points to the extreme scenario whereby the free-market economic system produces globally the vast, caste-like social inequalities associated with the worst aspects of Brazil. In football, Brazilianisation occurs through the extreme spatial segregation of different social castes within the stadium, to the extent that the poorest communities are excluded. The decision by Brazil's football club presidents to raise the minimum admission prices to league fixtures in order to attract wealthier fans at the expense of poorer supporters provides empirical support for the eponymous thesis (*The Guardian*, 17 December 2003).

Brazilianisation is at least a useful heuristic model against which we may focus analysis on heightening inequalities. However, in the study of South American football, it has ambiguous potential: should it always relate to Brazil's societal aspects (vast inequalities) or should we consider the partial, historical exception of football culture (traditionally cross-class and relatively unifying)?

Another variety of argument related to neoliberalism concerns *economic globalisation*. This analysis focuses on how economic globalisation from the 1980s onwards has led to the abandonment of the interventionist state, the diminution of public services, intensified inequalities, immense financial instability and the advanced political economic influence of Western corporations and institutions within South American nations. Consider the economic crises in Argentina, Bolivia, Uruguay and Venezuela, amongst others. In Argentina and Uruguay, currency collapses provoked major revolts among the middle classes. In Argentina, particularly, football played a symbolic role as the public turned to the national team's colours to signify solidarity in the midst of economic and social meltdown.

There are two other sets of arguments in the structuralist mould which require consideration, the first of which concerns *regional power systems*. Immanuel Wallerstein's 'world systems theory' divided the world into 'core', 'semi-peripheral' and 'peripheral' nations, with South American societies grouped in the latter (Wallerstein 1974). A more regionally focused analysis highlights the political imbalances *within* South America. Thus, in football, we find that the largest (or core) South American economies of Brazil and Argentina tend to exploit the smaller, semi-peripheral economies of Chile, Uruguay and Peru, and (less concertedly) the more peripheral economies of Bolivia and Paraguay — for example, through elite player recruitment. Moreover, within nations we find that the metropolitan cores, such as Buenos Aires and Porto Alegre, exploit semi-peripheral and peripheral locations, such as the interior of Argentina and North-East of Brazil, for players.

A different approach relates to the suggestion that in South America there is an especially *weak civil society*. In this approach, the absence of a strong civil society means that relations between elites and intellectuals are particularly important, notably at personal level and in terms of patronage. Elites are prone to 'cuddling' intellectuals as a proxy for public approval of political authority. Thus South American intellectuals ought to endeavour to build up the public sphere by opening up the rule of elites to democratic scrutiny and accountability. In South American sport, this means having open public debates and inquiries into issues such as hooliganism and corruption, rather than having consultation restricted to a few intellectuals or academics. This argument acquires greater acuity through the fact that Gramsci's work is particularly influential within Latin American social science.

Cultural Identity

There are two prongs to this, both of which point to South America's cultural disempowerment.

This first approach, *Orientalism*, involves developing the arguments of the late Edward Said (1995), and applying these to the non-Occidental setting of South America. In his variation of Foucauldian theory, Said argued that the West's long-standing cultural imperialism served to construct vast systems of knowledge about the 'Orient. In turn, Western myths about the Orient were internalised by Orientals as part of the latter's collective identity. As the West sees itself as rational, organised, scientific, cool and methodical, so 'Orientals' are presented as expressive, unpredictable, magical and hypnotic. In sport, the West sees itself as producing linear or patterned forms of play, whereas Orientals engage in rhythmic (circular) or haphazard shapes of play.

It is possible to apply Said's thesis to football in such a way that the 'Orient' includes South America, in particular the hybrid 'Lusotropical civilisation' of Brazil. The pioneering Brazilian sociologist Gilberto Freyre believed that Brazil's *mulatto* players possessed an exceptional technical skill at football (Freyre 1964). More broadly, the South American cultural emphasis on dribbling and balletic skills, technical magic and unpredictable team play can be seen as an Oriental football culture that stands in contradistinction to the more regimented, predictable and comparatively artless displays of European teams.

A different approach is that of *cultural synchronisation*. Arising from the arguments of Cees Hamelink (1983) and others, this indicates that globalisation is homogenising global culture, with Western cultural products rampant, thereby obliterating cultural difference in South America and beyond. In football, it might be claimed that playing styles and supporter practices are becoming homogenised. More seriously, and in line with Sklair's arguments, world football

may be synchronising around an increasingly consumerist relationship towards sport, dominated by the advertising images of Western
transnational corporations.

There is no doubt that the 'hypercommodification' of football is
advancing in South America as on other continents (cf. Walsh &
Giulianotti 2001), but one should nevertheless be sceptical about the
claim that cultural 'homogenisation' results, unless one restricts such
'synchronisation' to the shallow level of the banal axiom that 'football is the global game'.

There is no space to dissect all of these arguments in full detail.
However, as the discussion above indicates, there is significant
strength in arguments relating to the structural impacts of economic
globalisation upon South America, the need to recognise the
complexity of regional hierarchies within and between nations, and
the consequences of a weak civil society for democratic participation
and political reform. The Orientalism thesis at least accounts for the
social construction of cultural 'difference' with reference to power
relations, and it deserves stronger elaboration. An initial weakness in
the Orientalism thesis, however, is that the Orient's self-knowledge,
rather than weakening its relationship to the Occident, actually seems
to benefit the erstwhile 'dependent' region. After all, the
'Orientalised' South American sides have been most successful in
winning World Cup finals and inter-continental challenge matches at
club level. Moreover, the Orientalist thesis, like the other structuralist arguments outlined above, is inclined towards a deterministic
reading of football cultures, such that human agency appears as a
relatively marginal ontological phenomenon.

However, the limitations of that general deterministic stance are
highlighted when we consider the influential structuralist argument
that is missing, for empirical reasons, from those addressed above.
This is, of course, the *Americanisation* thesis — that is, the argument
that the political and economic hegemony of the United States at
global level is promoting the dominant position of North American
cultural products, practices and tastes across the world. Yet the
Americanisation thesis is absent here precisely because the United
States has not been able to determine popular sporting tastes within
its nearest spheres of influence, through the Americas, as well as in

Europe. While very popular at grassroots levels in the United States, football is not a 'national' sport compared with American gridiron football, baseball, basketball or even ice hockey. Conversely, the reluctance of other nations, including South American ones, to absorb passively these favoured US sporting practices provides strong empirical counter-evidence to refute the Americanisation thesis. If the world's dominant nation cannot purposefully shape or mould the cultural habits and identities of poorer peoples south of its borders, then we should conclude that we ought to explore more action-orientated analyses of football culture in South America, which give more attention to the agency of South Americans themselves.

Theorising Football's Globalisation: Socio-Cultural Approaches

Three of the more socio-cultural approaches that are significant to the academic study of South American football are considered in this section.

The first is what Jonathan Friedman (1994) terms the 'cultural life-force' or vitality that requires application and consideration within football, particularly in the South American case. Football is a game in which the exact activities of a match are largely unpredictable. Thus we need to consider in part the role of *improvisation*, as a reflection of playful human agency, in the everyday construction of football culture. Improvisation operates at different levels, most obviously in the corporeal creativity of players, the dribbling or balletic arts of the most renowned South American footballers. But we also have more collective social improvisation — for example, in supporter songs or team passing patterns or tactics. New interpretations and meanings surrounding football are generated, as marked through the emergence of new technical terms to describe play, or fresh forms of identity within the game. Such improvisation inspires the collective, processual articulations of the cultural life-force that pulsates through football.

One implication of such an approach concerns centre–periphery relations. It was noted earlier that the political and economic structures of the modern world broadly place peripheral cultures on the defensive. However, football allows the periphery to 'talk back', to reverse the apparent trend of meaning flows so that the erstwhile marginal societies become communicatively active. Thus, across the world, we have the imagined emulation of South American football culture, perhaps most humorously in Europe through the 'Blue Brazil' nickname that has been attached to the semi-professional Scottish league team, Cowdenbeath.

A second socio-cultural approach concerns football and the local–global interface. Socio-cultural terms such as 'glocalisation' (Robertson 1992), 'creolisation' (Hannerz 1992) and, perhaps most importantly here, 'hybridisation', capture the active role of local agents in interpreting and reinterpreting global cultural forms according to local needs and resources. Eduardo Archetti's superb study of Argentina provides a telling demonstration of this, through his reference to the 'hybridity' of Argentine sports culture — that is, where hybridity is understood as producing a new and vital form of cultural life from the fusion of British, Spanish, Italian and other cultural influences within the new material environment of South America (Archetti 1998b).

The third approach concerns deterritorialisation and the global imagination. Much of the theorisation of globalisation focuses on the disembedding of cultural practices from any 'fixed' territorial settings (Tomlinson 1996). The hybridity of South American football highlights the long-term nature of deterritorialisation. Migration and the international media promote this deterritorialisation through the interpenetration of South American and European football players, teams, images and ideas. But we need also to consider the making of South American football beyond its spatial confines. What of the millions of Latino football fans who live in the United States? How do they imagine their cultural and national identities in respect of their American context? And what about the cultural politics between these Latinos and those who have remained in the 'home' nations?

Concluding Comments

In symmetry with the cultural history of South American football, there is a strong case for a 'hybrid' theoretical analysis that combines structural and socio-cultural dimensions. Certainly, the impacts of neoliberal globalisation place South American football within a weak economic position compared with that of the game in the leading industrialised nations. The nature of regional hierarchies, the history of weak civil societies and the 'Orientalist' dimensions of Latin American play add a particular complexity to the manifestation of South American socio-economic relations with more powerful regions. Yet some empirical knowledge of football in South America draws us to appreciate the compelling importance of socio-cultural perspectives relative to contemporary globalisation processes. The hybridity of Latin American football cultures should be viewed not as a regionally specific curiosity, but as emblematic of broader trans-formations that are reshaping the global game.

The work of Nestor García Canclini (1995) has drawn particular attention to the cultural consequences of Latin American migration in North and Central America. García Canclini's focus is typically on the hybrid cultures that emerge in border locations such as Tijuana (on the Mexico–United States border). Yet, given the global impacts of migration, mediation and cultural hybridisation, we may all be said to inhabit some kind of border-style culture. Even among migrant peoples living in the midst of rapid urbanisation and highly unpredictable social changes, there are intensive attempts to 'reterritorialise' these spaces as cultural homes. As Latinos become the largest minority in the United States, we may ask how the hybrid culture of these migrant peoples is reflected within football. Do they work to construct new football clubs, cultures, and loyalties that represent these 'home' border identities? Or do we find that these migrants maintain their support for the old teams 'back home', to the extent that these clubs continue to be projections for the old 'structures of feeling' or 'imagined communities' within the neighbourhoods of Botafogo, Avellaneda, Santos, and so on? These are emerging questions that are particularly intriguing in the light of the global cultural complexity that is showcased within and beyond South American football.

Note

1   Appadurai (1996) deploys the term 'vernacularisation', particularly in regard to the 'indigenisation' of cricket in India.

3

From Dreams to Reality:
The Economics and Geography of Football Success

Alan Gilbert

Football, long a business of a kind, has become a much larger enterprise in terms of both turnover and the globalisation of transactions. Television coverage and international air travel have made this possible. Today, the best teams in Europe contain a majority of foreign players, are increasingly managed by foreign coaches, and are marketed rather like cars or fashion goods. Less affluent teams are tending to fall by the wayside and now compete only for scraps. This has implications not only for football itself, but also for local and national culture.

The globalisation of football has increased the sport's glamour and the publicity attracted to it. Much of this attention is focused on the *galácticos* in clubs such as Real Madrid, Manchester United and AC Milan, although there is still considerable interest in some of the smaller teams. Globalisation has also improved the quality of today's teams: the most successful are almost certainly better than any in the past. Unfortunately, the price that has been paid is high: teams from small towns have little chance of winning the major titles, teams from poor cities are unlikely to be successful, and in international competitions the odds against teams from poor countries are increasing. As such, football has ceased to be a game about dreams and has become more like investing on the Stock Exchange — uncertain in terms of results but certainly not a realistic option for the poor.

If football is more of a global business than it once was, how has this affected football in Latin America? This chapter considers three main issues: the relationship between size of city and football success;

the increasing tendency for players to earn their living abroad; and the impact of these processes on local interest in football.

Successful Football Clubs Come from Large Cities

Europe

One of the joys of football is — or at least used to be — that a successful team sometimes comes from a small city. Perhaps the best European examples over the last couple of decades have been Ipswich Town and Blackburn Rovers in England, Auxerre in France, and more recently Chievo Verona in Italy. Of course, even in Europe, teams from small cities have rarely won league championships. The champions of Scotland have nearly always come from Glasgow; the champions of Italy from Milan, Turin or Rome; and the champions of England from London, Liverpool or Manchester. In the past, this supremacy derived from gate receipts — the main source of club income. In this respect, large cities have always had a big advantage over other places because, with more inhabitants, they could expect to attract more people to watch a successful team. In some cities, of course, local rivalries might cut into this advantage because too many local teams emerged in a particular conurbation, spreading local talent and support too thinly. They competed fiercely with one another, and in the process cut the fan-base of each of the metropolitan clubs. In general, though, it was clubs from big cities that won.

Today, the advantages of big cities are even greater because the revenue threshold that has to be crossed before success can be achieved is much higher than before. Since the elimination of the maximum wage as a result of the Bosman Judgment in 1995, and the relaxation of European rules on non-national players in 2001, the minimum price of success has risen in line with the total wage bill (Polley 1997, p. 53).[1]

This is demonstrated by what has been happening in the English league. In the 25 years before 1979, teams from London, Leeds, Liverpool and Manchester won the (English) Football League Division 1 Championship regularly. However, there were seven instances of teams from smaller cities winning Division 1: Wolverhampton Wanderers (three times), Burnley, Ipswich Town,

Derby County and Nottingham Forest. Since 1979, however, only two teams from outside London, Leeds, Liverpool and Manchester have won the top league competition in England.[2] Since 1995, only Arsenal, Manchester United and Chelsea (like Arsenal, from London) have won the Premier League.[3] Today, teams like Burnley, Ipswich Town and Blackburn Rovers can only hope to win the league if they attract a very substantial paymaster and an effective manager/coach. Only Blackburn Rovers has managed to do that in the last 25 years, and then with the financial backing of a local millionaire, Jack Walker.

If there is a strong link between city size and football success in Europe, some big cities do not pull their demographic weight. In France, Paris has long been a football desert compared with Bordeaux, Marseilles, Lyon or Monaco. Liverpool and Manchester in England do much better in per capita terms than London, and still better when compared with Birmingham or Newcastle — metropolitan areas of much the same size and national significance. In Germany, Berlin performs badly compared with Munich, Hamburg, Dortmund or Frankfurt.

The same pattern is clear in terms of the winners of the European Cup/UEFA Champions' League. Virtually all of the winners have come from cities with more than one million inhabitants, and the few exceptions have come from cities that have not been very much smaller. Perhaps only Eindhoven (Netherlands) and Porto (Portugal) are real exceptions to this generalisation.

Of course, size does not guarantee success and, of the ten European cities with more than three million inhabitants in 1990, only Madrid and Milan have hosted champions (see Table 3.1).

Why some cities perform better than others is an interesting question, but local culture is clearly important. The populations of some cities are more interested in sports other than soccer, and some are perhaps not very interested in sport at all. Parisian business people with spare time and money are possibly more inclined to put their energies and resources into opera or art than those from Marseilles or Bordeaux.

Table 3.1: European Cup Winners, 1956–2006

City	Championships	Inhabitants in 1990 (thousands)
Paris	0	9,344
Moscow	0	9,048
London	0	7,335
St Petersburg	0	5,053
Milan	9	4,603
Madrid	9	4,172
Athens	0	3,492
Katowice	0	3,449
Berlin	0	3,288
Naples	0	3,210
Rome	0	2,965
Barcelona	2	2,913
Kiev	0	2,638
Hamburg	1	2,540
Stuttgart	0	2,485
Birmingham	1	2,302
Manchester	2	2,277
Warsaw	0	2,235
Munich	4	2,134
Bucharest	1	2,047
Lisbon	2	1,658
Belgrade	1	1,278

Table 3.1 continued

City	Championships	Inhabitants in 1990 (thousands)
Marseille	1	1,230
Amsterdam	4	1,053
Rotterdam	1	1,047
Porto	1	<750
Liverpool	5	<750
Turin	2	<750
Eindhoven	1	<750
Nottingham	2	<750
Dortmund	1	<750
Glasgow	1	<750
Total	**51**	

Sources: Figures from Goldblatt (2002) and UN (1995).

Latin America

If the most successful clubs in Europe nearly all come from big cities, in Latin America the clubs from the big cities have been almost totally dominant. The reason is simple. In most European countries, the urban system is mature and most countries contain several large cities. Although there are countries where the urban system is dominated by a single city (Austria, France and the United Kingdom, for example), most countries have a number of large cities. Almost all contain several cities with more than 500,000 inhabitants — arguably the minimum size for a successful football city in Europe.

In addition, more European countries are affluent and many clubs can charge high prices for entrance to games. The fans can also pay the high cost of the paraphernalia that goes with supporting the team: the scarf, and the now ubiquitous and ever-changing football strip.

Table 3.2: Urban Primacy in South America

Country	Population of largest city	Population of second largest city	Ratio of first city population/ second city population	First city population/ national urban population (%)
Argentina	11,256,000	1,198,000	9.4	39.9
Bolivia	1,119,000	697,000	1.6	28.0
Brazil	14,847,000	9,515,000	1.6	13.4
Chile	4,729,000	751,000	6.3	43.2
Colombia	5,231,000	2,264,000	2.3	23.1
Ecuador	1,591,000	1,101,000	1.4	28.3
Paraguay	1,177,000	134,000	8.8	55.8
Peru	6,321,000	610,000	10.4	41.9
Uruguay	1,591,000	94,000	16.9	55.6
Venezuela	2,773,000	1,350,000	2.1	15.7

Note: Data are for 1990 except for Bolivia and Paraguay, which are for 1992, and for Uruguay, which are from 1996. The 1990 figures are used throughout the chapter, rather than the latest available, because most of the tables cover a historical period of usually thirty years.
Source: Calculated by the author from UN (1995: Table A12) and UNCEPAL (2001).

Compared with Europe, clubs in Latin America have a huge disadvantage insofar as the region is both poorer and has a very different urban system. Whereas Europe has only a few dominant, so-called primate cities, many Latin American countries are dominated by such cities (Gilbert 1998). Table 3.2 shows that Argentina, Chile, Paraguay, Peru and Uruguay in particular have highly concentrated urban distributions.

Using the European cut-off point of 500,000 people as the minimum size for football success, only five countries — Argentina, Brazil, Colombia, Chile and Peru — stand much chance of generating a successful provincial team. But it could be argued that the threshold of 500,000 useful in Europe is much higher in Latin America because the countries in the latter are so much poorer. Arguably, the minimum size of a successful football city in Latin America is at least one million (see below).

Table 3.3 provides support for the proposition that winning teams come from large cities, and that teams from cities with fewer than one million inhabitants rarely win major championships. It lists the teams that have won the Copa Libertadores since 1963, with the population of the cities in which they are based.

Table 3.3 shows that the Cup has only been won by three teams from cities with fewer than one million inhabitants. Olimpia of Asunción won in 1979, 1990 and 2002, Estudiantes de La Plata did so three times in succession (1968–70) in the first decade of the competition, and the Colombian team, Once Caldas, managed to succeed in 2003 despite coming from a city with a population approaching only 600,000 people.[4] If the runners-up are considered, only Calama (Chile) is an exception to the one-million inhabitant test. Of course, as in Europe, the size of the city is a less than perfect indicator of football success. For. although most wins have been achieved by teams from Buenos Aires and, to a much lesser extent, São Paulo and Rio de Janeiro, before the late 1980s Montevideo competed well above its urban weight. Other cities certainly did not pull their demographic weight; clubs from Bogotá and Lima have never been successful and the same is true of those from baseball-obsessed Caracas.

Table 3.3: Copa Libertadores, 1960–2006

City	Championships	Runners-up	Population c. 1990
Buenos Aires	17	5	10,623,000
Montevideo	8	7	1,287,000
São Paulo	4	7	14,847,000
Asunción	3	3	630,000
La Plata	3	1	640,000
Porto Alegre	3	2	2,921,000
Belo Horizonte	2	1	3,339,000
Santos	2	1	1,075,000
Rio de Janeiro	2	0	9,515,000
Others	3*	19**	
Total	**47**	**46**	

Notes:
*   Santiago, Medellín, and Manizales.
**   Cali (6), Santiago (3), Calama (2), Lima (2), Rosario (2), Guayaquil (2) Curitiba (1) and Medellín (1).
*** Mexico City is excluded as Mexican clubs have only been allowed in the competition since 2000.
Source: Calculated from Goldblatt (2002) and UN (1995).

The dominance of clubs from a few cities in Latin America contrasts strongly with the situation in Europe, where teams from a number of small cities have done remarkably well over the years in the European Cup/Champions' League (see Table 3.1). Latin America seems to lack the equivalents of Derby County, Liverpool, Nottingham Forest and Porto.

Urban Primacy and Latin American Domestic Championships

If football success in South America, as measured by success in the Copa Libertadores, is strongly linked to demography and the structure of the urban system, the pattern is demonstrated even more strongly at the domestic level. It is rare for teams from cities with fewer than one million inhabitants ever to win anything.

Countries with Primate Cities

In Argentina, successful teams rarely come from anywhere but Buenos Aires (see Table 3.4). The only real exception is Rosario — although, if it is not considered as part of Greater Buenos Aires, La Plata, the home of Estudiantes, also qualifies.

Table 3.4: Argentine Championships, 1931–2006

City	Championships	Population 1991
Buenos Aires	65	11,256,000
Córdoba	0	1,198,000
Rosario	8	1,096,000
La Plata	3	640,000
Corrientes	1	258,000
Total	77	

Note: Since 1992 there has been an *apertura* and a *clausura* tournament, each of which have been credited half a point in the table.
Source: Calculated from Goldblatt (2002), UNCEPAL (2001) and recent online sources, supplemented by press coverage.

In Uruguay, it seems that no team from outside Montevideo has ever won anything. Peru is very similar, with clubs from outside Lima winning only three championships since 1960 (see Table 3.5).

Table 3.5: Champions of Peru, 1960–2006

City	Championships	Population 1993
Lima	44	6,321,000
Arequipa	1	610,000
Huaral	2	54,000
Total	**47**	

Source: Calculated from Goldblatt (2002), UNCEPAL (2001) and recent online sources.

Chile is only different insofar as Cobreloa comes from a small city (see Table 3.6). However, this exception, as I will argue below, only serves to prove the rule.

Table 3.6: Champions of Chile, 1960–2006

City	Championships	Population 1990
Santiago	36	4,729,000
Valparaíso/Viña del Mar	3	751,000
Concepción (Huachipato)	1	610,000
Calama	7	120,000
San Felipe	1	44,000
Total	**48**	

Note: Since 2002, the Chilean championship has been divided into an *apertura* and a *clausura* tournament: each has been credited half a point in the table.
Source: Calculated from Goldblatt (2002), UNCEPAL (2001) and recent online sources.

Football Success in Semi-Primate Countries

The football map is a little more equitable in countries with less dominant capital cities. In Ecuador, there is a genuine struggle between the
clubs of the two largest cities, although only two teams from outside
Quito and Guayaquil have ever won a championship (see Table 3.7).

Table 3.7: Champions of Ecuador, 1966–2006

City	Championships	Population 1990
Guayaquil	18	1,591,000
Quito	21	1,101,000
Cuenca	1	195,000
Ambato	0	124,000
Riobamba	1	95,000
Total	**41**	

Source: Calculated   from   <www.ecuafutbolonline.org/campeonatos/
historia.asp> and UNCEPAL (2001).

Brazil, with its well-developed urban system, is slightly different;
however, it still fits the broad pattern insofar as teams from the four
largest cities almost always win the championships. The occasional
interruption to normal service never comes from teams originating in
very small cities: since 1971, no team has won the Brazilian championship if it was located in a city with fewer than a million inhabitants.

Colombia, of course, has the most balanced urban system in
Latin America, and does diverge from the general Latin American
pattern of football success. Teams from small cities such as
Manizales, Armenia, Santa Marta and, most recently, Ibagué, Pasto
and Cúcuta have won the championship, albeit infrequently. As in
the rest of the region, though, the big clubs come from the big

cities, and even Junior from Barranquilla struggles against the might of the teams from the three main centres.

Table 3.8: Champions of Brazil, 1971–2006

City	Championships	Runner-up	Population, 1990
São Paulo	12	14	14,487,000
Rio de Janeiro	9	6	9,515,000
Belo Horizonte	2	6	3,339,000
Porto Alegre	5	4	2,921,000
Recife	1	0	2,772,000
Salvador	1	0	2,375,000
Fortaleza	0	0	2,193,000
Curitiba	2	1	1,894,000
Brasília	0	0	1,547,000
Campinas	1	0	1,339,000
Belém	0	0	1,269,000
Santos	3	3	1,075,000
Vitoria	0	1	1,068,000
Braganza Paulista	0	1	99,000
Total	**36**	**36**	

Source: Calculated from Goldblatt (2002) and UN (1995).

Table 3.9: Champions of Colombia, 1948–2006

City	Champion	Runner up	Population 1993
Bogotá	19	19	5,231,000
Medellín	10.5	13	2,264,000
Cali	19.5	18.5	1,697,000
Barranquilla	4.5	4.5	1,310,000
Bucaramanga	0	1.5	729,000
Cartagena	0	0.5	616,000
Cúcuta	0.5	1	505,000
Ibagué	0.5	3.5	340,000
Manizales	1.5	1	328,000
Santa Marta	1	0	270,000
Pasto	0.5	0.5	261,000
Armenia	1	2	216,000
Total	**58**	**58**	

Note: Since 2002 there has been an *apertura* and a *clausura* tournament, each of which have been credited half a point in the table.
Source: Calculated from Goldblatt (2002), UNCEPAL (2001) and recent online sources.

Exceptions to this Rule

In Europe, several clubs have managed to beat the dominance of teams from the large cities. The most obvious include Aberdeen, Blackburn Rovers, Ipswich Town, Derby County, Auxerre, Chievo Verona, PSV Eindhoven and Parma. All of these clubs have managed to win something significant, even though they come from small cities. There seem to be two explanations behind their success. Either they have attracted significant financial support from a major company or a rich patron and/or they have been fortunate to have hired an exceptional manager or coach. The successes of Blackburn Rovers and Parma were backed by major sponsorship, while those of Aberdeen, Ipswich Town, Derby County and Auxerre can be explained in terms of exceptional leadership. Arguably, PSV Eindhoven has enjoyed both.

In Latin America, the exceptions are so few that they are very easy to identify. Cobreloa in Chile has had spectacular success largely through its sponsorship from the state copper company. Similarly, Colombia's fortunes in the Copa Libertadores improved markedly when clubs such as América de Cali and Atlético Nacional of Medellín began to attract financial support from the drug cartels in the early 1980s (Taylor 1998). Initially, the new sources of income allowed the two clubs from Cali to attract football stars from Argentina. Atlético Nacional tended to stick to local talent, although it is possible that illicit funding allowed the club to develop its young stars. It is surely significant that the country's two major drug cartels were based in Cali and Medellín rather than in Bogotá.[5] Perhaps the Colombian state's campaign against the involvement of *narcos* in football clubs partially explains the recent successes of teams from outside the big four cities (Once Caldas from Manizales, Deportes Tolima from Ibagué, Real Cartagena and Deportivo Pasto). Equally, the splitting of the season into *apertura* and *clausura* championships may also have contributed by shortening the period over which smaller clubs had to maintain their success.

The Implications

It is argued here that it matters whether clubs only have a real chance of winning an important competition if they are based in large cities; it detracts significantly from the romance of the game if small-town teams are excluded from success.

First, it means that fans in smaller cities and poorer countries can rarely watch the very best players in the flesh. In Argentina, it is difficult to support a good team if you do not live in Buenos Aires, La Plata or Rosario. The most successful teams generally only visit once a season and, gallingly, usually win. The distance of most fans from the largest cities means that they are reduced to watching quality football on the television. With the growth of international competitions, the distances that the clubs travel for matches are growing all the time. Today, it is both difficult and expensive for fans to travel to away matches. This may be good for reducing hooliganism but it is arguably to the detriment of the atmosphere in the ground.

Second, if domestically more of the successful teams are drawn from the same cities, this implies that the genuine *clásicos* increasingly take the form of local derbies. Whether fans in Buenos Aires and Montevideo lose out by watching so many matches between local teams is also pertinent. Arguably, local derbies are sweetest when they are relatively few in number, but in Uruguay virtually all matches are local derbies because nearly all of the teams come from Montevideo. In England, London teams have complained in the past that their relative lack of success in the league can be explained partially in terms of the many frenetic local derbies they have to play.

Third, none of this may be relevant insofar as the rising cost of watching football may be excluding an increasing proportion of fans from attending matches. As Giulianotti (1999b, p. 106) observes: 'In the post-modern football world, top players earn more, directors and shareholders profit, and media stations generate new markets. A new class of disenfranchised fans appears, missing out on the club's profitability, unable to afford entry to grounds, and reduced to watching the spectacular game on pub television.' While he is referring to Europe, the same phenomenon is even more true of fans in many parts of Latin America. Perhaps for that reason, the number of people attending football matches in many countries is in decline. In Argentina, only two clubs — Boca Juniors and River Plate — attracted more than 10,000 spectators per game in the 2000–2001 season (Goldblatt 2002, p. 346) and the average attendance for the league as a whole was fewer than 6,000.

The Tendency for Players to Work Abroad

Globalisation is arguably also affecting affinity to local football teams insofar as most teams from the major cities no longer field many local players. In the past, British footballers came 'from the same backgrounds as those who watched the game; they could literally be next-door neighbours. They did move, of course, but generally not very far.' (Lanfranchi & Taylor 2001, p. 1) Today, clubs recruit from across the globe. More and more good footballers are being attracted up the urban and economic system to the richest clubs. This means that the rich teams employ talented foreigners. The most affluent teams employ foreign *galácticos*, lesser teams less famous foreign recruits, and only the weakest teams resort to local players. A dendritic pattern of feeder clubs has developed whereby talented locals leave local teams almost before they have kicked a ball (Goldblatt 2002). In Latin America, many players start with a team in their national league, and then quickly move to a leading club in Argentina, Brazil or Mexico before moving on to a larger club, nearly always in Europe. Increasingly, they are moving directly to Europe and are being signed at very young ages.[6]

Was it not more satisfying when Glasgow clubs won championships containing a majority of local players? Does it matter that in current Celtic-Rangers matches only two or three of the players are actually Scottish? Do the fans of Chelsea care that their team is composed almost entirely of foreign mercenaries and that on occasion the club has fielded a whole team of foreigners? Can it really be true that Barcelona's first-choice team in the late 1990s contained seven Dutchmen and three Brazilians and was managed by another Dutchman? Despite Catalunya's traditional openness to foreigners, were not the successes of the region's sporting icon somewhat diminished? Maybe it is pure nostalgia, but many older fans regret the passing of the time when young boys began, and often finished, their careers playing for the local team. The time when teams upheld the principle of recruiting only from their immediate area has virtually disappeared. Today, only Atlético Nacional in Medellín, which rarely draws players from outside Antioquia, and the Basque clubs of Spain even pretend to follow this tradition.

Most fans in Latin America do not have to suffer from the need to accept many foreign players because most countries are generally exporters of football talent. Most Peruvian and Chilean teams are formed from local players. Argentine teams still recruit most of their players from within the country, although the number of

Colombians, Chileans, Paraguayans and Uruguayans seems to be increasing. Elsewhere, large contingents of foreigners have been recruited only at times of economic, or at least footballing, prosperity. The Golden Age of football in Colombia (1949–54) attracted major stars from Argentina, Uruguay and even England (Lanfranchi & Taylor 2001; Taylor 1998), and the drug-fuelled prosperity of the 1980s and early 1990s also attracted many players from Argentina and Uruguay. With economic recession, the outflow of players increases, and the attractions to a player of earning a salary in a hard currency become irresistible (Lanfranchi & Taylor 2001, p. 221).

With the traditional gap in wealth between Western Europe and Latin America growing as a result of the economic problems of the latter, the outflow of players is increasing by the day. The pattern is clear from the recruitment of overseas players in the English Premier League. In 1992, 15 foreign players appeared on the first day of the season; 11 years later, that number had risen to 127. In May 2007, there were 340 foreign players eligible to play in the Premiership (http://www.premierleague.com/en/faq/faqlanding. jsp#4). The haemorrhage of playing talent from Latin America is more obvious when recruitment into all the European football leagues is considered. The number of South Americans playing in Europe tripled from 140 to 417 between 1980–81 and 2000–01 (Lanfranchi & Taylor 2001, p. 103; Goldblatt 2002, p. 477). In the past, most of the stars stayed at home; in 1978, all but one of the Argentine World Cup squad played for local teams and in 1982 all but three did so. By the late 1990s, however, everything had changed. In 1998 only six were playing at home, in 2002 only two and in 2006 three (Lanfranchi & Taylor 2001, p. 103; Hancock 2006). The pattern is less marked in Brazil, although the trend is in the same direction (see Table 3.10).

Table 3.10 shows how the stars of Colombia have tended to move first to other countries in Latin America rather than directly to Europe. Several top Colombian footballers have passed through Argentina on their way to Europe, including Juan Pablo Angel and Mario Yepes via River Plate, Ivan Córdoba via San Lorenzo and Johnnie Montaño via Quilmes. The Peruvian midfielder Nolberto Solano followed a similar path via Boca Juniors, and the international strikers Diego Forlán and Marcelo Salas, of Uruguayan and Chilean origin respectively, both moved to Europe via River Plate.

Table 3.10: Members of World Cup Squads from Argentina, Brazil and Colombia Playing Abroad, 1978–2006

	1978	1982	1986	1990	1994	1998	2002	2006
Argentina								
Home	21	19	15	8	10	6	2	3
Europe	1	3	6	12	9	16	21	18
Latin America	0	0	1	2	1	0	0	2
Brazil								
Home	22	20	19	10	12	9	13	2
Europe	0	2	3	12	10	11	10	21
Latin America	0	0	0	0	0	0	0	0
Colombia								
Home	n.a.	n.a.	n.a.	20	18	10	n.a.	n.a.
Europe	n.a.	n.a.	n.a.	2	2	3	n.a.	n.a.
Latin America	n.a.	n.a.	n.a.	0	2	8	n.a.	

Notes: When numbers do not add up to 22 (1978-98) or 23 (2002 and 2006), the remainder are mainly registered elsewhere.
n.a. Not applicable because Colombia did not qualify for the finals.
Source: Lanfranchi and Taylor (2001, p. 103), supplemented by figures from Goldblatt (2002, p. 477) and Hancock (2006).

All this, it can be argued, means that globalisation replaces the romance of the 'local' game with a veneer of international glamour. Instead of boys growing up to play all their lives for the local team, they now begin their careers in the best national team or even the best foreign team. Fans can no longer watch the local stars at the local ground. If they want to watch them, they have to turn on the television. In this sense, football is becoming part of the international entertainment industry and fans have become consumers. Through television, Richard Giulianotti writes: 'The new spectator may elect to "shop round" the football market place to find the team with winning traits. It is likely that viewing football on the television will cut the fan base of most small football clubs.' (Giulianotti 1999b, p. 95)[7] The latter will no doubt survive, but many will have to give up large squads and even employ semi-professional players.

Conclusion

Football today is arguably much more glamorous than it once was, but at the same time it is far less romantic. Today, Cinderella would never win the hand of Prince Charming, and only Miss Berlusconi, Miss Murdoch or Miss Abramovic stands a realistic chance of matrimony. Even they will increasingly have to emigrate to find a suitable groom. Football today is all about hype and glamour. The top stars become instant millionaires while the majority of players struggle. Clubs at virtually every level face financial problems, lesser stars face increasingly unstable careers, and most players seem to be constantly on the move — from one city to another, from one country to the next.

Almost all good clubs now come from large cities, and typically from affluent large cities. Of course, not every big city maximises its advantages: cities like Caracas, Paris or St Petersburg are simply not heartlands of football. But, if economic and urban weight is not a determinant of football success, it is certainly a vital ingredient. The figures presented in this paper demonstrate that link, and suggest that the relationship between city size, affluence and football success is becoming stronger. Today, it is virtually impossible to win the UEFA Champions' League or the Copa Libertadores if the team plays in a city with fewer than one million people.

The problem for Latin America is obvious. With globalisation, more talented Latin American players are working abroad. The great clubs of Argentina, Brazil and Uruguay have been turned into football nurseries.

In turn, teams from smaller Latin American countries are providing many of the players who turn out for Boca Juniors, River Plate and Palmeiras, often before they in turn are sold on to Europe. Latin American football can perhaps be explained in terms of dependency theory (Cardoso 1972; Frank 1969; Kay 1989). While the simpler versions of dependency theory were based on assertion more than reality, football dependency is arguably very real. The core–satellite relationship described by Frank (1967) is seemingly alive and well. Great footballers tend to be reared in conditions of poverty and are sucked out to play in rich cities as soon as they hint at their greatness. No doubt countries and cities bask in their reflected glory, but is it the same if you have never seen your best players in the flesh?

The fate of Montevideo is illustrative. The clubs of a city that won so many South American championship titles no longer win very often. Montevideo is not only growing slowly and losing out in the demographic contest with other capital cities in the region, but most importantly it no longer has the economic weight to retain local players. Globalisation is clearly producing football teams of amazing quality, but if local fans cannot see the local stars play, if everyone is a mercenary and is living abroad, if success is determined purely by financial clout and the great stars are accessible to no one except their sponsors and agents, glamour has arguably replaced romance. For some of us, at least, that is a shame.

Notes

1   In the case of Jean-Marc Bosman, the European Court of Justice determined that a selling club could not demand a transfer fee from a club in another European country once a player's contract had finished. It also outlawed the restrictions that the European Union of Football Associations (UEFA) had imposed on the inclusion of 'foreign' players in European club competitions and, by implication, similar restrictions in domestic leagues.

2   Aston Villa (the major club in Birmingham) won the First Division in 1981 and Blackburn Rovers won the Premier League in 1995.

3   In 1992, the 22 leading clubs split from the Football League to form the FA Premier League, under the auspices of the Football Association. Chelsea's victories were due largely to the massive injec-

tion of cash to finance its annual losses by the Russian billionaire
Roman Abramovic.

4   This win was achieved by a team without many stars, which was
arguably helped by the fact that formerly prosperous teams in
Argentina and Brazil have been denuded by European teams of most
of their international players. Presumably the success of Cienciano,
the leading team from the Peruvian city of Cuzco, in the *Copa
Sudamericana* in December 2003 could be explained in similar terms. A
further explanation is that playing at altitude helped both clubs,
although it would not explain why neither had been successful previously. The inclusion of La Plata in the list of small cities is debateable
insofar as it clearly forms part of Greater Buenos Aires and — like
Santos, with respect to São Paulo — might be considered to reinforce
the argument here. This is perhaps even more true now that
Estudiantes play their home games in Quilmes, unquestionably a
suburb of Buenos Aires.

5   Although in the 1990s Millionarios of Bogotá was the beneficiary of
funding from drug-trafficker José Gonzalo Miguel Rodríguez Gacha.

6   The migration of Latin American footballers to Europe is nothing
new, particularly for Argentines and Uruguayans who could claim
nationality in Spain or Italy. What is different today is the sheer
number of Latin Americans playing in Europe.

7   It is only necessary to walk down a street in practically any city of the
world to find many children bedecked in the shirts of foreign teams
— the names Beckham, Ronaldo, Ronaldinho and Zidane seem to be
everywhere.

PART III:

FOOTBALL, IDENTITY AND CRISIS

4

Transformations in National Identity through Football in Brazil: Lessons from Two Historical Defeats

J. Sergio Leite Lopes

In many Latin American countries, football has been central to the formation of identities in the twentieth century, whether these be national, ethnic, local, generational or gender identities. In this light, a comparison between the explanations given for the Brazilian defeat in the 1950 World Cup, which took place in Brazil itself, and that in the 1998 World Cup Final in France can serve as an illustration and starting point for a consideration of some transformations in the construction and the sentiment of national identity through football in Brazil.

If imagined communities are built upon specific regional elements of local traditions, these collective movements are, on the other hand, greatly inspired by ideas that circulate internationally.[1] This type of construction affected European countries, starting at the end of the eighteenth century and continuing throughout the nineteenth century. The national identity of Latin American countries, on the other hand, was consolidated only in the twentieth century. This was the case for Brazil during the first half of the century. Like its neighbours, Uruguay and Argentina, the country went through an intense period of nation-building and invention of tradition. At the same time, football was appropriated and diffused throughout the country while, on the international scene, the World Cup was created in 1930.[2]

In instances of international competition such as the World Cup, as well as regional tournaments — for example, the Copa América

— the public representation of nationality finds adequate support for the elaboration of its qualities. The impact of victories in such tournaments on the display of national traits is well known.[3] However, what can be said about the impact of exemplary defeats such as those of Brazil in the 1950 and 1998 World Cup Finals? What reflections and collective fantasies derive from such results?

There is a considerable body of journalistic and academic literature in Brazil regarding the 1950 World Cup defeat. However, although the 1998 defeat received a significant amount of journalistic coverage, only a handful of academic essays have been published on it.[4] Comparisons between these two defeats have also been elaborated, but in a somewhat unsystematic fashion. The tentative comparison presented here aims to offer at least a first look at the transformations which affected Brazilian football between 1950 and 1998.[5]

The 1950 World Cup: Collective Self-reflection after a National Tragedy

The 1950 World Cup represents the culmination of an earlier process of football democratisation. The defeat affected this exemplary course of things in a negative manner. Brazilian football was ready to be presented to the world in 1950 as a greatly improved version of a British product — that is, an example of import substitution *par excellence*.[6] The seventeen years of improvement in the standards of Brazilian football from 1933, when the top level of Brazilian football officially became professional, to 1950, the year when it hosted the World Cup, were marked by the linear progression of football modelled on Europe and, closer to home, on Argentina and Uruguay.

Although Brazil participated in the first two World Cups, it was in the games of 1938 that it stood out with a team that already reflected the democratising improvements of professionalism. This occasion, 12 years before the 1950 World Cup, encouraged intellectuals, representatives of the cultural industry and the expanding public to begin a collective process of constructing national identity through football.[7]

Attentive to the process of discovery and invention of national traditions, Brazilian intellectuals pointed out national folkloric traits in football. These reached the international sphere of competition where Brazil's national qualities were underscored (see Leite Lopes 1999a). The traits which folklorists since the 1930s had regarded as the principal qualities of Brazil's popular art and traditions were precisely those that were recognised in the body movement and techniques of football players (such as the dance evident in popular religious feasts — see Vilhena 1997). During this period, a semi-clandestine type of self-defence called *capoeira*, which was created by slaves and ex-slaves, was also slowly being developed as a sport (Röhrig Assunção 2005). None of this went unnoticed by intellectuals such as Gilberto Freyre and writers such as José Lins do Rego. After the 1938 World Cup, these intellectuals — with the help of the insights of the journalist Mario Filho — developed two original interpretations of the country based on the practice of football and its diffusion in Brazil: first, the actualisation of the country's African heritage; and second, the incorporation of music and dance into a particular style of playing.[8]

The analogy with music gave football the necessary legitimacy to become a cultural representative of nationality. In the same way as modernist intellectuals from the 1920s had detected in music the criteria and sources of Brazil's national character, some of these intellectuals now recognised football as a new field that brought together modern urban practices and the traditional authenticity of the recently discovered popular culture (Buarque de Hollanda 2003, p. 40).

While this incorporation of invented traditions by Brazilian football was beginning at the time of the 1938 World Cup, it became consolidated as a particular national style of football only in the 1940s. The 1950 World Cup was seen as the perfect opportunity to show this style to the world, and possibly as an occasion for a marriage of style and victory. Brazil had presented its candidature as host in 1938, after a good performance in the competition that year, and during the postwar period this proposal seemed opportune to a Europe undergoing reconstruction. Taking on the challenge of constructing a stadium in the capital, Rio de Janeiro, when a group of stadiums already existed in other cities, confirmed Brazil's responsible organisation of the event even before the team's performance on the field. The inauguration of the Maracanã, the biggest stadium in the world — which was ready only one week before the World Cup started — demonstrated the confidence of the organising committee in meeting such a great challenge.

Flávio Costa, the coach of the national team, had been responsible for two of the most popular teams in Rio de Janeiro in the 1940s: first Flamengo, which won three state championships between 1942 and 1944, and then Vasco da Gama, which won three championships in the next five years.[9] The rivalry between Rio de Janeiro and São Paulo was strong and influenced the politics of team selection. São Paulo has competed with Rio de Janeiro — the capital of the country at the time — for control over the sport ever since the arrival of football in Brazil. After a drawn match against Switzerland that disappointed supporters in São Paulo, in the games that followed — which took place in Rio — the team improved, winning matches against Sweden and Spain by a large margin. A new form of cheering based on a much larger crowd of supporters than was usually present at the games between regional teams came into being. The presence of children and women or whole families contrasted with the normal crowds, composed mostly of men, which usually filled the stadiums. Besides this, the size of the Maracanã — which could hold ten per cent of Rio's 1950 population — produced a new and extraordinary demonstration of collective sociability which could instantaneously be visualised. The carnival melodies improvised and adapted for the context of the matches, along with a tentative organisation of supporters, brought about a collective dramatisation of a cultural and playful sentiment of nationality dissociated from politics and from the habitual military and patriotic context.[10]

The defeat in the final game in 1950 was completely unexpected and traumatic for this collective construction. Having played much better than the team from Uruguay in the earlier matches, the Brazilian team, greatly influenced by the public — which had reached the anticipated pleasure of the collective sentiment of nationality — and by the press, was regarded as certain to emerge victorious. But imagination did not secure victory in the face of an experienced and determined adversary, and the team did not do as well as expected. Unlike the other games, which had been won by a large margin, the stalemate was broken only after half-time, when Brazil scored the first goal. The supporters finally erupted in an expression of joy, and everything suggested the result they expected — especially since a draw in the final match, under the rules of the competition in 1950, would mean a Brazilian victory in the World Cup as a whole.[11] But silence filled the stadium when Uruguay successfully counter-attacked, scoring a goal. The silence persisted, contributing to the sentiment of deception and failure in the face of what should have been a display of artistry. The sentiment of fear seemed to spread among the players, helping Uruguay break the tie with another goal. The end of the game, after Brazil's desperate attempts to score again and obtain the draw that would be enough to win the trophy, was marked by collective silence and the display of intense social mourning through the following days, months and even years. No other World Cup finals represented a tragedy on this scale for the supporters of the team hosting the event.[12]

A defeat can also be an important marker of the sentiment of nationality. It is often a way of collectively sharing a profound culturally constructed loss. It is not a coincidence that many national monuments are built after traumatic defeats (the most common being those that result from military failures). This was the case in the 1950 defeat. Various reasons were given to explain the defeat, one of which ended up greatly affecting the construction of national sentiment that was underway before and during the World Cup.

Many explanations for Brazil's failure were produced, ranging from the excessive optimism of politicians and the press, which supposedly affected the concentration of the players, to the coach who advised the players not to react to the provocations from Uruguay's team, which might have suppressed the aggressiveness of the Brazilian players too early. The coach counted on the fact that, if there was fair play, the best team — Brazil, that is — would naturally win. Ironically, it was the public that, at the end, showed fair play and civility by staying in the stadium while the winning team received the trophy, and then silently leaving the Maracanã in a state of enormous grief (Perdigão 2001; Moura 1998).

This display of civility was suspended only during an isolated moment when the bust of Rio de Janeiro's mayor, situated at the entrance of the stadium, was violently destroyed. But at the same time, the self-restrained behaviour of the team during the match was viewed as displaying a lack of will and energy. To this claim of a lack of energy were added conservative explanations from Brazilian social thought about the inadequacy of Afro-Brazilian players in achieving favourable results and victories in competitions.

It was not a coincidence, according to these claims, that the two goals scored by Uruguay supposedly resulted from the mistakes of two specific defenders and the goalkeeper, all of whom were black. Such explanations — which are hardly present in the written records (see Table 4.1 later in this chapter) — were related to the earlier practice, during the period of amateur football in Brazil, of excluding players from the lower classes from teams. While this practice had continued in some of the elite clubs after professionalisation, it seemed to have diminished due to the success of the most lower-class clubs of the 1930s and 1940s. Mario Filho draws attention to this type of explanation, and highlights it critically. The explanations of this journalist and militant for the democratisation of Brazilian football have been followed by other journalists and social scientists such as Roberto Da Matta, among others (see Da Matta 1982; Vogel 1982). The difficulty of pointing out the weight of stereotypes resides in the fact that these frequently constitute very subtle forms of commonsense knowledge. Anyway, this type of observation was present in the formulations regarding the Brazilian team prior to and after the 1950 World Cup (see Table 4.1). It was against the background of these stereotypes that an intellectual such as Gilberto Freyre had gained the motivation to interpret the entry of outsiders the other way around. Based on the exploits of the Brazilian team in 1938, Freyre became the prophet of the success of a new style of football, linked to national traits that he was constructing positively.[13] The old stereotypes, however, make a strong comeback in 1950 with the defeat bringing about collective self-blame on the one hand (resulting from the social Darwinism present in Brazilian social thought in the beginning of the century), and a commentary on the deficiencies of the Brazilian people's mixed ethnicity on the other.[14]

The effects of the World Cup victory finally achieved in 1958, and repeated on two further occasions in the next twelve years — in 1962 and 1970 — were incorporated into Brazilian consciousness as a strong sentiment of nationality, due in part to the collective suffering and reflection that the 1950 defeat had provoked. This contrast between an opportunity lost at home (elaborated as tragedy) and the victories abroad (attributed to a special style of football) ended up providing an opportunity for the display of national qualities, where cultural characteristics could be detected in physical techniques — within, of course, the limitations and possible variations permitted by the rules of football.

The 1998 World Cup and the Politicisation of the Defeat That Denies Tradition

The interpretation of the 1998 defeat, Brazil's only other loss in a World Cup Final, is very different from that of 1950. This time there was no process of blaming players who had traditionally represented the flaws and needs of Brazilian people or nationality. In the case of the defeat in 1998, the explanations were directed towards globalised professionalism and football commercialism, as well as the inadequate use of this structure by the sport's administrators in Brazil.

In the 1998 World Cup, the process of player internationalisation which had begun in the 1980s reached its peak (Giulianotti 1999b, Ch. 6). The great era of Brazilian football had taken place when players spent their entire careers at home. From the second half of the 1980s and through the 1990s, however, most of the biggest Brazilian stars were playing abroad.[15]

Much like the 1950 World Cup finals, the days prior to the 1998 World Cup final were decisive. While in 1950 the team's concentration was disturbed by politicians and journalists who were certain of a victorious result, the defeat of the Brazilian team in 1998 had its beginning on the same day, during the players' rest period after lunch. The striker Ronaldo was exhibiting signs of stress due to the globalised football being experienced by the whole team. First there was the pressure of contracts with many different companies which divided the team, such as when players had to go to Nike's sports centre in central Paris during time set aside for training. Second, Ronaldo was feeling the pressure of his injured knee and the close interest shown by the press in his girlfriend. And finally, there was his personal history of somnambulism. This disturbance in his sleep provoked a dramatic convulsion, controversially diagnosed, which was witnessed by his team-mates and, as a result, disturbed the team emotionally. The lack of communication between the managers and the players during the crisis provoked a complete disorientation of the team (for details, see Caldeira 2002).

In contrast to the game in 1950 against Uruguay, Brazil played in 1998 in front of a predominantly French public. In 1950 Brazil had been on course to win the World Cup until the 34th minute of the second half, when Uruguay scored its second goal with only 11 minutes of game left. In 1998, Brazil started out very differently from all its previous games and was already losing 2–0 before half-time. The team was not able to reverse the situation after the interval, and the game ended with yet another goal for the French. The whole team played poorly; no specific player could be made responsible for the flaws in the game, unlike 1950 when a goalkeeper and two defenders were blamed. Nonetheless, Ronaldo attracted attention as the icon of the defeat due to his health problem prior to the game, which created the perfect conditions for defeat, even before the game had begun.

It is worth pausing here to outline the peculiar trajectory of this player. Ronaldo presents many of the traditional characteristics of the Brazilian players from past World Cup teams. Brought up in a peripheral, lower-class neighbourhood of Rio de Janeiro, Ronaldo endured financial difficulties in order to play indoor football and then regular football for the São Cristóvão team, a traditional second division starting-place for many players from Rio. In this team he came into contact with the 1970 World Cup champion Jairzinho, who pointed Ronaldo out to the Brazilian Football Confederation (CBF), which then chose him as a forward for the Brazilian team taking part in the South American under-17 tournament. As a result of this, Ronaldo went to play for Cruzeiro, a team from Minas Gerais, where he was coached by Pinheiro, an ex-player from the 1954 World Cup team. Ronaldo progressed from the Cruzeiro junior team to the first division team, where he played very well. Like Pelé in 1958, Ronaldo went to his first World Cup in 1994 at the age of 16. But, unlike the icon of Brazilian football, Ronaldo did not play on that occasion. The great difference between this player's career and that of traditional players was the fact that Ronaldo's managers (initially connected to Jairzinho) prepared contracts for Ronaldo's image to be linked to brand names early in his career. Even before Ronaldo was called to play in the national team, his managers were able to transfer him to PSV Eindhoven, a move to which he agreed on the advice of the leading Brazilian striker Romário, who had also played there. Romário also indirectly mediated the arrangements for Ronaldo's medical care. Romário had taken the specialist Nilton Petrone (Filé) from Rio de Janeiro to Eindhoven, and Filé was subsequently hired by PSV to treat Ronaldo's knee problem. The physiotherapist diagnosed a disproportion between Ronaldo's upper leg muscles due to the accelerated muscle development of the young athlete. The player was later transferred to Barcelona and then to Inter Milan. Ronaldo signed contracts with the beer brand Brahma (as did other players from the national team from 1994), and with Nike, Pirelli and Parmalat. Nike had just abandoned basketball as the basis of its globalisation campaign strategy and was looking at football, investing greatly in the Brazilian team. However, Ronaldo was the only Brazilian player to sign a lifetime contract.

The 1998 defeat in France took place when Ronaldo symbolised the contradictions of globalised football for the Brazilian public. High salaries represented good performance in clubs, and occasionally in World Cups, but the contradictions of globalised football, with its excessive demands in terms of training time, matches and business commitments, had a strong impact on Ronaldo's body — his knee especially — not to mention his mind.

Moreover, Ronaldo was a radical and successful illustration of what was happening with a great number of young footballers from Brazil and elsewhere. The increasing commercialism associated with the era of global television transmission sustains this international market of well-paid players and in various countries ends up disturbing the balance between the lower football divisions, comprising semi-amateur and semi-professional football, and the top-level divisions. This disrupts the ordinary communication and circulation of players between these divisions, which normally emphasises the importance of a sport practised by a large part of society's young population. The selection of a small group of youths who learn and train in the big European clubs from a young age and thus stand out from the average good players in Brazil ends up creating a restricted circuit of well-paid super-players, eliminating the channel which connects local football with its sources of renewal.

Another remarkable illustration of the globalisation of football was the fact that many of the Brazilian spectators in France wore green and yellow shirts displaying names of powerful companies, whether state-owned enterprises or more recognisable multinationals (Coca-Cola, McDonald's, Panasonic, Cyanamid, ABN-Amro, etc.). Many of these companies brought employees or clients to France, such as ABN-Amro, which brought 900 clients in all, 300 at a time, to watch two games of the national team each, staying in France for two weeks with all expenses paid. These clients, for the most part employees of the car dealer financed by this bank, were rewarded for their productivity and sales efficiency. Other companies brought employees of intermediate status, providing in this way a kind of salary bonus which in some ways resembles, under different historical conditions, the extra-monetary concessions to workers and employees that maintained factory football clubs and their worker-players during the early period of football expansion in Brazil. In fact, in its early days, football owed its rapid process of appropriation by the popular classes to company sponsorships, especially from the industrial sector.

The reasons given for the 1998 defeat by the press and people in daily conversations during the days after the game were also different from those given for the previous defeat. In 1950, journalists and intellectuals manifested disappointment regarding Brazil's incapacity for international distinction even in an activity at which the country was good, the defeat being a consequence of the flaws of the whole population as represented by the players. In the days after the 1998 defeat, the arrogance that had anticipated certain victory was criticised in the same manner as in 1950. But the arrogance in France was at least backed up by a successful history of victories (1958, 1962, 1970 and the most recent reinvigorating one of 1994). This favouritism was further increased by the promotions of the Brazilian team which were done by the international press and sponsors such as Nike. Brazil's team was a special attraction in the World Cup, appearing in countless publicity campaigns. Brazil also held a special place in the hearts of the public, since it was the only team whose practice sessions in a small stadium in the suburbs of Ozoire-la-Ferrière were open to the public.[16]

However, this time the reasons given for the defeat — unlike in 1950 — were directed not so much at the players as representatives of a people with low self-esteem and in search of a collective expression of national identity as at the administrators who had made poor use of the team's position as favourites for the trophy and of Brazil's well-known expertise in football. Ronaldo, who was positioned at the centre of the drama of the incomprehensible defeat, could be seen as the broken piece of a much bigger structure made up of an opaque administration and a budget full of secret contracts with Nike that eventually cost the team victory. The players were also criticised as mercenaries without sufficient love for their nation, playing for high salaries in foreign countries.

The disappointment with the results of the 1998 finals ended up triggering a politicised flood of explanations as a consequence of a collective football history which had slowly formed in Brazilian thought. National identity through football had already been consolidated, and was no longer at stake. As already noted, the stylish success of the 1970 team (the 'beautiful team', as it became known across the world) had marked the consolidation of national character through football by reversing, as in 1958 and 1962, the situation which Brazilians had experienced in 1950. In 1970, the first live television broadcast of the matches gave the general public the same visual access that those who had been in Maracanã in 1950 had enjoyed. In 1970 there was even a celebrated victory, or 'revenge', over Uruguay earlier in the tournament.[17]

The rivalry between Rio and São Paulo also decreased during this period as a consequence of the good performance of important teams and World Cup players from Minas Gerais and Rio Grande do Sul after the 1970s. The defeats in the World Cups between 1974 and 1990, which were received with sadness — especially in 1982, due to the quality and performance of the team that went to Spain — did not in any measure reproduce the reaction to the 1950 defeat. There was no longer a threat to national identity. Pelé's prestige, for example, persisted well beyond the occasion of the athlete's retirement, as Brazil retained its status as the 'country of football' throughout the world, despite having achieved no World Cup victory since 1970. In 1994, the team won although there was a lack of emotion as a result of its defensive strategy in the final game. This victory is also remembered for its difficult penalty kicks, during which the hero was the goalkeeper Cláudio Taffarel. The 1994 victory also contributed to Brazil's status as favourites in 1998. It was because 1998 brought on another defeat in the World Cup final that questions relating to national character arose once again. But this defeat did not bring about any kind of negative judgement on the population in the light of the performance of the players. The question of representation was no longer in the forefront. On the contrary, the questioning arose about the manager's decisions, the lack of transparency, the accusations of corruption and the lack of will on the part of the players. The 1998 defeat, the loss at the Olympic Games shortly thereafter, and accusations that the coach had profited from the participation of certain players in the team, led to two investigating committees in the National Congress — one concerned with the CBF-Nike contract and the other with alleged illegal contracts among the administrators of Brazilian football.

Epilogue: The Victory of 2002

Although Brazil's participation in the 2002 World Cup occurred in the context of the further globalisation of the sport and a recent crisis in the administration of the country's football, the problems that the national team had to deal with from the previous World Cup paradoxically strengthened it, leading it to a final victory against Germany. The failings of the national team between 1998 and 2002 seemed to reflect the political crisis that plagued Brazilian football. The weak performance of the national team in the qualifying games was the culmination of a long trajectory marked by failure, from the constant change of coaches to the final choice of Felipão, a pragmatic and disciplinarian coach who had been successful in recent years. The pressure and discredit that surrounded the team at the beginning of the World Cup in 2002 exposed it to a situation of apparent inferiority, requiring perseverance to overcome the difficult conditions it faced. This promoted unity among the players and attenuated the internal privileges and rivalry that characterised the work conditions of the globalised players (which was the case in 1998), reproducing in part the situation of 1958, 1970 and 1994 when the team also had to overcome unfavourable conditions (the ghosts of 1950 and 1954 in 1958; the failure in 1966, present in the preparations for 1970; the long series of failures with an emphasis on the 1982 defeat before 1994).

There was also the drama lived by Ronaldo who, after the 1998 defeat, had to face the threat of retirement due to problems with his knee, subsequent surgical operations and a spectacular rupture of his patellar tendon in April 2000. The player served as a symbol of the tenacity of all the players, the coach and the medical team, highlighting the attempts at recovery by players such as Rivaldo and Roberto Carlos, as well as reinforcing the team's spirit of unity. All of these difficulties, lived out by renowned players with high salaries who had experienced a fast ascent to wealth and fame, reminded us of the low-income origin of most players, represented by the emblematic '100% Jardim Irene' which the captain of the team painted on his shirt before holding the trophy over his head. 'Jardim Irene' is the name of the poor neighbourhood in São Paulo where Cafu came from, like the other peripheral suburbs such Bento Ribeiro in Rio de Janeiro or Paulista in Recife, where Ronaldo and Rivaldo originated. These neighbourhoods were under the spotlight on the day of the final game. The 2002 team presented to the public what the 1998 team had not offered: asceticism, tenacity, team spirit, sacrifice and homage to their modest origins as a sign of allegiance to the majority of the Brazilian population itself.

Thus, in different ways, the 1950 and 1998 defeats brought about a collective reflection that would only come to dramatise and valorise the later victories. The reverberations resulting from the reflexive moment that arose from the 1950 defeat gave a pessimistic and guilty tone to the optimism that had followed Brazil's discovery of football since 1938 as a type of 'emergent folklore' incorporated as a national sport. But the force of the democratisation of talents in football and the improvement of the technical and administrative departments of the team led to victories that were highly valued due to the former difficulties. Also, the political implications of the interpretations of the 1998 defeat put Brazilian football under the scrutiny of two parliamentary investigations that aimed to recover the honour and tradition of the most victorious football of all times. The idea was to recover the quality that had characterised Brazilian football between 1958 and 1970, and even in 1982 and 1994. The wealthy, globalised

Brazilian football had to return symbolically, in 2002, to the modest origins of most of its players in order to recognise the myths that surround the origin of the victorious Brazilian football of the 1950s.

Table 4.1: Significant Contemporary Comments on the Causes of Brazilian National Defeats in World Cup Finals

1938

The Brazilians, mostly with black faces and mixed blood of black input, have possession of marvellous natural qualities that make them born football players. Unfortunately, the idea that football is a team sport did not arise in their brains. (Gabriel Hanot, *Miroir des Sports,* 1938, cited in *L'Équipe Magazine*, no. 837, April 1998, p. 38)

I think that one of the conditions of the Brazilian victories in European matches is due to the fact that we had the courage this time to send to Europe a team frankly Afro-Brazilian (Gilberto Freyre, writing in *Correio da Manhã*, 15 June 1938)

Our style of game contrasts with the Europeans' by its qualities of cunning, surprise and slightness, by an individual spontaneity through which we show our mulatto characteristics. (Freyre 1943, pp. 431–32)

1950 and 1954

Brazilian football champions 'are generally lads of mixed blood, badly fed and with irremovable perverted health (*taras de saúde*)'. Soares attributes defeat to the fact that players would have been 'infected people, who in the way that they practise their sport compensate for their lack of force and health with agility'. The journalist of *Jornal dos Sports* replies, stating that some of our great players 'are men of pure blood and some even have blue blood'. This would be the only explicit reference where the idea of an inferior mixed race is clear in the aftermath of 1950 cup. (Moura 1998, p. 144)

The Brazilian players lacked what is lacking for the Brazilian people in general ... The causes ... touch on the foundations of social science in the comparative study of races, environment, climate, eating habits, spirit, culture, and individual and common living processes ...

Our people's psychosocial state is still *green* [i.e. immature or unripe], and the athletes emerging from amongst the people cannot improvise the conditions and tools for overcoming [such immaturity] in athletic contests, requiring the mobilisation of greater organic resources and reserves ...

Given the state of the Brazilian people, only by chance or contingency might we become world football champions and establish hegemony in this sport ... In Brazilian football, flashy trim lends artistic expression to the match, to the detriment of yield and results. *Exhibition* jeopardises *competition*. It would be easy to compare the physiognomy of a Brazilian all-star team, made up mostly of blacks and mulattoes, with that of Argentine, German, Hungarian, or English football. (Lyra Filho 1954, pp. 49–64).

1998

Maybe this was the final World Cup of nationalism. The supporters painted their faces with the colours of their flags in order to say a tribal farewell to any notion of a country. In the future the supporters will be composed of false savages and World Cups will be what this one was in a disguised manner, a tournament of trade-marks or *griffes*. (Luís Fernando Veríssimo, writing in *Jornal do Brasil*, 17 July 1998, p. 11)

Put into jail those who have stolen from the street cleaner the joy of brandishing the national football shirt to the whole world. Put into jail those who have shot at our major glory. Yes, I know, it's only football. But it is only football that makes mad the only genuinely *mestizo* country in the world, where we are proud of being the demoralisation of this stupidity which is the notion of race, when we proudly have descendants of people from Nigerians to Finnish, from Japanese to Arabs; and now they shamefully take away our football. (João Ubaldo Ribeiro, writing in *O Globo*, 19 July 1998, p. 144)

I hope that the defeat has served to finish with some myths. Players that think that life can be summed up in jewellery and the latest model cars. Maybe it is their distance from the reality of the country. Maybe it is to ignore what it means to be a world champion for the guy in the street corner [for ordinary people]. (Sergio Noronha, writing in *Jornal do Brasil*, 13 July 1998, p. 11)

Acknowledgements

I would like to thank Leslie Bethell, Rory Miller and James Dunkerley for their invitation and hospitality during the Football in the Americas conference. I would also like to thank the late Eduardo Archetti for my first introduction into the international football academic fraternity, through which I was able to collaborate in some of Richard Giulianotti's projects. I would therefore like to dedicate this article to the memory of Eduardo Archetti, an old friend since the 1970s, a great anthropologist uniting colleagues from Europe to Latin America, who sadly is no longer among us.

Notes

1   It is well known that the construction of a national identity is, paradoxically, mediated by international factors such as shared social and historical transformations, common channels of communication and a sharp attention to what other countries consider to be markers of nationality (see Hobsbawm & Ranger 1983; Anderson 1983; Thiesse 1999).

2   Prior to 1930, the only significant international football competition involving teams from different continents took place during the Olympic Games.

3   For the importance of Germany's victory in the 1954 World Cup for its national identity after World War II, see Gebauer (1999). For the Italian victories in 1934 and 1938 World Cups in the context of the fascist regime, see Papa & Panico (1993, pp. 185–201) and Milza (1990); for the case of Argentina, see Archetti (1994).

4   For the journalistic literature about 1950, the most complete account is in Perdigão (2000); the most important items of academic literature are DaMatta (1982); Vogel (1982); Guedes (1998); and Moura (1998). For a journalistic account of 1998, see Caldeira (2002), and for academic interpretations of its significance, see Leite Lopes (1999b) and Guedes (2000).

5   At this early point in the essay an important change that occurred during this period should be identified. Between 1958, the date of its first World Cup victory in Sweden, and 1970, when it won its third victory in Mexico, Brazilian football became increasingly prominent on the international scene, but Brazilian players still based their careers at home. However, during the 1980s and 1990s, a period of global professionalism, there was an intensification of player circulation around the world, especially to European teams.

6   The process of Import Substitution Industrialisation (ISI) was central to Brazil's economic development from 1930 to 1964. Such a process, which in the 1930s and early 1940s seems to have been unintentional, but which then became an official policy of industrialisation, supplied the population with increased confidence. On Brazilian football as an English import, see Hamilton (2001); for the rapid spread and diffusion of football from elites to working classes and the ways in which it was appropriated in the outskirts of Rio de Janeiro from the early 1920s, see Pereira (2001).

7   Competitions such as the Olympic Games or the World Cup offered emergent countries a context for the display of national qualities that would otherwise go unnoticed due to the peripheral position these countries held in the economic, political and cultural realms. Unlike the European nations, which had gone through a process of nation-building earlier, in Brazil this process happened simultaneously with the impressive diffusion of football among the country's urban population.

8   See Freyre's preface to Filho's seminal book (Rodrigues Filho 1964); see also quotations from Freyre in Table 4.1.

9   Both teams went into competition after hiring the best players from
     the working classes who were making the transition from amateur to
     professional football. Most of the players on the team in 1950 were
     from Vasco; the remainder came from other clubs in Rio de Janeiro
     and São Paulo. The national team of 1950 replaced the 1938 genera-
     tion, which had been relatively successful with players of the quality of
     Leônidas da Silva and Domingos da Guia.

10   The actual construction of the Maracanã during the period of democ-
     racy that followed the end of the authoritarian Estado Nôvo in 1945
     was different from the construction of the Pacaembu stadium in São
     Paulo in 1940. The latter was a project carried out by the dictatorial
     government of Getúlio Vargas in order to appease the regional upper
     classes who had just lost a civil war.

11   On the reasons for the unusual organisation of the 1950 event, see
     Glanville and Weinstein (1958, pp. 122–30).

12   The only other defeat suffered by the host team in the final match of
     the World Cup was when Sweden lost to Brazil in 1958. In that case,
     the Brazilian team was considered to be superior; therefore, it was
     expected to win. Moreover, Sweden did not rely on football for the
     construction of its nationality in the same way that Brazil depended on
     it in 1950. All of the other countries that hosted the World Cup either
     won the final match or did not reach it.

13   The commentary of Gilberto Freyre, about Brazilian football being a
     marker of national traits, can be interpreted as being homologous to
     the physical techniques resulting from a socialisation process that
     included traditional practices usually defined as folkloric. Our appro-
     priation of these revolutionary arguments must nevertheless guard
     against the possibility that an essentialist interpretation could also be
     made of the contribution of black ethnicity to Brazilian football as a
     response to racist adversaries. The use of this interpretation must
     emphasise relationships rather than intrinsic properties and qualities.

14   It is not a coincidence that the writer and journalist Nelson Rodrigues
     defined this self-deprecating sentiment as a 'stray-dog complex' in
     order to extinguish it prior to the 1958 World Cup and to recover the
     success of Brazilian football. The performance of the Brazilian team
     during the 1958 World Cup signals its internal changes — that is, an
     inversion of the prior stigmatisation with the progressive 'darkening'

of the players, with the presence of Pelé, Garrincha, Vavá, Zito and Djalma Santos (see Leite Lopes 1997).

15   This tendency has been increasing and spreading: in a little over a year in the late 1990s, approximately 700 footballers left Brazil 'to take their chances in 59 countries' (*Le Monde*, 4 July 1998). Also, Brazilian coaches and assistants, who had less chance of making it in Europe than the players, started going to the Middle East in the 1970s, opening a secondary field of possibilities for players. Coaches of Brazilian national teams such as Zagallo, Parreiras, Telê Santana and Felipão worked in the East where they built or consolidated good careers. Soon afterwards, Japan also started hiring Brazilian players.

16   I was present at these public training sessions, and was able to observe that admission tickets sponsored by the Brazilian airline, Varig, were distributed by the city authorities, which also improvised a restaurant in a tent next to the training ground. Besides the Brazilian supporters and the local population, children accompanied by their parents would come from all over Paris to see their Brazilian idols play. In another tent, the postal service received and displayed an enormous number of letters sent to the Brazilian players. There was also a press conference centre sponsored by Coca-Cola and equipped with 400 qualified journalists near the training ground.

17   Since the military dictatorship was then at its peak, some authors highlight the paradoxical participation and autonomy of the players in relation to the technical staff and officials of the 1970 team. The participation of the players in important decisions perpetuated the little tradition of experiences that had began in the 1958 World Cup, and had continued in teams such as Botafogo and Santos in the 1960s, culminating in the profound and explicit 'democracy' of Corinthians, a team from São Paulo, in the 1980s, when the country went through a process of social movements and redemocratisation.

5

Football Fans and the Argentine Crisis of 2001–02: The Crisis, the World Cup and the Destiny of the *Patria*

Pablo Alabarces

While I was finishing my book, *Fútbol y patria*[1] — an analysis of the relations between football and narratives of the nation in Argentina during the twentieth century that was eventually published in Buenos Aires in 2002 — the country was shaken by an unprecedented economic and political crisis, which led to mass demonstrations and ended with the resignation of two presidents in a fortnight. Those demonstrations showed, surprisingly, the everyday pervasiveness of a football culture that seemed to become politicised (in terms of songs, the shirts of both local and national teams, and confrontations with the police). A few months later, while the continuing political and social instability illustrated the deep fragmentation of society, the World Cup in Korea and Japan allowed the emergence of contradictory discourses. Some believed that success in football would be the route to escape the crisis and lead to an eventual reconstruction of society, while many others believed that defeat for Argentina in the World Cup would instigate a new social crisis. Both predictions failed to materialise. This work aspires to read that process, through participant observation and the analysis of the media (printed, radio and television), and to postulate some hypotheses for the interpretation of a — perhaps new — role for football identities in Argentina.

The Crisis: Armed with a Thesis[2]

I finished writing *Fútbol y patria* in November 2001, at that time in the form of my PhD thesis. On the evening of 19 December, I was editing the English version when I stopped to listen to an address to the country from the Argentine President, Fernando De la Rúa, via national television and radio. It had been a dramatic day, with news that the desperately impoverished popular classes had been looting shops and that the middle classes had been on the streets demonstrating. Their savings, which were theoretically protected by the 1:1 linkage of the Argentine peso to the dollar, were being held in insolvent banks, and there was no possibility of being able to withdraw them (this was known as the *corralito* or fence).[3] Rumours accompanied the news: the declaration of a 'state of siege' (that is, the restriction of the constitutional right to hold meetings and public demonstrations), repression and deaths from police bullets.

The President spoke at about 11.00 p.m., and announced the latest news: shops had been looted, people repressed and killed (at that stage there were 16 dead across the country). De la Rúa assured the nation that the situation was under control, and claimed that in order to avoid further incidents instigated by 'organised groups', it was necessary to decree a state of siege. A few minutes later, everything took off.

I lived in the Congreso district of Buenos Aires, a few blocks from the Argentine parliament building. Although I lived in an apartment, I could hear people banging saucepans (or *cacerolas*) in the streets below. I imagined the latest demonstration by angry savers over their money, which lay 'seized' in the banks, and I decided to see what was happening on the streets. I thought that it would only take me a few minutes. I took my thesis with me in order to continue working on it while sitting in a bar. In Avenida Rivadavia, thousands of people banging saucepans began to gather. I joined the protestors. In the Plaza del Congreso in front of the parliament building, there were already thousands of people banging their pans and chanting abuse at the government, demanding the resignation of the President and his Treasury Secretary (Domingo Cavallo) and chanting abuse against the state of siege, under which that very demonstration was illegal.[4] The *cacerolazo*, as the demonstration was known (because of the banging of the pans), was at its most fervent.[5] Demonstrators continued to arrive in droves. Many waved Argentine flags and wore the replica shirts of the national football team. I looked towards the Parliament steps and thought: 'It looks like a football terrace.' The colour — a plethora of light blue and white — along with the body language of the demonstrators, waving their arms rhythmically in time with the songs, and variations of the typical songs of the stadiums, all reminded me of the popular terraces of Argentine football. Several thousand demonstrators began to move towards the Plaza de Mayo, where the presidential palace — the Casa Rosada — is located, fifteen blocks away from Congress. When they arrived, the plaza was already full of crowds chanting the same songs — with one addition, the old (Peronist) chant, 'If this is not the people/where are they, then?' At approximately 1.00 a.m., the police began to use tear gas to control the crowds. Then military reinforcements arrived. We had to make our way back towards the Congress building. On the way, the demonstrators began to throw stones at the buildings and shops along the Avenida de Mayo. Still with the draft of my thesis under my arm, I continued to take part in the demonstration, which gathered once again on the steps of Congress, and still reminded me of a football terrace. At 4.00 a.m., the police forced the demonstrators to disperse again. One demonstrator was seriously wounded and died a few days later.

The following day, after Cavallo's resignation, the demonstrators returned for more. They were stronger now. Demonstrators appeared in an orderly fashion, and stood with people who had been trying to protest in the Plaza de Mayo (those who had been violently evicted by the police, time and time again, because of the paralysing fear of the authorities who refused to resign 'just' because a square had been taken over by a popular protest). They stood alongside members of left-wing political parties and several unions.[6] There were clashes in the nearby streets, with police blocking the way to the Casa Rosada. Tear gas gave way to bullets. During the day, the police murdered five demonstrators. Beyond those belonging to unions and political parties, groups of youths tried to break into the fenced off area next to the Plaza de Mayo. They were trained in combat with the police from their experience in the football stadiums or on the picket-lines of the unemployed — an important form of political protest in Argentina since 1994. Armed with handkerchiefs and lemons to resist the tear gas, they demonstrated their ingenuity by breaking off pieces of paving stones to use as missiles. At 5.00 p.m., abandoned by his party and by the

Peronist opposition, President De la Rúa resigned and left the Casa Rosada. The news calmed the atmosphere somewhat, although signs of the battle remained in the form of looted shops and the burnt-out premises of multinational companies.

What happened next can be explained quickly. The government was in the hands of the President of the Senate, Ramón Puerta (a Peronist), who was superseded a few days later by the Governor of the province of San Luis, Adolfo Rodríguez Saa (also a Peronist), who was chosen by Congress. Rodríguez Saa declared default on the interest payments on Argentina's huge foreign debt. A week later, with the continuation of the *cacerolazos* and a lack of political support, Rodríguez Saa resigned. In the demonstration of 29 December, three more young demonstrators were murdered by police in Buenos Aires, 10 kilometres from the Plaza de Mayo. Puerta refused to assume the presidency again, leaving the post to Senator Caamaño (also a Peronist). Then, on 1 January 2002, Senator Eduardo Duhalde, former Governor of Buenos Aires (and, predictably, a Peronist) was nominated as president by Congress. He promised that presidential elections would be brought forward. In early January, Duhalde decreed an end to the 'convertibility' plan (the economic plan which had linked the value of the Argentine peso to the US dollar since 1991). A devaluation of 40 per cent took place immediately; this devaluation in fact reached 400 per cent in just a few months. The end of the Argentine neo-conservative experiment brought with it (as well as five presidents within two weeks) an explosive rise in the rate of unemployment and poverty. The number of people classified as 'living in poverty' in Argentina doubled (from 27 per cent in January to 54 per cent in September 2002) and, while the official unemployment rate stood at 25 per cent at that time, it was estimated by journalists that the real figures were more likely to be around 40 per cent. Furthermore, industry was devastated by a lack of competitiveness. The working class was resigned to structural unemployment or under-employment in the black economy. The economy was left in foreign hands (98 per cent of the mining industry, 93 per cent of the fuel industry, 92 per cent of communications, 89 per cent of manufacturing industry, 76 per cent of food and tobacco sectors).[7] Public services were privatised and in the hands of multinational companies (Cicalese et al. 2002, p. 7). At the same time, however, the middle and upper classes — global travellers who had savings in dollars — had been seduced by false richness. They had surrendered to excessive consumerism and famous international labels thanks to the over-valuation of the peso. Argentina was known by some as Belinda: a third of its inhabitants lived as if they were in Belgium; two thirds as if they were in India. Moreover, the events of December 2001 had left 25 dead on the streets of Argentina.

My thesis was finished: I defended it in February 2002, and it was published in July. After all that happened, and with the proximity of the FIFA World Cup in Korea and Japan in 2002, I feared that I would have to rewrite it completely.

Football and *Patria*: The Return of Politics

Fútbol y patria focuses on football as a 'discourse' of tribal identity in contemporary Argentina. At the same time, a weakness of football lies in the difficulty it has in articulating new and evolving discourses or expressions of national identity. The mass media are unable to mediate a successful discourse. In conclusion, I argued for the need to re-read the political ways in which civil society in Argentina could articulate new expressions of identity, in spite of its weaknesses and the country's peripheral and subordinate status in a globalised world. A lengthy sociological debate preceded my conclusion that football in Argentina consists of depoliticised discourse, as do the mass media, and that this is typical of neo-conservative societies. All social change or progress should necessarily be political, and therefore not within the realms of football or the media (Alabarces 2002, pp. 209–13). These conclusions undoubtedly deserve an extended analysis.

In *Fútbol y patria*, I presented the difficulties of contemporary political discourses in producing new and efficient national 'narratives' — narratives that could produce new social practices. The withdrawal of the state, which had been the great 'narrator' throughout the country's history once Argentina had adopted neo-conservative policies in the early 1990s, left this task to two different actors. The first was the mass media — a machine that produces stories which are geared to the maximisation of economic profit (that is, aimed to produce consumers rather than citizens). The other actor was civil society, profoundly weakened after the experience of the military dictatorship of 1976–83 and the subsequent failure of the Radical government of Raúl Alfonsín to bring those responsible for the dictatorship to justice during the subsequent democratic transition.[8] This weakness was further exacerbated by the deep ideological shift of Peronism, the dominant political movement in Argentina, which transformed its discourse and policies from progressive populism into a conservative revolution with the election of Carlos Menem in 1989.

The military terror of 1976–83 and political betrayal of 1987–89 weakened society, with the exception of certain pressure groups connected to the most privileged sectors of the middle classes, such as certain consumer or environmental protection groups. The other exception was the reaction to specific cases of state excesses, such as police repression. The only organisations that survived this period with some symbolic importance were the human rights groups born during the dictatorship. These included the group known as the Mothers and Grandmothers of the Plaza de Mayo, as well as the group of Children of the Disappeared (HIJOS). However, these groups were not representative of society as a whole, but limited to their specific demands.

In this context, football's attempt to provide the discourse of a new national story must necessarily fail, because it is a discourse based on sporting heroes, and Diego Maradona's retirement represented the end of the last sporting hero in Argentina. In addition, the conditions imposed by the media transformed this discourse into a commodity, making it incapable of producing new political practices. The current social, political and economic conditions of Argentine society make it a country of football fans, united by the Argentine shirt, and sharing an impossible dream of imaginary success — but one that is sporting, not political or economic. National identity — a phenomenon always imagined but never imaginary — must be based on specific elements that indicate belonging (Anderson 1982). If being Argentine does not include the right to work, food, health care and education, then it is not worth it. Identity must be inscribed in a physical, not an imaginary, way (Jenkins 1996). The chauvinist tales of sports presenters do not involve any physical inscription (Sarlo 2001, p. 18).

The events of December 2001 confirmed this analysis. National symbols, such as flags and Argentine football shirts, had been revived. However, the popular movement, influenced by the practices learnt in football stadiums — the spontaneous creation of songs and chants, but also the tactics of resisting police oppression — became purely political. Thus an act of displacement (in which football's practices were placed in new contexts in order to produce new meanings) provided the only opportunity for a weakened and marginalised society to produce new meanings of identity. As Thompson (1979) argues, identity is an experience, but it is an experience that involves constant struggle and conflict. In this confrontation, for example, the globalised conditions of Argentine society were perceived as economic issues. That the attacks were directed specifically at banks and at private companies highlights the fact that globalisation was beginning to be interpreted as a process that concentrated wealth and involved the loss of political autonomy, and not as the illusory access to global symbolic goods. In addition, the fact that later demonstrations in January 2002 targeted the mass media also indicates that the public was distancing itself from journalistic discourse.

The politicisation of football routines mentioned above (their displacement and replacement into a political context) also needs further explanation. As María Graciela Rodríguez points out:

> Although it is certain that consumerism itself holds a dominant position as long as a consumer, by definition, is not a producer … cultural consumerism occupies a secondary position and relates to the legitimacy or not of the product concerned. For the *motoqueros*,[9] for instance, who were particularly visible during the events of December 2001, cultural consumerism justified their position in the confrontation as the staging of an identity: 'I come from *escraches*[10] against the military, from the rock festivals of Los Redondos, from the football ground, and I am a lorry-driver,' comments Sebas[tián].[11] This statement demonstrates the convergence of diverse practices which took place during the events of December of 2001 in Argentina, in the realisation of a socially situated political action. Practices of cultural consumerism, of political activism and of work, all constituted from relatively subordinated positions and with some

degree of illegitimacy that were articulated in a political symbolisation of an 'Other' in a particularly critical context. (Rodríguez 2003, p. 8).

However, this analysis merits further discussion. The testimony of Sebastián provides a random list of topics whose only feature in common is their subordination. It names several issues: politics (from the *escraches* against the military), socio-aesthetic identities (the rock festivals of *Los Redondos*), the football stadium, employment ('I am a lorry-driver', a job that is low in status but also autonomous, belonging to the black economy in the world of work in the popular classes). For this young militant, politicisation is a consequence of a practically apolitical world. The *aguante*[12] is understood to be a simple objection towards a world they do not understand — and there is probably no attempt to understand it.

Another interviewee, also quoted by Rodríguez, states:

> I have been going to see *el bicho* [the club Argentinos Juniors in Buenos Aires] for a long time. I realised that the guys [the police] aren't as violent repressing a *banda*[13] as they are in a political demonstration. It is also certain that the *banda* itself is more violent, while in a [political] demonstration, apart from the fact that they carry sticks, as far as I know, there are no real problems. (Carlos, 30 years, courier). (Rodríguez 2003, p. 9)

This adds a further perspective. The comparison between football and the world of politics becomes explicit. On one hand, the perception is that politics receives a greater punishment ('the guys aren't as violent repressing a *banda* as they are in a political demonstration'), and implies that the political world is taken more seriously than the football world. However, at the same time, the interviewee adds: 'It is also certain that the *bandas* tend to be more violent.' The interpretation is clear: the police punish most those who resist least. The football world, although depoliticised, is more resistant to the police than the political world. Add to this the symbolic power of football: if violence in sport is basically expressive, symbolic rather than functional (this is the hypothesis which explains the *aguante*), then according to the interviewee, football's battle with the police appears to be more symbolic, but also more emotionally charged.

What is certain is that 25 deaths in a few days of repression (and two more were still missing on 26 June 2002) are equivalent to several years of fighting in football stadiums.

Football is Always There (Thank God)

The fact that the Argentine national football team was a favourite to win the World Cup in 2002 stimulated high expectations in the country, and these were fuelled by the media. A survey published on the day of the first match against Nigeria revealed that 85 per cent of Argentines thought that Argentina would win the tournament (*Página 12*, 1 June 2002). It was not surprising which countries those polled did not want to see as alternative winners: England (33 per cent), Brazil (21 per cent) and the United States (12 per cent). England's place at the bottom of the popularity stakes confirmed other statements in *Fútbol y patria* (Alabarces 2002, pp. 190–95). The legendary status of hostilities against the English surpasses any other rivalry in Argentine football. The position of Brazil in second place, of course, represents a local rivalry. It was the third team that was more surprising, since there was not even a remote possibility that the United States would win the World Cup. The only possible interpretation of this dislike of the US team lay in politics. In mid-2002, Argentina's sporting rivalries were tinged with anti-imperialism. At the same time, however, 17 per cent of those questioned preferred Brazil as an alternative winner of the tournament, while 14 per cent preferred Uruguay. A sense of solidarity seemed to appear, as intercontinental ties were stronger than the historical sporting rivalries.

In the same article, journalist Raúl Kollman reminded the readership that 80 per cent of people believed that the political, economic and social situation would worsen, and that 70 per cent described Duhalde's government as 'bad' or 'very bad'. Football aspirations, then, led to a kind of apocalyptic prophecy, as the article suggested that football success would provide a magical solution to the political crisis: the suspension (if not the end) of the conflict, and the extension of a 'honeymoon' period for the government. However, that prediction was always credited to others. There was no one who would admit to that belief themselves, yet it was attributed without hesitation to others — to 'cultural zombies', to use an old expression of Stuart Hall (1984) who, blinded by sporting triumph, would imagine a world of roses and a victorious country.

However, at the same time there was also circulating what might be called the revolutionary 'counter-prophecy'. In the same article, Kollman stated that the Governor of the province of Santa Fé, Carlos Reutemann, had said in a meeting with the President: 'It's necessary to resolve the matter of the *corralito*, because if we are knocked out of the World Cup and we don't solve the issue of the *corralito*, who knows what can happen in this country.' (*Página 12*, 1 June 2002) The 'counter-prophecy' therefore considered the possibility that a social uprising would take place if Argentina were defeated in the World Cup. After the team's elimination, the reaction of angry *piqueteros* and savers combined, incited by defeat on the football pitch, would inevitably lead to a social revolution and the lynching of politicians in the Plaza de Mayo.

Argentina's failure on the pitch (the team was eliminated from the competition after the first phase with just one victory, a draw and a defeat, and only two goals scored) did not allow the first prediction to be tested, but the second prediction proved to be wrong as well. So why had there been so many incorrect predictions? Basically, the explanation lies in the suggested cause–effect relationship between football and politics: the unproven link between sporting achievement and political success. Without any doubt, the political, economic and social climate encouraged exaggerated expectations. Success on the pitch would have been welcomed by a population who had been hit hard by the devaluation of the peso, inflation, unemployment, hunger, poverty, the collapse of the illusion of being part of the First World and the betrayal of the political classes (the seven plagues of the neo-conservative inheritance). However, Argentina's exit from the World Cup actually demonstrated that football is … well, football.

The discourse of the mass media turned the prediction into a yearning. Players were asked repeatedly how they related their predicted success to people's 'hard reality'. Juan Pablo Sorín, perhaps one of the more politically active players, stated: 'When I listen to our national anthem I try to think about the true Argentine people

… Among others, I think of those in Catamarca, Formosa and in other cities where they don't have even one peso and perhaps the only happiness for them could be given by us.' (*Crónica,* 3 June 2002)

Quotations attributed to the Argentina coach, Marcelo Bielsa, were also very interesting. He deliberately and carefully distanced himself from substituting sport for politics and emphasised the aesthetic nature of the sport:

> What we offer might be evaluated in an inappropriate way. This is about football — an aesthetic, visual, artistic game — and we are being given the impression that we can offer everything to the Argentine people. In no way can we assume that football is a substitute for anything. You seem to imply that it is a substitute for something else, but in my view it is not a substitute for anything … We have a big responsibility that we don't ignore — that is, to fulfil our potential. And, if we succeed on the pitch, we deserve only one reward: popular recognition. And if we don't make it, we also deserve only one punishment: popular disapproval … What I mean is, if the people in our country were prosperous, we would not be exempt from fulfilling our obligation: to try to play football well. (*Clarín Deportivo,* 25 May 2002)

However, the broadcasters of matches, on radio as well as television, insisted on making the link that Bielsa denied so emphatically. Some of the best examples could be heard on La Red, the radio station with the largest audience during the 2002 World Cup, and a subsidiary of Torneos y Competencias, the owners of Argentine football.[14] Sport presenter Sebastián Vignolo, in the preview to the match against England on 7 June, said: 'It is a pleasure to find our colours in every corner [of this country], the colours of the national flag in every neighbourhood, in every street, on every traffic light … Today the *patria* is united, the football team and the flag …' Or, on 2 June before the match against Nigeria: 'I can see a First World team representing a Third World country … this team will look for victory to give happiness to people who are going through a bad time … In the most difficult time for the country, this has to be Argentina's World Cup. They have to bring us some happiness.'

Meanwhile, in the preview to the England clash, the presenter kept mentioning 'our dear but suffering country', emphasising the 'need' for a sporting victory to cheer up the people: 'Fortunately, Argentines have the chance of at least 30 days, I don't say to be unaware of the reality that surrounds us and rips apart our daily lives … but … where we can feel part of the First World is in football. And today, for that reason, Argentina wants to raise its flag, the football one, you know what I mean …' (*Radio La Red*, 7 June 2002)

However, after the defeat, the leading journalist of Torneos y Competencias, Fernando Niembro (a member of Menem's government, a former official and connected to the right wing of the Peronist Party), was concerned to distance himself from the consequences beyond the strictly sporting: 'If Argentina had won, the country's problems would not have been solved. It is a strictly sporting disappointment.' (*Radio La Red*, 12 June 2002). He added the following day: 'We are sad, but this doesn't change our lives. People in Argentina have the same problems as yesterday and continue to worry about getting a job and avoiding being mugged on street corners.'

Marketing and the *Patria*: The Nation and Transnational Businesses

Another interesting area for analysis is that of the businesses which exploited football and patriotism in their advertising campaigns during the 2002 World Cup. Their investment — despite the severe downturn in consumerism — was important. Direct TV, a satellite television company, paid US$400 million for the broadcasting rights for the 2002 World Cup in Argentina, Chile, Colombia, Mexico, Uruguay and Venezuela. Coca-Cola invested US$2.5 million in marketing and publicity in Argentina (*Clarín Económico*, 26 May 2002). The official sponsors of the Argentine national team were Carrefour (a French supermarket chain), Coca-Cola, Quilmes (a brewery), Visa, adidas and Repsol-YPF (an oil company).

Carrefour was the exclusive sponsor of the national teams of both Argentina and France (despite being pre-tournament favourites, both were eliminated after the first phase). Coca-Cola, as is widely known, sponsored several teams, as did Visa and adidas. All are transnational companies, as are McDonald's, Gillette and Mastercard, which also rolled out campaigns. The most interesting cases, though, are the other two sponsors.

Quilmes, traditionally a national brewery, was sold to the Brazilian company, Brahma, a few days before the beginning of the World Cup. This allowed a competitor in the Argentine market, the German brewing firm Isenbeck, to carry out an aggressive campaign in which it questioned the legitimacy of Quilmes in exploiting Argentina's football patriotism. Isenbeck's first advertisement (a full page) had an image of Brazil's national flag where the sun had been replaced with the cap of a bottle of Quilmes. It was accompanied by the slogan: 'The Brazilians bought Quilmes. Just before the World Cup? How do you say "sold" in Portuguese?' And then: 'Isenbeck. We sell good beer. Nothing else.' This advertisement questioned the association of national feelings with the product (*Página 12,* 20 May 2002). The second advertisement was highly amusing and questioned the commitment to Argentina's cause. It also occupied a full page. Isenbeck claimed: 'The Brazilians bought Quilmes. Now, they cannot stop making new songs.' They included slogans which imitated football songs:

> We'll be back, we'll be back, we'll be back again
> We'll be champions again
> As in '86, '58, '62, '70, '78, '94
>
> We have to win, we have to win,
> But not against Brazil
> Against them, we'd rather draw.
> (*Página 12*, 27 May 2002)15

The case of Repsol-YPF deserves special analysis because for many years, since its foundation in the first half of the twentieth century, the oil company YPF had been the pride of the Argentine public sector, and had guaranteed Argentina's self-sufficiency in petroleum products for decades (it had also been a tool through which the government regulated gasoline prices). Its privatisation under Menem's government was highly suspicious and corruption was strongly suspected. Apart from that, it meant the end of government price-fixing, and the price of gasoline subsequently rose markedly. It also led to the disintegration of communities where YPF was located

— towns that were heavily reliant on the employment the company provided, such as Cutral Có and Plaza Huincul in the province of Neuquén, and Tartagal and General Mosconi in the province of Salta. Significantly, the most important social unrest at that time, when the *piqueteros* emerged, was in precisely those places. The memory of the role played by the public sector in the generation of employment and in the organisation of community life is still very strong in these towns, and the political practices of their inhabitants are organised along these lines. To make things worse, the privatised YPF was bought in 1999 by Repsol, the Spanish state oil company. This changed the deep national association for a foreign one, yet Repsol-YPF unfolded a huge publicity campaign during the World Cup, claiming: 'When the national team plays, we all play. YPF, more than a sponsor, official fan of the national team …' The slogan hid Repsol's logo.[16]

All these companies therefore dedicated their campaigns to the trivialisation of patriotism, and proposed a recurrent national argument. However, in all the cases the advertisements showed a marked difference compared with the previous World Cup. They acknowledged the fact that there had been a crisis and social unrest in Argentina. The main character of Repsol-YPF's advertisement said his prayers and asked for 'at least something to be happy about', praying for the ball to enter the opposition's net. Coca-Cola's slogan suggested 'Let's all hug each other again', implying that Argentines had stopped doing so.

All the sponsors, then, acknowledged the crisis. Something had happened in the country, but the market operators were beginning to believe in the possibility that the familiar discourse, the old heroic tale of football, victorious on the field, could replace a *patria* whose economy had significantly reduced in importance in the eyes of the IMF and Washington. Citizenship as a form of consumerism entered academic discourse (García Canclini 1994), and was at the basis of advertising campaigns. But here was also the wish that sporting success would heal the social, political and economic divisions, too real to be overcome by symbolic gestures, and that a magical displacement (from added value to 'football passion') would allow the transnational corporations to reap their rewards.

Conclusion: The Nation, the Politics and the (Still) Tribal Fans

This analysis has contributed to an interpretation of the role of football and Argentine identity. It seems that the crisis, people's behaviour, print media and radio discourse during the 2002 World Cup and Argentina's elimination from the competition provided further evidence to confirm all the hypotheses included in *Fútbol y patria*. Football was again only football, and politics only politics.

So what happened after the World Cup of 2002? In the political sphere, the middle classes seem to have recovered from their original indignation and from their street militancy, and brought a cautious end to their public protests. Apart from providing extra work for academic colleagues in social sciences who were frantically dedicated to analysing the events, the crisis of December 2001 produced a healthy repoliticisation of society and a growth in the discourse of progressive politics. Today the population is much more optimistic.

And football is still only football. After politicisation peaked during the crisis (the national team appeared with shirts defending the old public airline, Aerolíneas Argentinas, and its workers, and also supporting the teachers' pay demands), the waters calmed. Tribalism reappeared. Between World Cups, nobody cares about the national side. At its extreme, local football plays the role of a non-governmental organisation: it worked in collaboration with the organisation Missing Children, or with the Red Solidaria (Solidarity Network) — in the latter case helping to collect funds and goods to help those affected by floods in the city of Santa Fé in April 2003. The biggest 'contamination' with macro-political intervention was during the invasion of Iraq. Demands for peace were expressed in some stadiums, and some flags were waved in support of Saddam Hussein, as a means of complaining about the imperialist Anglo-Saxon invasion. But these examples also highlight persistent tribalism. When the war began, Colón fans, from the province of Santa Fé, waved a banner that read: 'Bush, in the stadium of Unión [from the same city] there is oil', with the (metaphorical) objective of hoping their rivals would be bombed. But after the floods the stadium of Colón was seriously affected, and the fans of Unión responded with: 'In Colon's stadium there is … water.' Even political issues, such as the war, are reinterpreted as tribal banter.

This chapter closes with two final observations which illustrate a marked separation between football and political worlds. Of course, the description and interpretations are only temporary, and relationships might change in the future. Football discourse complemented the political national one for many years, and was its basic support at some historical moments, the climax being the case of Maradona. That scenario could be repeated in the (unlikely) event of a new 'Maradona-style' figure emerging.

These final examples differentiate the two worlds. The first one was the celebration of the twenty-fifth anniversary of the 1978 World Cup victory, in July 2003. Most journalists insisted that at the time the military dictatorship was credited with Argentina's success and that football itself was not given a high enough profile. Some of the players involved in the organisation of the celebration (in particular Ricky Villa, who had played in the World Cup, and Claudio Morresi, brother of a *desaparecido*) tried to balance the debt that football had with the memory of the dictatorship at the River Plate stadium, involving a tribute to human rights organisations. However, the Mothers of the Plaza de Mayo were not invited to be part of the ceremony, and attendance was also low. The football establishment was not willing to accept a recognition of its complicity with the military governments of 1976–83 — and nor were the fans prepared to recognise that.

Finally, on 26 June 2002, in a *piquetero* demonstration in the Puente Pueyrredón, which forms the border between the City of Buenos Aires and the rest of the province, the police killed two young militants. Politically motivated murder continued to be only politics. On the other hand, the River Plate *barra brava* killed two fans of Newell's Old Boys of Rosario in April 2003. The fans were still, and persistently, killing each other, and not fighting those who held political power. It was not surprising.

Acknowledgements

The research for this paper was financed by UBA, FONCYT and CONICET (Argentina). It was made possible by many contributors: first María Graciela Rodríguez, with whom I presented an ad hoc seminar in the Department of Communication (FCS-UBA) and discussed several of my hypotheses: she generally disagreed with me, so I cannot make her responsible for what this chapter contains. I am also grateful to the students of Communication and Sociology who gathered the sources and remained upbeat during the pitiful World Cup in 2002: Andrés Accorinti, Vanina Celada, Luis Cicalese, María Eugenia Curto, Fernando Czyz, Ariel González, Santiago Marino, Santiago Pernín, Bettina Presman, Camila Quaglio, Malvina Silba, Mauro Spagnuolo, Federico Torres, Mariana Torres Day. Thanks also extend to Mariana Conde, Christian Dodaro, José Garriga Zucal, Daniel Salerno, and Verónica Moreira, who always contribute, with their support and talent, to my general confusion.

Notes

1   I have preferred to use the Latin term *patria* instead of 'fatherland', because it represents more accurately the meanings of a legal and institutional community and its associated connotations. This is in line with the usage of Smith (1991).

2   On the Argentine crisis, see also Carranza 2005 and Auyero 2006.

3   In order to defeat hyperinflation, the Peronist government of Carlos Menem pegged the Argentine peso to the US dollar in 1991. It became increasingly impossible to sustain this exchange rate, and from the middle of the decade a deepening economic crisis due to over-valuation led to increasing unemployment. The crisis deepened after the devaluation of the Brazilian *real* in 1999, which made Argentina more uncompetitive and diverted the attention of the international currency markets to its worsening economic problems. In December 2001, the De la Rúa government imposed the so-called *corralito*, freezing bank accounts in a final attempt to stave off the collapse of the currency and of the country's domestic banking system.

4   In a demonstration formed largely by the Buenos Aires middle classes, an unsuspected solidarity was formed with the suburban popular classes, the people against whom the state of siege was directed (since the lootings had taken place primarily in the poor neighbourhoods of the suburbs of Buenos Aires and in other provinces of Argentina). Those same middle classes seemed largely to withdraw from the public protest after De la Rúa's resignation and the devaluation that would happen a few days later.

5   The *cacelorazo* is not an Argentine invention. There have been many antecedents, a famous one being the protests of Chilean (right-wing)

housewives during the last days of Salvador Allende's socialist government in 1973.

6   My own participation became more organised. No longer with my thesis under my arm, I joined the teachers' unions who, lacking training in this sort of exercise, were easily repressed.

7   Figures are taken from Cicalese et al. (2002, p. 7). A chart of the Argentine situation under the neo-conservative order can be seen in Alabarces (2002, p. 21).

8   In 1987, the radical government had to stop the trials against the military because of their pressures.

9   *Motoqueros* is the popular expression for couriers who travel through downtown Buenos Aires by motor-cycle. As Rodríguez points out, in the events of 20 December they played an important role, attacking the police on their motorcycles and establishing quick communication between the groups of dispersed demonstrators. One of them was killed by the police.

10   *Escrache* is a type of political action performed by left-wing demonstrators and consists of visiting the houses of military to protest, making sure that the neighbours know who they are living next to.

11   Rodríguez draws this from M. Blejman: 'Moto bronca', *Radar*, 6 January 2002, pp. 20–21. Los Redondos was one of the most popular rock bands.

12   *Aguante* is an Argentine word (originating among young people from the popular classes and specially linked to football) that defines resistance by means of a physical fight against someone considered as 'other' and understood as an opponent (another group of football fans or the police). The *aguante* is also a radical form of reaffirming masculinity. See Alabarces et al. (2000) and Alabarces et al. (2005).

13   The *bandas* are the groups of fans known as *barras bravas* or organised groups from the *barras*.

14   Torneos y Competencias is a sports marketing and media company with extensive interests in Argentine football. In 2001 it held the TV rights to the Argentine national league and the merchandising rights for all the teams in the top division, as well as operating its own television station and studios. In addition, it owned the oldest Argentine sports periodical, *El Gráfico*, as well as several sports apparel stores and sports bars.

15   Thus combining the dates of Brazil's World Cup victories (1958, 1962, 1970, 1994) with those of Argentina (1978, 1986).

16   On YPF, its privatisation and its influence on crisis and *piquetes,* see Svampa (2005).

6

Football Fandom and Identity in Mexico: The Case of the Pumas Football Club and Youthful Romanticism

Roger Magazine

The Mexican professional football league consists of 20 clubs, four of which are known as 'national teams' since they attract a nationwide rather than a regional following. Each of the four 'national' clubs represents for fans a different identity and set of values — or what I prefer to call an 'ideal vision' for Mexican society.

América, a team owned by the powerful television conglomerate Televisa, represents the promise of a free global market and capitalist competition, paying high salaries to international and national stars. Perhaps because América represents the currently dominant social vision in Mexico, all three of the other national teams consider América to be their biggest rival.

Las Chivas of Guadalajara, the only national team located outside Mexico City, follows a creed of *puros mexicanos* (pure Mexicans), fielding only Mexican players and exemplifying an ideal of national autonomy. Guadalajara is the largest city in the region from which many of Mexico's national symbols have come — tequila and mariachis, for example. This social perspective matches a vision for Mexican society of import substitution and revolutionary nationalism, one that constituted the dominant state strategy from the 1930s to the 1970s.[1]

Cruz Azul, the third national team, is owned by the cement cooperative of the same name and symbolises working-class identity and values. Its nickname, appropriately, is *la máquina azul* (the 'blue machine'). Like the inward-looking nationalism of Chivas, the working-class vision represented by Cruz Azul enjoyed strong state support in the recent past in the form of state corporatism, with its government-backed cooperatives and unions, the majority of which have been weakened or disappeared entirely since the switch to neo-liberal policy in the early 1980s. In the rivalries between América and these other two teams, therefore, we can read the tensions resulting from recent and dramatic shifts in national political economic strategy.

This paper focuses on the ideal vision for society represented by the fourth national team, Pumas, which represents the National Autonomous University of Mexico (UNAM). Pumas follows the philosophy of *puros jóvenes*, or pure youths, which refers to the fact that the team fields only young players. Most of the Pumas fans also see themselves as youths, and explain that they are attracted to the team because of the perspective on life and football that they share with the players. Among these fans, the importance of being young is that they and the players are closer to something inherently and basically human, for they have not yet been dulled by scientific objectivity or democratic rationality, or influenced by corruption and clientelism — by which I mean the long-term relationships between powerful patrons and weaker clients in which the former provide material benefits and protection in exchange for the latter's political loyalty.[2] Without these negative influences that come to transform and dominate older people after they have spent time in the world of work and politics, they are free genuinely to experience emotions such as love, passion or joy. Thus their practices on the pitch, in the stands or in life in general are guided by these emotions and not by dependence on others, as in clientelism, or by external objective rules or logic as in modern democracy or the free market.[3] Thus, if Chivas fans look to what is most Mexican for their vision of football and society, Cruz Azul fans to the working class, and América fans to the best that money can buy (whether Mexican or foreign), then the Pumas fans look to the emotional capacity they see as inherently human. While Pumas fans see América and what it represents as their greatest rival, they do so in a way that also opposes them to Chivas and Cruz Azul, which both represent a style of being Mexican that is closely associated with corruption and clientelism. Also, unlike Chivas and Cruz Azul, the ideal vision of the Pumas did not enjoy a dominant position in Mexico's past — or at least not in most historians' portrayals of that past.

This chapter begins by discussing how Pumas fans conceptualise their ideal vision for society through the idioms of styles of play and of fans' support. Subsequently, it describes how one group of Pumas fans — a supporters' club — put this ideal vision into practice, formulating a critique of the processes of democratisation, corruption and commercialisation that were affecting them directly. In conclusion, a comparison is drawn between the ideal vision of Pumas fans and the Romantic movement of the late eighteenth and early nineteenth centuries, in an attempt to contextualise the former within a broader framework that extends beyond the world of football.

The data presented here were collected during 18 months of intensive ethnographic fieldwork in 1996 and 1997, and then during short periods of additional research in 1998 and 2000. The period of intensive research consisted of participation in all of the activities of the supporters' club, including gatherings before and after home games, chanting during the games themselves, trips to many of the away games, club meetings, gatherings to paint flags and banners, and parties in members' homes. In addition, I taped interviews with over 40 *porra* members at my home, at theirs, or at their places of work or study.[4] Subsequent research in 1998 and 2000 consisted of attending home games with members of the supporters' club and conducting informal interviews with them, focusing on how the fans, supporters' club and team had changed.

Contrasting Styles of Play and Support

Pumas fans contrast the playing style of the team and their styles of support with those of other teams. They state that Pumas always play an attacking, aggressive, entertaining, creative style, moving their players up the pitch in an attempt to score goals even when they are winning. One fan described the Pumas' style as: 'Such a harmonious form. For me, how football should be played: with flair, attacking, moving forward. Not like Necaxa or América who defend and then suddenly score. I prefer a style of football with a lot of passing; an open game.' (Héctor, a 25-year-old Pumas fan and accountant, 11 December 1996)[5]

The fans explain that this risky, entertaining style is inspired by the players' love of the game and for the team's shirt and colours. They contrast this with the defensive style of the other teams in the league. At best, they claim, this defensiveness constitutes good strategy, but it is boring. At worst, what passes for strategy is really a product of clientelism. Players defend, playing passively, because they are more focused on maintaining their clientelistic relationships with the team management than with the game itself. This loyalty is usually expressed off the pitch — for example in interviews, when players are expected to praise their team and its management. Meanwhile, Pumas fans claim that what happens on the pitch is seen as inconsequential as long as players make a minimal effort. Playing aggressively would only expose a player to the risk of threatening the patron–client relationship, and thus his job, by drawing attention to himself, either as an independent individualist craving attention or as a failure. For example, Gerardo, a 21-year-old *porra* member and student at UNAM, once highlighted the playing style of the Pumas' midfielder, Braulio Luna, as an example of someone under the effects of clientelism. He claimed that Luna played as though he was more concerned about his stylish long hair than the game, rarely tackling or doing anything else that might cause injury or even get his kit dirty. He stated that Luna and América were a perfect match, and that the player would soon be transferred to the other team (which in fact occurred the following season).

Pumas fans draw a parallel contrast between their chanting style and that of other teams' fans. They say that they 'cheer' to support the team, and thus to aid the attempt to produce goals. They contrast this active cheering with the passive cheering of other fans, who only chant after their team has scored a goal. Furthermore, they posit that this cheering after a goal is a less heartfelt way to demonstrate loyalty to their team. They claim that these other fans are so accustomed to patron–client relations in other areas of life that they cannot help but see their relationship to a team in these same terms. The Pumas fans add that the influence of clientelism denies other fans the possibility of expressing passion and of doing so in a creative manner. They state that these other fans recite the same simple nonsensical chants over and over again, and that they do so sitting — or, at best, standing fixed to one spot. In contrast to what they portray as blind obedience among other fans, they point out that they are continuously composing their own new chants and songs, which allows them to express creatively what they are feeling for the team. They add that they sing these chants (rather than simply reciting them) while swaying from side to side or jumping up and down, which they say constitutes a bodily expression of their joy.[6]

The *Porra Plus*

My research among Pumas fans focused on one supporters' club, or *porra*, known as the *Porra Plus*. This club consisted of over a hundred members, mostly males between the ages of 16 and 30. It also included a few women of the same age and a few older men. The members were from all corners of the sprawling city, but with a higher concentration from middle-class and lower middle-class neighbourhoods. While most of the former were studying at UNAM and many of the latter expressed aspirations to do so, both groups were struggling to maintain the class position or class aspirations of their parents' generation, who had benefited from Mexico's 'economic miracle' — a period of rapid economic growth that lasted from the 1950s until the 1970s, before a series of economic crises hit in the 1980s and early 1990s. Most of the informal peer leaders in the club were from this group of middle-class university students. These informal leaders most clearly and naturally expressed the philosophy of the Pumas fans.

While in ideal terms the stadium, and in particular the supporters' club, constituted islands of pure passion for the team and the game in a sea of corruption and democratic rationality, to the *porra* members' constant frustration this was not the case in reality. Thus the *porra* itself was, for its young members and for me, a context for experiencing and confronting the effects of corruption and democracy at first hand. This direct confrontation with precisely what their philosophy was supposed to replace made it apparent that this philosophy was not simply an inert tradition, passed from generation to generation of fans, but rather something in a continuous process of formulation. Wider political and economic processes occurring during the intense period of my earlier ethnographic research, 18 months in 1996 and 1997, meant a particularly intensive confrontation of this sort. The whole country was immersed in the rhetoric of democratisation as the 70-year rule of the Partido Revolucionario Institucional (the PRI) appeared to be nearing its end. It was also a time of rapid commercialisation set off by the North American Free Trade Agreement (NAFTA), which had been ratified a few years earlier and entered into force at the beginning of 1994. Both of these processes had direct effects on the *porra*, which will be discussed in order to illustrate how group members put their philosophy into action, not simply as an act of resistance but as the consolidation of an alternative. The reactions of *porra* members to these processes culminated in 1998 in the formation of a new *porra* called the Orgullo Azul y Oro (the 'Blue and Gold Pride') and nicknamed *El Rebel*.

A Critique of Democracy, Objectivity and Corruption

Just months before the research began, the *porra* was still unofficially — though indisputably — led by Javier, a charismatic man in his late thirties. *Porra* members remembered him as a sort of benevolent dictator who made all the decisions for the group, including which songs and chants they would recite during games. They stated during interviews that no one even thought to question his leadership. When Javier left the group, Ernesto, a middle-aged lawyer, became the *porra*'s first president. Drawing on the wave of democratic rhetoric sweeping the country, he called for an election to choose a president for the group, and for meetings to reach decisions collectively. Ernesto himself won the election. While *porra* members admitted that Ernesto's democratic leadership made possible the critical perspective they never thought to develop under Javier, they soon directed their criticism toward Ernesto, his democratic rationality, and the corruption they claimed that his democracy served to obscure.

For example, they expressed dissatisfaction with Ernesto's manner of including new members in the *porra*. Ernesto claimed that, during Javier's time, decisions about including new members were personalised and arbitrary, as he himself admitted those he liked and excluded those he did not. Thus Ernesto set about establishing a set of objective rules for membership. He proposed that new members would be admitted when they could demonstrate that they had attended a minimum number of consecutive games and that they knew all of the chants and songs. He asked the current members for photographs and printed up identification cards, so that only those with a card would receive the benefits of membership — that is, permission to sit in the *porra*'s segregated area of the stands and free or discounted tickets for games. *Porra* members noted, however, that Ernesto used his supposedly objective criteria to legitimise his personal decisions to admit new members in exchange for their loyalty. While they expressed disgust at his clientelistic practices, they laughed at his attempts to rationalise membership, using it as evidence that he — no longer a youth — had forgotten the true meaning of Pumas fandom. They explained that for them, new membership is a process of mutual attraction between the group and the potential member. Potential members are drawn to the *porra*'s section by their heartfelt affinity for the club's passionate support, just as previously they were drawn to the team and the stadium. After the newcomers have been sitting on the margins of the *porra*'s section for a few games, the *porra* members are drawn to the passionate support shown by these new fans and invite them to sit in the section. Thus emotive expression and heartfelt affinity determine membership, not simply attendance or knowing lyrics, and fans who ask what they have to do to join are inappropriate members since they don't understand that passionate support leads to membership and not the reverse. With the establishment of the *Orgullo Azul y Oro*, the young fans (while still gathering in a specific section of the stadium) eliminated the clear boundary and formal distinction between members and non-members, letting passion draw new fans towards the section and towards its physical and emotional centre.

The young *porra* members also grew frustrated with Ernesto's attempts to organise their chanting in a more rational manner. Previously, Javier had stood on the wall forming the limit of the upper deck, held on to a speaker post, and led the *porra*'s support. In addition, he himself had decided which chants to use. In contrast, Ernesto placed an energetic young member, one with a strong voice, in this same place. He said that any *porra* member could request a cheer through him, and he would inform the 'cheer leader'. Ernesto posited that his system was efficient since an able leader would coordinate the singing of the group, making it clearer and louder, while at the same time it was democratic since all could request songs. The young group members complained, however, that he ignored their requests, using those favoured only by him and his close friends — or really clients, as the *porra* members saw them. They noted that he tended to favour the same old chants, resisting the addition of their new compositions. In reaction, they began to break into their own compositions, drowning out the leader as well as Ernesto's protests. Soon they came to see this undirected support as an end in itself, claiming that beginning a song or chant through a spontaneous outburst was a better means of expressing heartfelt emotion than following someone else's directions. They argued that this manner of starting a chant also better reflected the group's feelings as a whole, since a chant that reflected other members' emotions would be taken up while an outburst that did not would simply die out.

This new manner of chanting frustrated Ernesto immensely. He began to argue with the *porra* members at meetings after games, reprimanding them for ruining the group's support of the team. These reprimands, and an inability to contradict the politically agile Ernesto during meetings, were a key factor in pushing some fans to form the new *porra*. They explained to me that they were happy to give up efficiency for spontaneous passionate expression, something that Ernesto didn't understand. In the new *porra*, the position of leader was eliminated and all singing was begun through spontaneous outbursts. I noted that these outbursts usually came only from one of a few core members, however — suggesting that the new group was not totally democratic. Yet there was also no notion of an obligation or commitment to a collective goal, no external, objective position from which the core members could reprimand non-participation or conflicting outbursts.

A Critique of Commercialisation

Alongside the imposition of democratic rationality, the *porra* members also experienced an increased commodification of the team and of their club. When this research began, interviewees noted that the Pumas team was unique in the league not only for its 'all-youth' philosophy, but also because of its distinctive form of ownership. They explained that Pumas was the only team in the league owned by a not-for-profit corporation, which directs all profits back to the team or to UNAM, while the alumni on the Board of Directors absorb any financial losses. They posited that this form of ownership protected the team from the forces and logic of the market, allowing it to maintain its all-youth practice, even if this were not the most profitable strategy. As evidence of this distance from the market, they pointed out that Pumas was the only team without the name of a sponsor on its kit and without advertising around the pitch.

During the period of this research, however, this distance began to shrink rapidly. Rotating perimeter advertisements were added at the side of the pitch and the name of a corporate sponsor appeared on the players' shirts and at other places around the stadium. The most visible sponsor was Nike, which began an intensive advertising campaign. Nike representatives appeared during half-time to throw t-shirts and kick footballs into the stands. They set up displays of Nike products in the carparks together with free games, such as kicking a ball through a target, for which winners were awarded Nike products, and all participants received key-chains and other trinkets with the Nike logo. They also distributed posters and collectors' cards with the best and best-looking Pumas players sporting Nike products, thereby commodifying another aspect of their youthfulness. These were most popular among female fans, whose evaluation of players' youth was somewhat different from the male fans, since it took into account the personalities and physical attractiveness of specific players, both on and off the pitch.

Nike's onslaught was also directed at the *porra* as a group. Through Ernesto, the company attempted to establish itself as the club's sponsor. They gave him trinkets and hats with the Nike swoosh and the Pumas logo to distribute to the *porra* members. Then it provided him with t-shirts and a banner, made especially for the *porra*, to hang over the wall of the upper tier in front of the group.

At first, *porra* members were happy to receive the trinkets and t-shirts. It seems likely that Nike's novelty value, both in Mexico and in football, gave it a youthful feel that appealed to them in contrast to more established brands. A look around the stadium at that time revealed most fans wearing Nike trainers or walking boots, and many with Nike hats or t-shirts. In addition, *porra* members were never against commercialism, but rather in favour of allowing emotional expression. The first complaints I heard about Nike were related to clientelism and corruption. They protested that Ernesto was giving more of the paraphernalia to his clients rather than distributing it evenly and openly, and some even claimed that he was receiving financial compensation from Nike when it was really the whole group that should be rewarded for its advertising potential. However, it was not until they felt that Nike's sponsorship began to affect their passionate support of the team in concrete ways that they grew critical of commercialisation in itself.

This began when Ernesto informed them that one of the conditions of Nike's distribution of t-shirts was that they all wear the shirts to every game. He added that the uniformity would create a superior collective appearance which would be conducive to coordinated supporting. After hearing this, some of the *porra* members refused to wear them at all, often preferring to wear the Nike jerseys that they had purchased themselves, since this obligation contradicted their expression of love for the team through clothing. Now conscious that such commercialisation could affect their most valued practices and beliefs, other critiques emerged. Many complained that the Nike swooshes on the t-shirts, banner and hats were bigger and more visible than the Pumas logos. They commented sarcastically that they felt like they were supporting Nike rather than Pumas. A group of these *porra* members made a collection and gathered volunteers to sew and paint another banner without the Nike swoosh. When it was finished they hung it so that it covered the Nike logo on the other banner. When Ernesto saw this he reprimanded them and had it removed, which suggested to the *porra* members that he cared more for his relationship with Nike than he did for the team, once again encouraging plans for a new *porra*. Once the new *porra* was established, the members explained that after what they had learned through the experience with Ernesto and Nike they would refuse any offers for sponsorship, either from advertisers or the team itself. Thus, by cutting themselves off from the products provided by sponsors and even the free tickets provided by the team, making regular entrance into the stadium difficult or impossible for some members, they eliminated the danger of having their practices affected by entanglements with actors with different interests.

During the research, *porra* members also developed a critical awareness of when the team itself was over-influenced by financial interests. For example, over a period of a few months, when the team was playing poorly — both in the sense of losing games and of playing a rather boring style of football — many of the group members grew angry and frustrated. They began to boo, insult and criticise the coach and the players during games; however, they explained that their criticism was mostly directed at the team management, who were selling too many of the good players too soon. Although they did not understand why, they felt that the management was neglecting the team and the fans, and was focusing instead on increasing earnings. The coach and players asked the *porra* members to stop expressing their critical stance during games. Ernesto and his followers supported this stance and began pressurising the other *porra* members to stop. Ernesto stated that they should help the team through the difficult period with supportive chants, suggesting that their passionate support would rub off on the team and help to alleviate the problem on the pitch. He also accused the critical *porra* members of having given up on the team and having lost their passion. They responded by positing a separation between the Pumas ideal and the actual team, coach and management at any specific time. They stated that the team, coach and in particular the management were the ones who had lost their passion, while they were remaining faithful to the Pumas ideal and their passion for it with their critical stance. They added that they had not given up, and in fact could wait patiently, since they knew that they would still be around, supporting the team, when the current players, coach and managers had moved on to other teams. Once again, Ernesto's attempt to impose his position on the majority of young *porra* members helped to convince the latter of the necessity of separating from Ernesto and the team management and forming another *porra*.

Conclusion

In this chapter, I have described the ideal vision for Mexican society represented by the Pumas football club, one of four 'national' teams in the Mexican league. In this ideal vision, action on the football pitch, in the stands or anywhere else is guided by heartfelt emotion, and not by an external objective logic (as in the context of scientific, democratic or market-based rationality) or by other people (as in clientelism). I have also tried to demonstrate that this vision was strengthened among the young members of a supporters' club in the face of recent processes of democratisation and commercialisation. The democratisation of Mexican politics and of the club itself in the mid- to late 1990s provided the young members with the opportunity to develop and express a critical perspective regarding not only clientelism, but democracy itself. Club members became aware of the fact that the new objective and democratic rules for determining club membership and for guiding their styles of support were inhibiting their expression of heartfelt emotion for the team, just as clientelistic relations had done previously. Meanwhile, a wave of commercialisation in Mexico following the inauguration of NAFTA brought club members into contact with the increasing commercialisation of the game of football, of Pumas, and even of the club itself. At first, they eagerly received the free paraphernalia including t-shirts and banners provided by Nike, but when the company's representatives made demands upon their use of these gifts, they began to feel that their expression of love for the team through their clothing and their decoration of the stands was being restricted and controlled. In reaction to the encroachment of the processes of democratisation and commercialisation upon their passionate support for the team, a group of young club members decided to form a new *porra* whose organisation was specifically conceived to promote behaviour guided by heartfelt emotion and to protect from the inhibiting effects of clientelism, democracy and commercialisation. In the new club, objective rules, leadership and sponsors were conspicuously absent. It should be noted, however, that this new club was observed in 1998 and 1999, during its first two years, and that other forms of social organisation such as clientelism, democracy or sponsorship could very well have emerged since then — even despite the club members' concentrated efforts to prevent it.

In conclusion, I would like to draw attention to the broad social significance of one aspect of Pumas fans' ideal vision for society, related to the similarities between the Pumas fans' vision of an ideal world and the Romantic movement of the late eighteenth and early nineteenth centuries.[7] Both visions demand freedom from tradition, hierarchy and dependence on others. While this notion of freedom is derived from Enlightenment philosophy, these ideals reject the Enlightenment standpoint that reality is to be experienced through (and action guided by) reason or objectivity. Thus both positions claim that scientific objectivity, democratic rationality and even freedom are important as means to an end, but that they are not ends in themselves. Like the Romantics, Pumas fans believe that life should reflect authentic, spontaneous heartfelt emotion, and that scientific objectivity and democratic rationality should only serve as a means to achieve this end. On the one hand, the two positions are inherently oppositional, defined in contrast to both traditional hierarchy and democratic rationality. On the other hand, meanwhile, the Pumas fans' and the Romantics' stances are potentially and ideally universal since they derive from the basically human rather than the partisan loyalties of nation, region or class. These similarities between Pumas fandom and literary romanticism are not due to the former's imitation of the latter. Rather, they are reactions to parallel circumstances — that is, to scientific objectivity and democracy that are on the rise but not yet dominant. While these circumstances can be found throughout the contemporary world, they are prevalent throughout much of Latin America, and more attention to this type of fandom in research might well reveal numerous examples of it throughout the region.

The comparison between the Pumas fans and artistic Romanticism is not an attempt simply to categorise the former. Rather, the intention is to show that Pumas fandom is one example of a more generalised phenomenon in the modern world, and thus to suggest that it deserves the kind of consideration given to the versions of this phenomenon expressed in poetry and other artistic forms, which have been treated not only as significant contributions to art, but as major forms and factors in modern society and history. These football fans, and others like them, should be taken seriously as a primary source of Romanticism and its emotional, passionate alternative in the contemporary world. In other words, the telling of Mexican or even Latin American history should include the ideal vision for society represented by the Pumas alongside those repre-sented by the Chivas, Cruz Azul and América.

Acknowledgements

Funding for the research on which this chapter is based and for its writing was generously provided by the Wenner-Gren Foundation for Anthropological Research, the Fulbright Foundation and the Universidad Iberoamericana.

Notes

1   For further discussion and analysis of Chivas fans, see Fábregas Puig (2001).
2   For more on clientelism in Mexico see Lomnitz (1982); Fox (1994); Pansters (1997); and Wolf (1966).
3   This connection between passionate, creative play and youth recalls the Argentine *pibe* described by Archetti (1998b). In fact, the Argentine Renato Cesarini, a former *pibe* himself, brought the 'pure youth' philosophy to the Pumas in the 1960s (Eduardo Archetti, personal communication).
4   A *porra* is a supporters' club, equivalent to a *barra* in Argentina or Peru.
5   This and all other fans' names used here are pseudonyms.
6   Here I should note that only a few of the fans actually compose chants and songs that are used collectively, and that these are composed by putting new words to popular songs, or to chants they hear South American fans use on television.
7   My understanding and description of Romanticism derive principally from the work of Talmon (1967) and Grenier (2001).

7

¡Arriba Perú! The Role of Football in the Formation of a Peruvian National Culture

David Wood

The study of football in Peru, in line with the situation in many other countries of the sub-continent and more widely, remains a field with relatively new and few players. Indeed, it was only in the late 1970s that the first tentative analyses of the country's footballing tradition were published (in newspapers and journals); the same decade saw the production of several works of literature that drew on football as their raw material. This convergence of events has to be understood against the backdrop of profound changes in the country's social and political structures, as a left-wing military regime sought for the first time to incorporate traditionally marginalised sectors of society into the project of the nation as subjects rather than simply objects. In the wake of the emergence and acceptance of cultural studies as an academic discipline, arguably with similar aims, the early 1980s saw an ambitious project in Lima to study the cultural practices of working-class Lima in the early twentieth century under the direction of Steve Stein, a US historian of Peru. This project gave rise to a two-volume publication (Stein 1986a), but another decade was to pass before the study of football established itself as a subject of academic study in Peruvian universities, in large measure thanks to the efforts of Aldo Panfichi, for whom the key importance of football 'lies in the fact that it is a central instrument in the imaginary construction of socio-cultural identities' (Panfichi 1994, p. 18).[1]

The origins of a socio-cultural identity that can be considered Peruvian are to be found, as might be expected, in the decades around the time of Peru's independence in 1821, when local creoles sought to mark their break from Spain. Despite the formation of the new republic and the expulsion of the Spanish colonial authorities, Peru's identity remained in the hands of a white elite, whose vision of the nation 'was founded on the colonial concept of "castes", based on a racial and cultural hierarchy where what is white and European is superior to what is native and American' (Rebaza Soraluz 2000, p. 33). One such white, European group constituted the British, who sought to exploit the trade and finance vacuum left by the Spanish, although of even greater importance in the context of this study was their exporting of football to Peru in the mid-nineteenth century, when it was played in exclusive expatriate British (and later Italian) clubs. Not until the late nineteenth century and the defeat of Peru at the hands of Chile in the War of the Pacific (1879–83) was the vision of the country's identity as intimately connected to the white elite questioned; in the wake of the elite's failure to defend 'their' country, an alternative national identity was given voice by Manuel González Prada. In what can be seen as a founding statement of the *indigenista* movement, González Prada argued that: 'The real Peru is not formed by groups of creoles and foreigners who inhabit the strip of land between the Pacific and the Andes; the nation is formed by the masses of Indians spread along the eastern slopes of the mountain range.' (González Prada 1976, pp. 45–46)

In the first decades of the twentieth century, *indigenismo* was championed in the political field by José Carlos Mariátegui, the principal Marxist ideologue of 1920s Peru, and by a variety of cultural producers and intellectuals, while the hegemonic *criollo* culture incorporated cultural practices of Lima's Afro-Peruvian population such as the religious procession of El Señor de los Milagros and the *marinera* dance. At this time, the two cultural traditions occupied spaces (be they geographical, ethnic, economic or cultural) that were clearly separated, but mass migration — primarily from the Andes to the coastal cities — led to a blurring of the demarcations between these traditions in the middle decades of the twentieth century, and to attempts to reconcile them through the concept of *mestizaje*. By 1970, the dominant national cultural identity, promoted by General Velasco's military government (1968–75), was *cholo*, foregrounding Andean ethnic and cultural characteristics on the national stage as never before, and at the start of the twenty-first century the crisis of hegemony that has characterised diverse aspects of Peruvian public life has led to a growing acceptance of the heterogeneity of the country's cultural landscape.[2]

In the late nineteenth century, football in Peru was markedly English, played by members of the expatriate community and the Anglophile elite on grass pitches in clubs that were physically separated from the daily reality of Lima, although there is also evidence that sailors played impromptu games with local workers around the port of Callao. It could be argued that the predominantly elite associations of the game at this time made it representative of the country's identity — at least as a reflection of its institutional structures and recognised cultural production. However, this changed markedly in the early twentieth century as the appropriation of the game by the capital's working classes and the emergence of mass-based political parties in the 1920s led to Alianza Lima — intimately associated with the district of La Victoria, which was home to a high proportion of the city's black population — becoming accepted as the best team in the country.[3] The adoption of the sport by the popular classes at the start of the twentieth century meant a break in the association between football and the socio-economic elite but, faced with the risk of football becoming a form of popular culture with autonomous characteristics of organisation and practice, and of it serving to form class bonds among the growing urban proletariat — which was increasingly mobilised by a nascent trades union movement — the elite did not allow this rupture to last long. It is worth highlighting at this juncture that Alianza Lima's associations with Afro-Peruvians and the working classes have afforded it a privileged position with regard to academic studies, while analyses basing themselves on other clubs have been almost non-existent.

Steve Stein describes the first decades of the twentieth century as a period of 'significant institutional growth' at the level of government (Stein 1986b, p. 13). The culmination of this tendency may be seen in the regime of President Augusto B. Leguía (1919–30), who sought to undermine the new mass-based political parties through populist measures, including the channelling of support for football into institutional structures that saw the state, for the first time, assume the role of organiser and promoter of sport. Leguía also oversaw the formation of the national team, which played (and lost) its first matches in the 1927 South American Championship, held in Lima in the brand new Estadio Nacional — constructed by the Leguía administration after the land had been donated to the Peruvian state by the English expatriate community in 1921 to commemorate the centenary of the country's independence. It is no surprise that Deustua, Stein, and Stokes and colleagues should describe this period in terms of 'the institutionalisation of football and its recognition as the official sport' (Deustua et al. 1986, p. 147).[4]

Another means by which Leguía sought to channel popular expression into his regime via cultural production was cinema, and numerous documentaries made about the regime and its works received government funding. Indeed, from 1924 the state gave a monthly subvention to one production company with the express aim that it 'produce propaganda for the nation through cinema images' (Bedoya 1997, p. 45). The 1927 South American Championship held in Lima provided the first images of football on the cinema screens, as Leguía used the sport to promote his regime as both modern and cosmopolitan. Further football scenes appeared on the big screen in a documentary that recorded events of the Independence Day celebrations in July 1928, as the sport was once again linked to national identity. Football, then, served to bind together notions of the popular, modernity and a sense of the nation as an imagined community constructed for the first time by the mass media. This is further illustrated by the founding of Peru's first radio broadcasting organisation in 1925. By the mid-1930s, it was possible to listen to commentaries of local matches as a regular feature of certain stations. It was even possible to follow matches played overseas, as was the case with the quarter-final match between Peru and Austria in the 1936 Olympic Games in Berlin, when some 5,000 people gathered in front of the offices of *El Comercio*, the leading newspaper in Lima, to listen to Peru's participation in the international sphere, with a sense of national identity generated via the mass media and football as national cultural practice. Once again, however, we are dealing with an audience limited to the socio-economic elite and middle classes and, rather than representing a means by which football spread among the popular classes, radio constituted a symbol of modernity in the mediation of popular cultural practices.[5]

By contrast, popular songs of the 1920s and 1930s — a good number of which were devoted to football stars of the period — were spread among the less privileged classes by word of mouth and performance in public spaces and at private parties. The *canción criolla* was Peru's equivalent in many ways to the Argentine *tango* and Mexican *ranchera*, spread by mass media in the 1930s in such a way that it enjoyed national and international recognition and was subsequently adopted by the middle classes as a symbol of national culture. The forms of this musical tradition have their origins in the nineteenth century, and are typically appropriations of European forms such as the waltz and the polka, which gave rise to the *vals criollo* and *polka criolla* respectively. The leading exponent of *música criolla* in the 1930s was Felipe Pinglo, whose keen support for Alianza Lima and friendship with the team's stars ensured that Alejandro Villanueva (the centre-forward), Juan Valdivieso (the goalkeeper), Juan Rostaing (fullback) and the team itself were all the subject of one-steps, *pasodobles* or *marineras*. Such treatment was not restricted to Alianza Lima, however, and Lolo Fernández of Universitario, Valeriano López of Sport Boys and the club Atlético Chalaco all enjoyed similar homage. An interesting case of this process in reverse is that of Alianza Lima's winger, José María Lavalle, who was famous for dribbling the ball to the rhythm of the *marinera* playing in the crowd, and whose goal celebrations involved extracting the hand-kerchief that the dancer traditionally waves to accompany his steps. If the *canción criolla* came to national prominence in the 1930s, with foot-ball a significant element in the repertoire of popular experiences it depicted, its popularity has lasted well beyond that period, and the ongoing relationship between this musical form, football and national identity is illustrated by the optimistic *polka criolla*, 'Perú Campeón', dedicated to the team that took part in the 1970 World Cup finals.[6] The examples considered here indicate that, at the time when *criollo* culture incorporated aspects of Afro-Peruvian culture — which thus became identified with national culture — football was a cultural practice that was able to bind together notions of popular forms of creativity and participation with a national and international perspective.

To return to the use of football by the state as a means of legit-imisation, another way in which the elite regained control of the burgeoning practice of the sport among the capital's population was via the establishment of an organisational structure that would oversee competitive matches. The Federación Peruana de Fútbol (FPF), founded in 1922, assumed control of the local leagues following the demise of the Liga Peruana de Fútbol, formed a decade earlier by gentlemen amateurs from Lima's exclusive clubs, and the close relationship between the hegemonic classes and the FPF is reflected in the fact that all of its 39 presidents since then have been white. Moreover, all have been lawyers, businessmen or senior military officers — occupations traditionally the reserve of the country's elite. The tensions between the traditional oligarchy and the popular classes who now excelled in football were exemplified in an infamous episode in 1929, when Alianza Lima was expelled from the league following the withdrawal of the club's black players from the national squad in protest at their segregation and general poor treatment during preparations for that year's South American Championship. Despite the threat of poor results at the tournament, however, the absence of the black stars was not lamented by many members of the elite, who feared giving an impression on the international stage that Peru was a country whose cultural production was dominated by blacks. Following their expulsion, Alianza Lima was forced to play unofficial matches in the area around Lima, and according to Stokes: 'It is no exaggeration to say that, in some ways, the Alianza players chose a popular and national form of football, rejecting the version of the Federación that was centralised and oriented overseas.' (Stokes 1986, p. 245) This situation is symptomatic of the tensions that existed between contending visions of national identity in which the traditionally hegemonic white model sought to continue to impose itself. However, this version of *peruanidad* was losing out, both on the pitch (the 'whitened' Peruvian team lost all three of its games in Buenos Aires in 1929, conceding 12 goals and scoring only one) and in society more widely. The following year, Alianza Lima was re-admitted to the League, albeit with a high-ranking official of the Municipalidad de Lima as club president, which for Deustua meant that the club 'had to abandon its own football, which somehow represented autonomous popular culture — the only form of popular culture that in our view would have allowed a space for the emergence of the solidarity and collective consciousness of the popular sectors through sport' (Deustua et al. 1986, p. 161). This episode shows that while the structures of the hegemonic sectors of society were attempting (with some success) to check popular autonomy — thus maintaining the status quo (at least superficially) — the entry of the popular classes into the national sphere could not be denied. In the team that beat Austria in the quarter-final of the Berlin Olympics, several of the stars were black, mulatto or mestizo, and on returning to Peru, Alejandro Villanueva, Alianza's centre-forward, was welcomed by President Oscar Benavides as a hero. Football at this time thus served as a barometer of the oligarchic state's attempts to use the sport to bolster its position and simultaneous attempts by popular classes to establish a place and a voice in national society.

The 1940s and 1950s were less significant in terms of the development of football, although professionalism was introduced in 1951 and the ongoing management of the game by the national elite can be seen in the FPF's decision in 1952 to impose a lifetime ban on the black centre-forward, Valeriano, for insulting the Peruvian ambassador in the changing rooms following a defeat by Chile. Of more transcendental impact at the national level was the mass migration that took place during this period, which saw the ratio of rural to urban population exactly inverted from 72 per cent rural in 1950 to 72 per cent urban by 1993, blurring the dichotomies and binaries of Peru's traditional cultural identity. Although the population of Lima increased by 500 per cent between 1961 and 1993, according to the censuses of those years (compared with a national increase of 260 per cent over the same period), the capital's hegemonic position as a seat of cultural power underwent a thorough questioning as it also became home to a broad spectrum of cultural practices habitually considered 'Other' by the traditional coastal elite. As mentioned above, this is the time when *criollo* culture, essentially based on the culture of the white coastal elite with the incorporation of some aspects of Afro-Peruvian popular culture, was challenged as the official national culture by *mestizo* and subsequently *cholo* culture. Successive governments introduced measures that gave unprecedented prominence to the provinces and recent migrants: President Fernando Belaúnde Terry (1963–68) undertook massive public works that included irrigation programmes and a planned highway to the east of the Andes, while General Juan Velasco Alvarado (1968–75) undertook an extensive agrarian reform programme, recognised Quechua as a co-official language, and sought to involve the migrant masses in political and cultural institutions.

These processes can also be studied via an analysis of the country's cultural production during this period, in which the growing recognition and acceptance of football as emblematic cultural practice of the traditionally disenfranchised classes became increasingly apparent. Although state-sponsored cinema documentaries of football matches and sports journalism were features of the 1920s and 1930s, the presence of football in other cultural media at this time was all but non-existent, as art and literature were dominated either by *indigenismo* or avant-garde tendencies imported from Europe. Indeed, the only football literature produced that could be considered Peruvian was the 'Polirritmo dinámico a Gradín, jugador de football' ('Dynamic Polyrhythm to Gradín, Football Player'), written by Juan Parra de Riego, who had been born in Peru but was resident in Uruguay and had been inspired by one of that country's stars. There are also several references to football in *Duque*, a novel written in the late 1920s charting the decadence of members of Lima's elite. In this work, it is worth noting that football is either a point of reference to periods spent in England, a subject of patronage or a spectacle that arouses the passions of women and of men whose masculinity is called into question. Football here, then, would already appear to have lost its appeal as a sport practised by the upper classes, who instead play tennis, golf and polo (unlike football, all destined to remain elite sports as a result of the requirements of equipment and land), at least on the evidence of this work. In the following two decades, football retained a markedly low profile with respect to its representation in the country's cultural production, appearing in José María Arguedas' seminal 1958 novel, *Los ríos profundos (Deep Rivers)*, but only serving to symbolise the conflict between the cultures of the coast and the Andes, thus continuing the dualistic visions of the country's cultural experience. Further slim evidence of the penetration of football into the traditional cultural forms of the elite during this period is found in art. As *indigenismo* waned as a political and cultural discourse from the 1950s, arguably having fulfilled its purpose, artists turned their attentions from the country's indigenous inhabitants and their activities to the marginalised sectors of society more widely. Examples of this are Julia Codesido's *Muchacho de pelota roja* and Aquiles Ralli's *El Taquito*, both of which convey the enjoyment of football by boys on the street, barefoot yet agile and skilful, framed by a gaze that recognises them to be as much a part of the national culture as the canvas art that depicts them.

Indeed, it was not until the late 1960s, and especially the 1970s, that football came to adopt a more central space with regard to its representation and mediation through other cultural forms, with works such as Mario Vargas Llosa's *Los cachorros (The Pups)* and Alfredo Bryce Echenique's *Huerto cerrado (Closed Orchard)* portraying football as an important component in the re-creation of the experiences of urban, middle-class adolescents. Bryce's 1970 novel, *Un mundo para Julius (A World for Julius)*, which deals with the life of the oligarchy, offers some interesting and revealing points of comparison with *Duque*, written 40 years earlier. While in the earlier novel football features exclusively as a spectacle for the oligarchy, in *Un mundo para Julius* it is portrayed as a daily practice among the boys at the elite school, and as an important tool in the creation of identities. In this regard, comparisons can also be made with *Los ríos profundos*, for in Julius's school in Lima it is acceptable for the boys from the white elite to support Alianza Lima, despite it still being the club of the black working classes. By 1970, then, football had become accepted as part of the nation's cultural landscape and as a means of forging identities that went beyond the traditional dualistic visions of previous decades, facilitating associations between formerly antagonistic sectors of national society.

The first text devoted entirely to football was not literary, however, but cinematic. The 1972 film *Cholo* is a biography of Hugo Sotil, a first-generation migrant to Lima who went on to play for Barcelona and the national team at the height of its success, and this film, along with a number of journalistic essays and interviews with star players, saw the penetration of football into national cultural production as never before. Indeed, as the Peruvian sociologist Abelardo Sánchez León noted in 1981: 'Only a football match allows the *cholo* and the black to appear on the television cameras or on the front page of the newspapers, to wrap themselves in the flag bare-chested and be, just for once, the representatives of Peru' (Sánchez León 1981a, p. 115).

The 1970s and the early 1980s also saw the publication of the first works of literature centred on football, reflecting the simultaneous foregrounding of the popular classes in the political arena. This can also be seen as a continuation of a process that had begun with educational reforms in the 1960s, which opened up literature for consumption and production among sectors for whom the written word had not hitherto been an option as far as cultural production was concerned. Guillermo Thorndike's 1978 novel, *El revés de morir (The Opposite of Dying)*, focused on the career of Alejandro 'Manguera' Villanueva to re-evaluate, from the perspective of the *apertura* of the time, the contribution of Afro-Peruvians to the country's footballing tradition and national prestige.[7] Historical footballing events also provide the basis for Jorge Salazar's novel, *La ópera de los fantasmas (The Opera of Ghosts)*, published in 1980. Football itself, however, is not so central to this work: the author uses the tragedy of several hundred people crushed to death at a match between Peru and Argentina in the Estadio Nacional in 1964 as a starting point to denounce abuses by the authorities and social injustices in Peru at the time. More interesting — both for its footballing content and its literary value — is *Tiempo al tiempo (Time to Time)*, a novel published by Isaac Goldemberg in 1984 which uses football as a metaphor for the Jewish-Peruvian protagonist's problematic integration into national society. Via the alternating narration of an imaginary match between Peru and Brazil and the recalling of episodes from Marquitos's schooldays the competing expectations of Peruvian and Yiddish cultural traditions are explored, with the protagonist ultimately unable to assimilate the two of them. The novel's structure also borrows from football, divided into a 'first half' that sees Marquitos in a Jewish school and a 'second half' that sees him in a Peruvian military academy. Moreover, the work comprises 12 chapters that may be seen to represent a football team, including a substitute. Such a reading may seem tenuous, but is borne out by the fact that in the novel Marquitos takes to the field against Brazil as a second-half substitute, unable to play from the start as a result of injuries following circumcision. The effect of his introduction is dramatic, as he scores a hat-trick that earns a draw although Peru still loses the South American Championship on goal difference. His contribution to the match already limited as a consequence of his participation in Jewish cultural practices, his chances of scoring the winner are again frustrated by Rabbi Goldstein, this time as he commits a cynical foul on the protagonist from his new position at the heart of the Brazilian defence, ending Marquitos's involvement in the game and symbolically preventing his full participation in Peruvian culture.

Following several years of relative silence in the late 1980s, both in terms of cultural representations of football and international success on the pitch, the 1990s saw something of a resurgence in the fortunes of Peruvian football. As was the case in the 1970s, this mini-boom can usefully be seen in the context of socio-political conditions, as the election of President Alberto Fujimori in 1990 gave renewed prominence to the popular classes, and saw the emergence in a variety of institutional structures of members of social groups not typically associated with the ruling elite (for example, Protestants, ethnic Japanese and women). Oscar Malca's 1993 novel *Al final de la calle (At the End of the Street)* is about Lima's disenchanted middle-class youth, written by a member of that class. Football serves as one of their main cultural practices (together with rock music and drug-taking) in the construction of a convincing picture of urban youth culture, at the same time providing a key to the forging of neighbourhood and national identities. The animated discussion of football and its often violent practice contrast with the generally lethargic and stagnant existence of the main characters to suggest a dynamic role for the sport amid the social problems experienced by Lima's younger generations. *Al final de la calle* was also made into a film, adapted by Giovanna Pollarolo under the title *Ciudad de M (City of Sh..)* confirming the potential of the film and its subject-matter for conveying action, as well as offering another example of the penetration of football into national cultural production.

Often considered a form of elite culture, but highly dependent on features shared with music, poetry has also given expression to football as another dimension to the democratisation of the country and its literary production. Examples from the work of Juan Parra de Riego and songwriters of the 1930s have already been cited, but the late 1970s, early 1980s and 1990s saw further developments in this field as poets — male and female — used football as a means to their poetic ends. The internationally renowned Carlos Germán Belli's 'Estadio vaticano' ('Vatican Stadium') from 1972 substitutes classical warriors at the heart of epic struggles with football players on the receiving end of a 6–0 thrashing, while in Carmen Ollé's 'Damas al dominó', from her powerful first collection *Noches de adrenalina* (*Nights of Adrenalin*), published in 1981, football is portrayed as marking a divide between the sexes, and indeed as sexual sublimation. A group of young men watch a match on television, oblivious to the provocative sensuality of the female narrators who sit opposite them, finding symbolic and vicarious release in their celebration of a goal on the screen before them. A similar role is played by football in Giovanna Pollarolo's 'El sueño del domingo (por la tarde)' ('The Dream of Sunday Afternoon'), included in her 1991 collection *Entre mujeres solas* (*Between Women Alone*). Here Pollarolo places her characters in the space that follows the family Sunday lunch, with the mother and daughter awaiting 'the click of the radio / to be sent off kitchen-side', while the husband/father listens to the match commentary lying on the bed, where 'he quivers for the passion of a goal / love long forgotten' (Pollarolo 1991, pp. 21–22). As well as football being represented again as sublimation of male sexuality, Pollarolo expresses through the daughter the hope that the changes in society discussed above will continue until sexual equality is reached and women replace football as the ideal partner: 'I swear that when I grow up / I won't be like her / and he, who I still haven't met / won't be like him: / in my days there won't be ironing / nor football nor regrets,' (Pollarolo 1991, pp. 21–22. Women authors may be less enthusiastic about football as social and sporting practice, but nonetheless recognise its power as a symbol of gender and power relations, and make good use of it in pointing up the inequalities ingrained in such relations.

The importance of the mass media in the construction of an imagined national community has already been mentioned in the context of the 1920s and 1930s, but it was not until the late 1960s, following the appearance of transistor radios, that radio in particular became accessible to the majority of Peruvians who lived in rural areas and to the urban population of lower socio-economic strata. The newfound accessibility of radio, and of sports journalism in the printed media as a result of greatly improved levels of education from the 1960s onwards facilitated attempts by the regime of General Velasco (1968–75) to construct a more inclusive national identity. The 35 radio stations operating in Lima alone by 1969 reflected the increasingly broad range of experiences and cultural practices that were coming to be accepted as part of national culture. By 1974 there were approximately 530,000 homes with radio, with an average of 6.5 listeners per household (Gargurevich 1987, pp. 159–77, 222). Such figures indicate that over a quarter of the population of Peru had access to radio broadcasts, including the numerous commentaries of football matches. In the realm of print media, 1962 saw Supercholo — a comic strip character in *El Comercio* who expressed the rising pride in *cholo* identity and cultural practices — assume a starring role in a World 11 football team whose victories in an inter-galactic championship were invariably the result of Supercholo's exploits.

The rise of television in Peru also dates from the 1960s, after the first images were shown in 1958. By 1969 (just in time for the national team's exploits in the 1970 World Cup) there were seven channels and 292,000 homes with television, of which 149,000 were lower class, according to traditional socio-economic categories (Gargurevich 1987, pp. 183–97). The general rapid expansion of the mass media, which created a series of links between football and notions of modernity, also made a crucial contribution to the sense of imagined national community, as football acted once more as a focal point for the convergence of diverse technical, political and social developments.

The sense of opening and expansion evident in the above has its equivalent in the birth of both the Campeonato Descentralizado (Decentralised Championship, the name given to the Peruvian national league) and the Copa Perú (Peruvian Cup) in 1966, as the country's footballing authorities responded to the higher profile enjoyed by the provinces under the developmentalist government of President Belaúnde (1963–68).[8] The Campeonato Descentralizado was instigated as the result of an agreement between the Comité Nacional de Deportes (National Sports Committee) and the FPF, but the concession to the provinces was more symbolic than real. The four clubs admitted to the Liga were from the coastal area, traditionally associated with the export oligarchy, and it was not until the following decade that teams from the Andean or Amazon regions made their way into the top flight of Peruvian football. The Copa Perú, on the other hand, did witness participation from the length and breadth of the country, as over a thousand teams competed for the cup, which would entitle them to entry to the national first division, at the same time playing an important role in the creation of Anderson's 'imagined community' (Anderson 1983). However, this community was doubly imagined, as the winners of the cup in its first five years came from cities on the coast, the seat of power since colonial times, and each season the team that was relegated from the national first division (often from the provinces) was replaced by the winner of Lima's second division. As in other areas of society, football's apparent decentralisation masked an ongoing attempt to cling to traditional power relations.

It is curious, but not coincidental, that the developments of the 1960s foreshadowed Peru's best ever results in the World Cup, as the national team reached the final stages of the competition in 1970, 1978 and 1982, losing in the quarter finals of Mexico 1970 only to the eventual winners, Brazil. Peru also won the Copa América in 1975, for only the second time in its history, while at club level Universitario de Deportes became the first Peruvian side ever to reach the final of the Copa Libertadores, losing the 1972 final to Argentina's Independiente. In attempting to account for this unprecedented (and unrepeated) period of success, one must consider the role of mass migration to Lima and other coastal cities in the 1960s and the impact of the sense of *apertura* and optimism of that decade on a generation of players. Of even greater significance, perhaps, was the impact on the national psyche of the incorporation of football (and other cultural practices of the popular classes) into the programme of a highly nationalistic government after 1968, and the sense of enfranchisement and recognition that the popular classes gained as a result of such measures, which culminated in the right to universal suffrage in the new constitution of 1979. For Peruvian sociologist Carlos Iván Degregori: 'Until the 1950s and 60s, Peru was a fragmented country, defined as an archipelago, as a dual country, as a nation in formation.' (Degregori 1994, p. 19) If the late 1960s and 1970s can be seen as marking a serious attempt to resolve these issues, the role of football in reducing that fragmentation and in contributing towards the formation of a coherent concept of nation cannot be under-estimated.

Finally, we turn our attention to one of the most obvious, yet perhaps most contentious, ways in which football is conjoined to the national, namely via the construction and definition of a national style of play. The successes on the pitch in the 1970s, together with the official recognition of the popular classes and their cultural practices described above, were the decisive catalysts in this process, first expressed in Thorndike's 1978 novel and in two essays by Abelardo Sánchez León, 'Fútbol: un espejo para mirarnos mejor' ('Soccer: A Mirror to See Ourselves Better') and 'Fútbol: casi un estilo de ser peruanos' ('Soccer: Almost a Style of Being Peruvian'), published in 1980 and 1981 respectively (Sánchez León 1980, 1981b). These were closely followed by an article by José María Salcedo, 'Así jugamos porque así somos' ('We Play That Way Because That's How We Are'), published in 1982. These texts mark a watershed in the consideration of the subject, spearheaded by sociologists who have tended subsequently to favour themes of identity and of violence as their object of study.

It is difficult to deny the significance of the sporting and political events of the 1970s in the creation of such a discourse, but the period that enjoys consensus as marking the origins of the national style is the 1920s, while the figure of Alejandro 'Manguera' Villanueva — the Afro-Peruvian centre-forward of Alianza Lima — is identified as its founding father, confirming the degree to which popular and Afro-Peruvian culture had been incorporated into national culture in the intervening decades. If the 1920s were characterised by the oligarchic state's use of football in an attempt to bolster its position, the 1970s looked back to the same period as a period of change and the beginnings of a new national identity. Such considerations no doubt play their part in explaining the fact that cultural representations of football are dominated to such a high degree by Alianza Lima and its players, while their eternal rivals, Universitario de Deportes (and others), are almost completely absent from this arena.

Peru has changed markedly over the course of the last century, from being a country with a white Europhile oligarchy that enjoyed political, economic and cultural hegemony to a more representative nation in which the heterogeneous nature of cultural practice and production is increasingly accepted. Football has undergone developments that are in many ways similar, moving from its origins among the European expatriate community to a sport characterised by the excellence first of Afro-Peruvians, such as Villanueva or Teófilo Cubillas, and subsequently of *mestizos* such as Hugo Sotil, Roberto Palacios or Nolberto Solano. President Leguía's attempts to harness popular support for football to his regime constitute the first political manipulation of the game by the country's authorities, and coincided with *criollo* culture being adopted by the middle classes and given a national value. However, this period also saw the practices of the popular classes contribute as never before to national identity, at the same time as Alianza Lima in particular provided a focus for the creation of popular, autonomous identities through football and through musical representations of it. From the perspective of the 1970s and 1980s, the same period is retrospectively considered to mark the foundation of a national style of play, as football thus made a significant contribution to a sense of national pride and to a shift in official visions of the country's cultural identity. A second era of government intervention in the sport in the late 1960s and 1970s, combined with the rapid spread of the mass media as a result of technological developments, used football to promote — arguably for the first time — a truly national community, with the Campeonato Descentralizado and the Copa Perú at the forefront of its efforts. During the same period, football penetrated various cultural forms, its incorporation to the range of national *dramatis personae* reflecting its presence within state institutions and at the same time furthering acceptance of the game — and its practitioners — in society more widely. As football has become more prominent, it has increasingly been recognised as a means of binding together disparate sectors of the national population and has been accepted by traditionally elitist cultural forms as a legitimate subject of representation. As it has entered cultural forms considered by their nature to be more elite, until the 1960s at least, it has rendered them more popular and has also made them reflect more accurately the country's culture. Football in Peru, then, has been in part defined by the country's national culture (elitist, *criollo* and *cholo* by turn), but at the same time —

as we have seen in the examples studied here — it contributes to the defining and refining of what it means to be Peruvian as the nation seeks a new cultural identity able to draw upon the various components of previously hegemonic — and homogenising — visions.

Notes

1   All translations in this chapter are the author's.

2   *Cholo* is a term used to refer to a *mestizo* who has adopted Western cultural codes to some degree, but who is perceived by the dominant social order as being more Indian than Western. It can be used affectionately, but its use is more often derogatory. See Aníbal Quijano's essay, 'Lo cholo y el conflicto cultural en el Perú', in Quijano (1980).

3   According to Stokes (1986, p. 13), La Victoria was home to 19.4 per cent of Lima's black population in 1908.

4   While on the subject of the Estadio Nacional, it is interesting to note that its reconstruction in 1952 was part of a programme of populist measures undertaken by the military government of General Odría (1948–56): the reappropriation of football by a regime that favoured the country's oligarchy found symbolic expression in the fact that when the new floodlights were turned on, many homes in the district of La Victoria, the home of popular football and of Alianza Lima, suffered power cuts.

5   On the development of the mass media in Peru, see Gargurevich (1987); on Peru's middle classes and entertainments in the first half of the twentieth century, see Parker (1998) and Muñoz Cabrejo (2001).

6   See Parodi (2002) and Villanueva & Donayre (1987).

7   The Peruvian military government that had come to power in 1968 ran into increasing economic and political problems in the late 1970s. After a widespread general strike in July 1977, President Francisco Morales Bermúdez announced that the country would revert to civilian rule and convoked a constitutional assembly.

8   Given the fractured and mountainous geography of Peru, which meant that the country did not have a national rail network, a national league would have been impossible before the introduction of regular and reliable air transport that allowed teams to travel for weekly matches.

8

Identity and Rivalry:
The Football Clubs and *Barras Bravas* of Peru

Aldo Panfichi and Jorge Thieroldt

This chapter explores the role of football in the formation of identities and rivalries among groups of fans in Peru. It demonstrates that these identities and rivalries have formed one of the main mechanisms of social and cultural differentiation in Peru since the early twentieth century. However, it also postulates that this has become more accentuated during the last two decades, in a context in which society as a whole has been affected by economic and political crisis, political violence and radical structural change. It examines the extent to which fanatical support of football clubs has become a cultural and organised response to its political and socio-economic environment, as well as creating a new form of social and cultural differentiation that cuts across traditional lines of class, ethnicity and even gender. A comparison is made between the origins of the mutually exclusive identities of Peru's two oldest football clubs and the evolution of their respective organised groups of fans or *barras*. Special attention is paid to the strategies, symbols and forms of confrontation that these two sets of fans use to face their rivals, both on and off the field.

Football Clubs and their Identities, 1900–1930

As in other Latin American countries, football emerged in Peru at the end of the nineteenth century, during a period of transformation from traditional Peruvian society. At that time, Peru achieved relative economic prosperity due to the favourable prices of some of its primary exports (such as copper, sugar and cotton). This allowed the development of early industrialisation, driven by British, US and Italian capital. The population of Peru's capital city, Lima, grew rapidly during this period, and its urban infrastructure became modernised. Philosophically, positivism planted strong roots in schools, universities and the developing media (Muñoz 2001; Panfichi & Portocarrero 1995).

The first football clubs in Peru were formed by British merchants who settled in Lima, along with members of the Peruvian elite who had studied in Europe. This spread quickly to the lower classes, who demonstrated an enthusiasm for this sport. Learning and playing the game were both simple; it was enough to fill a sock with old rags and find an open space in which to play. At the beginning of the twentieth century, the wounds of the War of the Pacific of 1879–83 (in which Peru and Bolivia were defeated by Chile) were still fresh, and the elite class was divided by fierce debates concerning the reasons for the failure of the war effort, and by questions about the very viability of Peru as a nation. For some, the problem was racial, with the local elite regarding the Chinese immigrant and the black and indigenous populations as inferior.

In this context, football spread rapidly from the exclusive private clubs made up of British immigrants and young members of the social elite to the state schools, factories and working-class neighbourhoods (Alvarez 2001). This early passion for football reflected the fact that the sport allowed individuals, organised into clubs, to compete under equal conditions regardless of skin colour, economic standing or social status. Hence football produced something previously unheard of in Peru: a forum governed by egalitarian rules of competition between diverse ethnic and social groups, who shared a passion for this sport, but who at the same time reflected the prevailing discriminatory cultural and class divisions that existed within society.

At that time, two major football clubs, Alianza Lima and Universitario de Deportes, emerged with contrasting identities. This rivalry increased significantly over the years, and the encounters between both clubs became known as the 'Classic of the Classics', one of the greatest polarising factors among all Peruvians. Black workers and *mestizos* (people of mixed race) supported Alianza Lima, while middle- and upper-class university students of European descent identified with Universitario. A loyal nucleus of spectators, journalists, club members and workers followed these clubs, each playing an active role in the production and reproduction of these initial identities.

Alianza Lima

Three social and cultural factors came together initially to form the identity of the Alianza Lima club: the sense of community in a neighbourhood or *barrio*; urban Afro-Peruvian culture; and the working-class status of the club's members. These factors integrated to produce a football identity for individuals who, at this particular time in Peruvian history, were governed by rigid criteria of social stratification and were considered inferior beings. Yet these same individuals, thanks to football and the ability to compete on an equal footing, had the opportunity to invert the current social and political order and obtain victories that were impossible to achieve in other spheres of daily life. The popular passion for Alianza Lima, together with the union activism and working-class struggles of the early twentieth century, were expressions of the desires of the poor and marginalised sectors of society for integration into the political and economic systems (Flores Galindo 1994; Tejada 1988).

From its early years, the founders of Alianza Lima directed the club. They were young manual labourers and workers from the poor neighbourhoods in the centre of the capital city, who were initially players and then later became directors. As the club gained recognition for its sporting success, Alianza became one of the few positive symbols of the black and *mestizo* population, as well as being a means to earn individual and collective respect. It was also a way of making extra money to complement the meagre income these individuals received as textile or construction workers.

Perhaps because of this, the club adopted an organisation that was both 'collectivist' and 'co-operative', where the players — increasingly worshipped by their fans — managed the club directly without significant definition of roles. A kind of community (or extended family) emerged, strongly united by bonds of friendship, *barrio* ties or quasi-family relationships. The first players were recruited through ethnic and neighbourhood networks, and their culture of collective participation led them to be known as '*Los íntimos de La Victoria*' (the friends from La Victoria), an allusion to the neighbourhood of La Victoria where they lived or worked. This was a metaphor for a group of close friends who had grown up together in the *barrio* making adobe bricks or working in factories, and who were capable of defeating anyone, including the employers. Apparently, during this period, Alianza maintained some organisational characteristics that emanated from the old religious brotherhoods of black slaves and the mutual aid societies of artisans and workers.

From this social and cultural environment, and thanks to the ability of its players, Alianza Lima became the most successful Peruvian football team of the 1920s and 1930s, defeating the other local clubs and also the foreign teams that passed through Lima on South American tours. The superiority of Alianza permitted black and *mestizo* individuals to claim the right to represent Peru on the pitch. In effect, when a foreign club won a match, or even scored goals against Peruvian clubs, Alianza Lima came to the fore to defend the honour of the country. However, Alianza's sporting success also provoked conservative and racist reactions at home. In 1929, the Peruvian Football Federation suspended Alianza from all competitions for one year. The motive: its players had refused to cancel a local championship match in order to allow the national team to prepare for the South American championship in Argentina, arguing that they needed the money earned from the ticket sales of local games for their livelihoods. Alianza players were accused of being 'anti-Peruvian', of being concerned only with money and not with the honour of representing their country. A sector of public opinion even celebrated the sanctions saying it was good that the *aliancistas* had not been selected because the Argentines might think that all Peruvians were black (Stein et al. 1986).

Universitario de Deportes

The Universitario de Deportes club was founded in 1924 by university students from the middle and upper classes. It quickly became the principal rival of Alianza, both on the sports field and in symbolic terms. Within a short period of time, Universitario de

Deportes came to represent the 'modernising' and cosmopolitan elite who were, more importantly, the educated population of white or European race — or who at the very least held pretensions of being white. There also remained on the sidelines some of the most conservative sectors of society who looked down on football completely, and who preferred traditional forms of entertainment such as carnivals, bullfighting and cockfighting. The modernising elite actively assumed the promotion of football, although frequently combining democratic ideals with traditional anachronisms such as racism, discrimination and the 'natural right' to be considered superior.

In effect, the social proximity of the university students with the modernising elite of the country permitted the Universitario club to obtain advantages and patrimonial favours not typically extended to clubs that came from lower-class origins. The first example of these advantages occurred in 1927 when the sporting authorities approved the incorporation of the recently formed Universitario club directly into Peru's First Division, waiving the requirement of playing in the qualifying championships, and as such violating the procedures instituted by the authorities themselves. The authorities decided that the *universitarios* were 'decent' and belonged to 'the best families', and thus had the right to compete in the higher division without passing through the lower leagues. With this decision, the favouritism displayed seemed to contradict the democratic principle of competing on equal terms.

During this period, the university youth movement emerged throughout Latin America as a social and political actor that questioned the traditional order and teaching at the region's major universities (Cueto 1982). It found in football an arena for the expression of its activities. The modernising discourse of the university leaders, with the support of influential journalists, preached the need to develop healthy young people, with a sense of honour and decency as well as the strength to defend the country in any military conflicts that might arise. The memory of the War of the Pacific and the reasons for Peru's defeat dominated the public interest. In this context, football was seen as a means to create a 'new Peruvian man', and the university elites would not merely be bystanders in this process. This process was even more important given that football — which had become the main public competitive forum — was dominated by working-class clubs whose players were black or *mestizo* and, according to many, did not represent the cosmopolitan modernity to which these young elites aspired.

In this manner, university students and modernising elites found in the Universitario club a means to enter into sporting competition with an organisation and an identity of their own, which at the same time allowed them to reclaim their prestige and superiority on an additional terrain — the football field. For this purpose, the club was institutionally structured from its foundation according to modern statutes of organisation and division of labour. In contrast with the informality and community orientation of Alianza Lima, Universitario had its founding constitution (*Actas*) legalised by a public notary. The club had a Board of Directors with clearly defined roles and responsibilities, and it had legal statutes that regulated the membership of the club. As such, Universitario was endowed with symbols of identification as well as sporting heroes who were the antithesis of the skilful but often 'bohemian' Alianza players, who were worshipped by working-class followers for both these qualities. Instead, 'La U' presented itself as a model of correct sporting behaviour, where physical effort and discipline on the pitch, along with decency and respectability on and off the field, were valued above all as 'civilising' traits.

The First Classic

The first match scheduled between Alianza Lima and Universitario de Deportes, on 23 September 1928, was abandoned 35 minutes into the second half when Universitario were (surprisingly) leading 1–0, and after a fight ensued between the players that resulted in the expulsion of five Alianza players and two Universitario players. These fights spread to the stands, when spectators located in the 'premium' seating area (the 'preferential' area) began shouting racial abuse and hitting Alianza players with their walking sticks as these players entered the stands to respond physically to the insults. This fight, along with the debates in the main newspapers and magazines, gave birth to what is today still considered the 'Classic' of Peruvian Football.

The interesting aspect here is that these matches were — and are — presented by the media as a clash between two football identities that, in turn, represent contrasting perspectives on life itself. These identities, furthermore, are associated with distinct playing styles. According to fans and sports commentators, Alianza's football style is characterised by a collective game where talent and skill on the ball predominate. Although Alianza's aim is to win, this should be accomplished by playing well, and it is by playing well, with flair, that superiority should be established. This football style reflects the idea that Alianza is a community or family, firmly united by close, intimate ties.

Universitario, on the other hand, relies upon rigorous preparation, strength and physical effort to gain advantage. From the start, physical strength and tenacity — or *garra* — was the central element of this club's identity. Former Universitario players from the period have indicated that, in order to face Alianza on the field, one needed to have drive to prevent them from playing and a willingness to harass them until their morale was dampened. This was precisely the strategy employed by Universitario to face the skilful and bohemian Alianza players and win the first historic 'Classic'. This result was not, however, accepted as valid by the Alianza fans, who argued that the referee and authorities were biased. These differing views regarding the validity of match results always re-emerge when a 'Classic' match is played.

Organised Fans and Modified Identities (1970–2000)

The end of the twentieth century in Peru was characterised by significant social and political transformation. Peru was transformed into a predominantly urban society, due to internal migration and the explosive growth of the cities along the Pacific coast, especially the capital of Lima.[1]

Between 1968 and 1980, an authoritarian but unorthodox military government implemented a series of measures to redistribute wealth, including drastic land, labour and industrial reforms. At the same time, the military attempted to reorganise society following a top-down, corporatist model. However, after a few years the military was confronted by massive social uprisings, headed by the supposed beneficiaries of the reforms. This led to a forced transition to democracy in the late 1970s, resulting in the return to power of conventional political parties in 1980. Political democracy brought with it enormous public expectations regarding improvements in social welfare. However, governments of both the centre-right (Acción Popular between 1980 and 1985) and centre-left (APRA between 1985 and 1990) brought profound economic and social crises, increased levels of poverty and widespread political violence.

In the early 1990s, the convergence of economic disaster, a rise in political violence and terrorism by the *Sendero Luminoso* (Shining Path) movement, together with the discrediting of all of the mainstream parties and ideologies, laid the foundations for the emergence of a profound anti-political sentiment among the population (Sanborn & Panfichi 1997). Alberto Fujimori took advantage of this situation, arising as an unknown candidate with no political party or formal organisation to achieve a surprise victory in the presidential elections of 1990. Once in power, Fujimori applied a harsh neo-liberal stabilisation programme (backed by the international banking system), and stepped up intelligence and military efforts against Sendero Luminoso.

Football began to gain greater prominence during this period as a means to channel social rivalries (see Panfichi & Thieroldt 2002). It became a space for physical and symbolic violence between young people — mostly poor — who were organised territorially into fierce gangs or *barras bravas*, and who held in common a declared loyalty to a particular football club and identity. In this chapter, the focus is on the cultural process that accompanied the formation and consolidation of the organised *barras* of fans that follow the two leading football clubs, Alianza Lima and Universitario de Deportes. Specifically, we analyse here the ways in which organised groups of fans inherit, but also adapt, certain aspects of the primal identities of both clubs — especially their class and racial identifications — in order to generate more general and inclusive identities that appeal to all social groups, and hence allow each of them to sustain claims of superiority and hegemony.

This process of adaptation of the original identities of the football clubs was strongly linked to social changes. Due to migration patterns, Lima had been completely transformed into a metropolis of seven million inhabitants. Both clubs extended their original social borders and enjoyed the support of fans from all social, economic and cultural backgrounds. As such, friends and enemies of each team are no longer differentiated by their economic status or by the colour of their skin, but rather by their adherence to or rejection of the significant elements that make up each of these newly inclusive identities.

The efforts of the fans to go beyond the initial restrictions of class and race, however, also produced generational struggles within the *barras*, forming antagonistic and irreconcilable bands within each group, where some claimed to defend 'tradition' and others proposed 'radical changes' — a process that to a large extent mirrored the contemporary political process in Peru. For the young *barristas* of the 1990s, the original ethnic and racial anchors of the clubs' founding identities had become obstacles in their struggle to recruit new fans and new members. The 'old-fashioned' *barristas*, on the other hand, believed that their roots and traditions should not be lost.

In the longer term, racial identification became less significant in the face of increasingly important symbols relating to feelings and relationships. Hence today, rather than race or class, what most distinguishes the typical Alianza fan is an attraction to the ideal of 'brotherhood' and community, and a football match that is, above all, well played. The 'intimacy' of the black and working class neighbourhoods in which Alianza was formed has been transformed into the slogan *Alianza Corazón* (roughly meaning 'Alianza from the Heart'), while the 'drive' of the original university students has become the *Garra Crema* (or the 'Cream Claw', in reference to the team's colours of cream and red). These 'reformulated' identities cross all social classes, groups and institutions, recruiting fans and converting them into one of the most important mechanisms of social and cultural differentiation in Peru today. The organised *barras* express this process, particularly in their violence.

Alianza Lima's Comando Sur[2]

The *barra* of Alianza Lima was founded in 1972, under the name of Asociación Barra Alianza, by a group of young middle-class fans who were bank employees and residents of Miraflores, one of the wealthiest districts of Lima at that time. These primarily white and *mestizo* youths, transgressing their own social surroundings, became members of the club, attracted by Alianza's playing style and bohemian spirit. Initially, these young people watched the game from the comfortable Tribuna Occidente (West Stand or executive seating area) of the National Stadium, paying the highest ticket prices, and it was here that they decided to establish the *barra*. Furthermore, this group was organised following the model of organised fans from neighbouring countries such as Brazil and Argentina. Yet the Asociación Barra Alianza subsequently moved, along with its banners and bands, to the more densely populated Tribuna Sur (South Stand), where the cheapest tickets were sold, the more plebeian fans congregated, and where Alianza's goals were celebrated most vociferously. When Alianza Lima inaugurated its own stadium in 1974, the *barra* moved to a location its members called 'The Temple'.

The idea of these young founders was to organise an official *barra* for the club — one that respected its original popular identity. With this in mind, they decided to seek and recruit more fans, concentrating their efforts on the district of La Victoria, long known for its poor, working-class and black inhabitants, and for being the mythical origin of Alianza Lima. It was through this first group of founders that the Alianza 'mystique' was cultivated in the popular stands. The *barristas* began to reproduce, on site, the religious rites that the historic Alianza players supposedly carried out before going out on the field: lighting 12 candles around the team uniform, praying to the Virgin Mary, dancing and entrusting themselves to El Señor de los Milagros (the Lord of Miracles), an image of a black Christ painted by a slave in the colonial period and believed by many to have miraculous powers. Furthermore, at the centre of the *barra* was the *bombo*, a type of drum that beats the team songs and chants with Afro-Peruvian rhythms.

During its first few years, the power of the *barra* was controlled by the initial group of founders and its youngest followers, many of whom were recruited from lower and middle-class neighbourhoods. These individuals were interested in reproducing, although in imaginary form, the historic roots of the Alianza identity. Yet other fans arrived on the scene and demanded changes. Members of a dissident group (of lower class composition), the *Cabezas Azules* (Blue Heads), were initially beaten and expelled from the stands. Another middle-class group, *Los de Surco* (the Guys from Surco), was more successful in proposing new fan styles. The changes proposed included the 'democratic' election of the leader of the fan group, the replacement of the older Afro-

Peruvian-inspired fighting songs for other war chants, and the adoption of a more aggressive and confrontational attitude towards the rival Universitario fans, who were also in the process of extending their influence into lower-income neighbourhoods.

The principal success of these innovators was changing the name of the *barra*. In fact, the members of *Los de Surco* decided to practise what they preached, and became a sort of 'commando' group in charge of browbeating the referees and rival players and fans. Following the example of an Italian *barra* known as *Comando Tigre*, *Los de Surco* brought flags with the name *Comando* to the stadium and insisted that all fans become 'commandos' defending the club's colours. Gradually, this belligerent style of fandom spread throughout the stands. Young people from all social sectors, although they identified with the symbol of the heart, identified even more strongly with another element of fandom: the emotion involved in violently confronting the fans from rival groups in order to steal their flags and later display them as war trophies.

The 1990s brought about significant transformation in the Tribuna Sur (South Stand) of the stadium. Parallel to the discrediting of the political system and an increase in terrorism, the Alianza *barra* became attractive to hundreds of young members of *pandillas,* or gangs, who were organised territorially. These young people took on the symbols and style of *Los de Surco*. As such, the actions of a small commando group were converted into multitudinous street marches where hundreds of youths armed with rocks, sticks and knives moved throughout the city in search of Universitario fans. The point here was to remove any Universitario symbols, steal flags, beat up those fans found around the stadium, and in general commit all kinds of attacks on private property and public authorities, both of which were perceived as being corrupt.

Currently, the strongest and largest of the Alianza *barras* is a coalition of small gangs from the district of La Victoria called the *Barraca Rebelde* (Rebel Barracks).[3] In 1997, this group participated in a *coup d'état* to remove forcefully those who had inherited the *barra* from the founders. From that point on, the *Barraca Rebelde* formed an extensive network of groups and gangs from almost all of Lima's districts, whether poor, middle or upper class. The leaders of the *Barraca Rebelde* proclaimed that all of these groups were now commandos, that there would be no more elite groups, but rather a new army of rebel warriors steadfast in their refusal to accept abuse from any leader or patron. Hence we can observe that the *barristas* have followed the symbols and styles imposed by *Los de Surco*, but they have done so by reformulating the 'intimacy' of the slave barracks that lie in the hearts of all.

Universitario's Trinchera Norte

The *barra* of Universitario de Deportes was organised in 1968 when a group of upper middle-class students from La Inmaculada school, run by the Jesuits, along with residents from the exclusive San Isidro district, decided to organise themselves along the lines of the *barra* of the leading Argentine club, Boca Juniors. As time passed, the group of fans involved became more numerous, and it was difficult to congregate everyone in the Tribuna Occidente (West Stand), the most exclusive area of the National Stadium. For this reason, these youths decided to migrate to the Tribuna Oriente (East Stand), previously recognised as the middle-class stand, where there were no restrictions on space or movement.[4] Unexpectedly, the students from San Isidro were joined by unknown groups of fans carrying flags and singing battle songs. As a consequence of this encounter, an official fan group was formed for the club, located in the East Stand of the stadium. This fan group was basically made up of middle- and upper-class youths and adults.

The principal problem for this fan group was the constant harassment it suffered at the hands of Alianza fans located in the cheap South Stand, who stole the club paraphernalia carried by the Universitario fans and attacked them near the stadium. The Alianza fans were much more numerous and seemed better prepared to handle violent and high-pressure situations. A decision was made by the leaders of the Universitario *barra* to avoid physical confrontation with the Alianza fans and instead differentiate themselves by being a group of decent and well-mannered fans. The Universitario *barra* believed that responding to insults and provocations meant lowering themselves to the uncivilised level of the mob. In this respect, in order to maintain the 'decency' of the East Stand, the leaders of the Universitario *barra* did not hesitate to carry out cleansing operations to expel any fan group that consumed alcohol or drugs, insulted the players, or responded violently to the provocations of the 'savages' from the South Stand.

In 1989, however, a group of young fans from the East Stand, discontented with an official leadership whom they accused of being passive and increasingly bourgeois, decided to break with the official group and migrate towards the cheaper North Stand. Until this time, the northern area of Lima's stadium had stood symbolically 'empty', as no specific group had laid claim to it. The aim of this group was to create a popular force capable of facing their Alianza rivals while dispelling the idea that Universitario was a club for rich white people. For this, it was necessary to make the identity of Universitario more mass-based, by rescuing a discourse and imagery linked to the original identity: 'strength' and 'drive' as part of a strategy for achieving success. This idea was radically represented with the symbol of the *garra*, or claw.

In some ways, this is the same strategy of strength that the Universitario players used in the first 'Classic' match of 1928 when they faced a rival which was widely considered to be superior. At the end of the 1980s, the goal of this group was to take forcibly the last cheap stand that did not already have a defined identity and to confront the enemy, Alianza Lima, from that vantage point. Many of these fans feel attracted to intolerant or radical emblems such as the Nazi swastika. This symbol still appears on the flags, shirts and graffiti that serve as identifying factors of this *barra*. *Holocausto* and *Ultras Cremas* (the Cream-Coloured 'Ultras'), terms with fascist overtones, also appear among the names of groups associated with the *barra*.

In the 1990s, however, the fans appeared fascinated by the extremism of Sendero Luminoso. In fact, in 1993 the *barra* was named *Trinchera Norte* (or the Northern Trench), inspired by Sendero Luminoso militants who from inside prison had resisted guards and authorities from what they called *trincheras luminosas* (luminous trenches). The following year, 1994, the directors of the *barra* named themselves the *Cúpula*, the same name used by the police and the press when referring to the central committee of Sendero Luminoso.

Equally, in 1995, another group assumed the denomination *El Buró*, the name of the political commission of Sendero Luminoso. Symbols with antagonistic political content were stripped of their political connotations and given a new meaning by the Universitario fans. In truth, these were all means of demonstrating the radical nature and violence to which the *garra* would resort in order to defend its colours.

Conclusion

One of the conclusions that can be drawn from this case is that the identities and symbolism that are constructed around football clubs form a type of cultural structure, one that can help to reduce the social complexity that may otherwise overcome individuals in distinct historical contexts.[5] In fact, in the early twentieth century, the founding identities of the principal clubs emphasised the factors of class and race, together with demands for social integration. These were the years of the so-called 'Aristocratic Republic', an early effort at capitalist modernisation that coexisted with an oligarchic state.

A loyal nucleus of spectators, journalists, club members and workers congregated around each of these clubs, and each played an active role in the production and reproduction of these initial identities. These nuclei generated unilateral explanations of the players' behaviour, reducing the complexity of social life by imagining a simpler and static society where blacks and whites, rich and poor, *aliancistas* and *universitarios* did not mix with each other, but instead laid claims of social inclusion or exclusion. The Alianza founding identity was based on the notion of brotherhood or *intimacy*, as a distinct form of relationship between members of a diverse but closed group, while at Universitario the central element was the notion of *force*, as a distinct form of relationship with other rival groups.

At the end of the twentieth century, organised fans gave new meanings to the original identities of these two historic football clubs, downplaying factors such as class and race which excluded some social groups, while strengthening their more inclusive cultural and emotional appeals such as the *corazón* (heart) or *garra* (claw), the iconographic symbols used most frequently by these rival clubs. In fact, the main actions of the *barristas*, both in *Comando Sur* and *Trinchera Norte*, had as their objective the extension of the mass fan-base of the clubs. The history of the *Comando Sur* is marked by the struggle between a younger generation that wanted to integrate 'modern' and 'white' elements against an older generation that felt comfortable with a tradition that was 'black' and 'patrimonial'. The result of this confrontation was a greater tolerance and acceptance of other races and groups, without abandoning the idea of 'intimacy' as a distinctive form of internal organisation. The founders of *Trinchera Norte*, for their part, sought to break the 'white' stigma and popularise their club, drawing it closer to black and especially the *cholo* sectors of society. This was achieved through strengthening the concept of the *garra* and the use of force in confrontations with rivals.

Notes

1 In 2000, 72 per cent of the population was considered urban, in contrast to 40.6 per cent in 1961. See NU — PNUD (2002).

2 This section is based on the authors' own ethnographic research undertaken in 2003 and 2004.

3 *Barraca* is the term that the Spanish conquerors gave to the dark and dirty wooden constructions in which African slaves were made to sleep after their long hours of work in the countryside.

4 The pitch in the National Stadium in Lima runs in a north–south direction. As at most football grounds, the cheaper terraces are located behind the goals, and the more expensive seats opposite the halfway line — in this case, in the centre of the East and West stands.

5 This idea draws from the concept of 'structures of reduction of complexity' proposed by Marcela Gleizer (1997).

PART IV:

THE BUSINESS OF FOOTBALL IN THE AMERICAS

9

Beautiful Game, Lousy Business:
The Problems of Latin American Football

Gideon Rachman

'Football is a crazy business all around the world,' observes Mauricio Macri, the president of the Boca Juniors club in Argentina (*The Economist*, 1 June 2002, p. 7). How true! Any survey of the problems facing football in Latin America has to start by acknowledging that many of the challenges facing the game in countries like Brazil and Argentina, the two countries on which this chapter will concentrate, are often replicated in the richer, more ordered environment of Western Europe. Football teams teetering on the edge of bankruptcy? Look no further than Parma of Italy or Leeds United in England. Football hooliganism? Fans have recently been killed in Italy, and European football still remains haunted by the memory of the Heysel Stadium disaster of 1985. Corruption? Think of all the rumours about games being thrown in Italy, or England's 'bung inquiries'.[1]

However, anyone attempting to compare the state of the football business in Europe and Latin America cannot but conclude that the problems in Latin America are far more severe than in Europe. Broadly speaking, the difficulties of the game there can be put into two main categories. There are those problems that are general to professional football around the world. These exist in Europe and are also present in Latin America, but in a much exaggerated form. In this category, one can put the inability to control the salaries of players; the problems of trying to run a football club as a business or at least as a going concern financially; the threats of hooliganism; and those of corruption. Then there is a second category of problem, unique to football in Latin America. These are problems which have no parallel in Europe, but rather are caused by Europe. The fact that there is so much more money in European football has a distorting effect on the game on the other side of the Atlantic. Specifically, it means that the continent is increasingly losing its star players at younger and younger ages, with negative effects on fan loyalty, interest in the game and even national teams. More generally, European money is undoubtedly a factor in the corruption of football in Latin America, which again leads to cynicism and loss of interest.

Of course, it must be acknowledged that to focus on the problems of Latin American football may seem a bit paradoxical — a bit like studying the crisis in US science, or the drawbacks of Paris as a tourist destination. For millions of fans around the world, Latin America remains the spiritual home of world football — with Pele and Maradona competing for the title of greatest player ever, and the Brazilian national team not only carrying off the World Cup in 2002 for a record fifth time, but also playing the kind of football that has made them icons all over the world. Tell any of the children wandering around London or Paris in a Brazil shirt that Latin American football is in crisis, and you are likely to be met with an uncomprehending look — and in many ways, rightly so.

Yet, while the signs of decline are not yet evident on the pitch, despite the relatively poor results of Brazil and Argentina in the 2006 World Cup, in the stands and the boardrooms Latin American football is in chaos, with financial and administrative problems that make the difficulties faced in Europe seem trivial. Jorge Valdano, who first became world famous as Maradona's striking partner in 1986 and was until recently the Director of Sport at Real Madrid, was unequivocal when he spoke about the decline of football in his native country: 'All the main teams are on the verge of bankruptcy,' he pointed out, 'and the stands are empty.' (*The Economist*, 1 June 2002, p. 12)

It is a similar story in Brazil. Crowds at football matches there have fallen by 40 per cent over the last 15 years. In 2002, a game between Flamengo and Corinthians — said to be the two most popular teams in the country — drew just 10,000 people to the Maracanã. Juca Kfouri, Brazil's leading football journalist and a campaigner against corruption in the game, says that he thinks that people are staying away from football as a 'Gandhi-type reaction, a passive protest against the state of Brazilian football which has lost all credibility because of mismanagement and corruption' (*The Economist*, 1 June 2002, p. 13).

Bankruptcy, mismanagement, even corruption — these are all laments that would be familiar to fans of leading European teams like Fiorentina, Lazio or Leeds United. The fact is that there are certain common themes which make football a notoriously difficult business anywhere in the world. European complaints about falling revenues from TV deals and rising player salaries are more than echoed in Latin America. As in Europe, television companies which found they had over-paid for football rights then tried to renegotiate deals, disrupting the financial plans of football teams. Although there is a lot of focus in both Europe and Latin America on the problems caused for football by unreliable television broadcasting deals, they are usually only a symptom of the underlying trouble. The truth is that no matter how much the revenues of football teams grow, clubs will almost always contrive to spend more than they earn. Deloitte Touche Sport calculated that, in the 1990s, the revenues of the clubs in the English Premier League went up by 500 per cent as television money poured into the game, but costs went up by 700 per cent — meaning that almost all teams, with the exception of Manchester United, were losing money (*The Economist*, 1 June 2002, p. 7). That is because many teams were prepared to lose money in the pursuit of the best players and the glory that it was hoped they would bring. The problem is even more acute in Latin America. It is summed up most succinctly by Mauricio Macri of Boca Juniors: 'We are all linked. When one club starts paying higher salaries than it can afford, sooner or later it will be a problem for your club.' (*The Economist*, 1 June 2002, p. 7.)

The difficulty that Macri identified is that football in most places around the world contains two sorts of teams: teams that need to make a profit — or at least break even — to stay afloat, and teams that are essentially funded by rich fans who do not mind losing money. The difficulty for the clubs that do not have a rich sugar daddy is that as soon as Roman Abramovic — or his Latin American equivalent — turns up down the road, they face an instant dilemma. Do they just accept that they will lose their best players and be condemned to sporting mediocrity? Or do they try to compete by raising salaries and paying high transfer fees in the hope that success on the field will eventually lead to the books somehow balancing? The difficulty for teams that adopt this strategy — which Peter Ridsdale, the erstwhile chairman of Leeds United, called 'living the dream' — is that it too often turns into a nightmare. The team unaccountably loses a few key games, financial calculations go awry, players have to be sold, fans revolt. Even teams that have the good fortune to find a sugar daddy often discover that this is only a temporary solution. When their benefactor loses his interest or his money, they can be plunged into crisis. In different ways, this has been the story at three big Italian clubs, Parma, Lazio, and Fiorentina.[2]

Indeed, Macri may arguably even be a symptom of the very problem that he describes. In 2002, he was quite open about using the visibility that football brings as a vehicle for his political ambitions. He planned to run for mayor of Buenos Aires and perhaps ultimately for president, noting that: 'There are many other people in the private sector who may have just as much talent as me, but they don't have the visibility that football brings.' (*The Economist*, 1 June 2002, p. 5) Macri, whose family had made its wealth in the construction and contracting business, insisted that he intended to run Boca in a financially prudent fashion. Indeed, part of his emerging political pitch was a stress on his businessman's ability to impose sensible financial controls — a potentially powerful appeal in a country still emerging from a disastrous economic crisis. But the fact remains that achieving success with Boca was part of a larger game plan. In certain circumstances, it often makes sense for a rich man like Macri to use a football team as a loss leader for the furtherance of other ambitions, whether they be political or indeed social.[3]

For teams in Latin America, the problem of controlling costs in an environment in which many teams are prepared to lose money is compounded by the fact that they are competing for talent not just with each other, but with the infinitely better-financed clubs of Europe. The 2002 list of the richest clubs in the world, drawn up by Deloitte & Touche, found no Latin American clubs in the top 30. Four teams — Boca Juniors, River Plate, Corinthians and Flamengo — made the top 40 (Deloitte & Touche 2002).[4] However, according to a report on Latin American football by *Soccer Investor* published in the same year, they were all being run at a loss — sometimes at a frightening loss. The *Soccer Investor* report, for example, estimated that in 2001 River Plate had a turnover of just over $40 million, and an operating loss of $28 million. Around the same time, the president of River Plate was quoted as saying that if player salaries and bonuses could not be cut, 'Argentine soccer will disappear' (*Soccer Investor* 2002).

Faced with desperate financial circumstances, the obvious solution is to sell players. The fact that so many of the leading players in the Brazilian side that won the 2002 World Cup, and all bar one of Argentina's starting line-up in that tournament, played in Europe is an important clue to one of the root causes of the problems in Latin American football. There is now a global market for players, and European clubs pay the best salaries. As they compete with the Europeans and each other for the best players, Latin American clubs have found their salary bills inflated beyond all logic. Before the devaluation of the peso in 2002, leading players in Argentina were being paid over a million dollars a year — yet a ticket to watch a big game cost around ten dollars. The predictable result of the wage spiral in both Argentina and Brazil is that many players are simply not being paid. There have been player strikes in both countries. In 2002, Romario — perhaps the most popular player then plying his trade in Brazil — was reported to be owed four million dollars in back-pay by his team, Vasco da Gama. The previous year he had to pay some of his team-mates' wages himself (Bellos 2002, p. 292).

Yet, despite bankrupting themselves in the pursuit of talent, most Latin American teams still end up selling their best players in a bid to keep afloat. Indeed, for many of the clubs, this has become their main commercial strategy. Boca Juniors raised 12 million dollars on the Argentine stock market by floating a fund which allowed investors to take a cut from the future sale of certain named players.[5] Moreover, the players are going abroad at a younger and younger age. Two-thirds of the Argentine team that won the World Under-21 Championships in 2001 were plying their trade in Europe the following year. As a result, the fans lose interest. No sooner have they discovered a new idol than he is on the next plane to Europe.

The fact that so many of Latin America's soccer idols are disappearing to Europe could even mean that the financial threat posed to Latin America's football teams may worsen. Teams like Real Madrid and Manchester United have been intent on turning themselves into 'global brands'. This has meant that — particularly in the case of Real Madrid under the presidency of Florentino Pérez — the purchase of players has frequently been tailored to the demands of the marketing department. José Angel Sánchez, Head of Marketing at Real Madrid, noted with satisfaction in 2002 that: 'We're content providers, like a film studio — and having a team with Zidane in it is like having a movie with Tom Cruise.' (*The Economist*, 1 June 2002, p. 9) A good geographical spread of players helps to build a global brand. For Real Madrid, Zinedine Zidane was not just a great midfielder, he also attracted support for the club from France and North Africa. Roberto Carlos and Ronaldo can perform a similar function in Brazil, while David Beckham is a marketer's dream in England and the Far East. It should be noted that in the period when Real Madrid was busy assembling its 'dream team', the idea of turning the team's worldwide visibility into worldwide revenues also remained the stuff of dreams. As late as 2002, both Real Madrid and Manchester United were still relying on their domestic markets for around 95 per cent of their revenues. But business strategists at both clubs had their eyes on emerging technologies which they hoped would help them target supporters and customers from all over the world. In the words of Sánchez of Real Madrid: 'Telecoms and globalisation are consolidating the global football market. Eventually you may just get six global brand leaders. People will support a local side and one of the world's big six. We have to position ourselves for that.' The idea, of course, is not just to attract support, but to generate revenue. Sánchez hopes that, in a few years' time: 'People will be watching a Roberto Carlos goal on their telephones in Rio and paying for it.' (*The Economist*, 1 June 2002, p. 9) By 2004, clear evidence was beginning to emerge that Sánchez's marketing dream was turning into reality. A Harvard Business School study showed that Real Madrid had become the first of Europe's super-clubs where marketing revenue now comfortably exceeded gate receipts and television money (Harvard Business School Case Study, 2004). In 2006, Real Madrid beat Manchester United to the top of Deloitte & Touche's 'Money League' for the first time (Deloitte & Touche 2006).

The globalisation of football poses a potential threat to the health of the Latin American game because it is clear that the would-be brand leaders of global football have an eye not just on the best players owned by Latin American clubs, but also on their supporters. In countries like Brazil and Argentina, where so much passion is spent on the national side and the vast majority of supporters follow the game on television, European sides featuring the best players from Latin America might indeed begin to make inroads on the fan-base of local teams. The warning signs are already there in the empty grounds of so many of Latin America's top sides. For a European paying a first visit to the continent that is the spiritual home of world football, the empty stadiums can come as a bit of a shock. Researching an article for *The Economist* in 2002, I went to a game in the Copa Libertadores between San Lorenzo of Buenos Aires and Peñarol, a visiting team from Uruguay. One end of the ground — the San Lorenzo end — was packed with a swaying crowd of singing, chanting, firework-releasing supporters. The rest of the ground was virtually empty. When I suggested to my companion that it might be fun to go and stand at the San Lorenzo end, he looked at me as if I was mad. He had once tried it, but had been swiftly identified as a *gringo*, hurled to the ground and stripped of all his possessions.

For it is not just the loss of star-players and economic crisis that is putting fans off going to games in Latin America. As anyone who follows the game in Latin America will know, there is also a real problem with hooliganism. That San Lorenzo game will be remembered for a long time. At the final whistle, supporters streamed on to the pitch and the players raced for the tunnel. A couple of unfortunates who did not make it in time were stripped almost naked. One player was left hopping about in his underwear and one boot. It was subsequently explained to me that the *barras bravas* (fan groups) liked to raffle the players' kit for profit after the games. Once again, hooliganism is a problem that clearly also exists in Europe. However, where Europeans (at least at club level) seem largely to have contained the problem — so that in England, for example, it is once again conceivable for families to go to games together — in Argentina, in particular, the problem seems to be worsening. There are many possible explanations, such as poverty or inefficient policing, but there is also clear evidence that many team-owners have struck a Faustian bargain with their most violent supporters. As Tim Vickery, a BBC correspondent in Latin America, wrote in 2003: 'It is an open secret in Argentina that club directors supply tickets, transport and finance to organised hooligans.' (Vickery, 2003) This may be done for political reasons, or simply for a quiet life, but the result is that ordinary fans can be very reluctant to go to a game.

The effects on gate revenues are predictably disastrous. Indeed, the bosses of Racing Club, another Buenos Aires team which is often held up as a rare example of sound business practice, told the author that they regarded hooliganism as perhaps the biggest problem facing the Argentine game, since it served as such an effective deterrent to their customers (Personal communication, March 2002). An inability to expand the number of paying supporters going through the turnstiles is a potentially crippling problem for a football club. For, despite all the hype about television money and shirt-sales, gate money is fundamental to the financial health of football teams, even in the most sophisticated markets. Take a look at the accounts of Manchester United, for example, and you will find that selling tickets to games at Old Trafford has remained the club's biggest single source of revenue (Deloitte & Touche 2002, p. 5).

Another problem which also exists in Europe, but which seems to be present in a sadly exaggerated form in Latin America, is corruption. Even the famously law-abiding English have long had problems with 'bungs' (bribes paid to football managers, players or agents, and often skimmed off transfer fees). Such corruption, as well as being morally objectionable, serves to weaken the finances of teams further, and to create disillusionment among fans. In Latin America, many football administrators are assumed to loot their clubs and federations. Pocketing the proceeds of the sale of players to Europe is a particularly popular, if poorly documented, pastime.

Once again, the gap in spending power between Europe and Latin America serves to accentuate the problem. The kind of money that European clubs are capable of throwing about inevitably creates huge temptations for shady individuals on the other side of the Atlantic. It must be said that European football teams, intent on getting the player they want and not too fussy about how the deal is done, are often complicit in the corruption. One leading European club that paid a multi-million dollar fee to buy a player from an

Argentine club told the author that it had had to pay seven different people who owned unofficial stakes in the player (officially all the money was going to his club). The completion of the transfer was delayed to allow all seven the time they needed to set up offshore accounts. The club in question did not blanche at doing business in that way, despite the fact that it was listed on the London Stock Exchange. Another anecdote told to the author (less well-sourced since it came from a football industry observer rather than a club involved in the deal) concerns yet another transfer from an Argentine club to a European side. In this case, the corruption was coming from the European end. The trick this time was to understate the fee. The figure announced was, let us say, £10 million. The real amount paid by the European club was £12 million. The difference was split between the personal accounts of the heads of the two clubs involved. This particular story may not be true, but there are so many similar stories circulating that it is difficult to believe that they are *all* false. Ezequiel Fernández Moore, an Argentine football journalist, argues that there are distinct parallels between the way Argentine football is run and the way the country as a whole was being managed in the run-up to its debt default in 2002. Both the country and the football clubs were living beyond their means, and corruption was widespread: 'Companies were privatised and yet a lot of the money would disappear off into Swiss accounts and never reach the government. It's the same when football clubs sell players. The money never reaches the clubs. This is a country which likes to break the rules.' (*The Economist*, 1 June 2002, p. 12)

In Brazil, the spectre of corruption and mismanagement hangs over not only the clubs, but also the beloved Brazilian national side and the Brazilian Confederation of Football (CBF), which runs the game. It is widely believed, for example, that the huge number of players who have been selected for the national side in recent years may have something to do with the fact that a player's transfer value will soar once he is a Brazilian international. As Sócrates, a much-loved former captain of the national side, told Alex Bellos: 'I think the team is being used much more as a negotiating table than for professional reasons.' (Bellos 2002, p. 361) After the Brazilian side lost the final of the 1998 World Cup, much of the initial criticism famously focused on Brazil's sponsorship contract with Nike, the sports goods manufacturer. Wild rumours circulated that Nike had insisted that Ronaldo, who had suffered something like an epileptic fit a few hours before the game, should nonetheless play. A congressional inquiry was set up into the matter in Brazil. It found no real evidence to support the idea that Nike had demanded that Ronaldo play in the final, although it did confirm that the Brazilian team had agreed to play an inordinate number of 'Nike friendlies' — exhibition games that were felt to be an unnecessary drain on the players. However, the real scandal hinted at by the congressional inquiry into the CBF was the question of what happened to all the money generated by Nike. As Bellos points out: 'From 1997 to 2000, the CBF's revenues quadrupled, but it did not pay off its debts. Ricardo Teixeira [the president of the CBF], however, did very well out of it. He and his directors received pay rises of more than 300 per cent.' Some of the expenditure authorised by the CBF also looks distinctly questionable. As Bellos adds: 'In 2000, the CBF spent $16 million on travel — enough for 1,663 first-class returns from Rio to Australia.' (Bellos 2002, p. 348)

So what hope is there for the future of football in Argentina and Brazil? The main hope for correcting some of the problems and abuses identified in this chapter is that football will increasingly be run on business lines. Lest that sound tiresomely like an *Economist* editorial, it should be pointed out that even people not in the pay of global capitalism seem to be coming to similar conclusions. Juca Kfouri, the best known and most respected football journalist in Brazil, dismisses the idea that Nike is the problem with Brazilian football. Indeed he reckons that ultimately business and capitalism may be what saves the game: 'There is just too much money in football now,' he says, 'for it to be run in the old, secretive amateurish way. Businesses will insist on transparency and proper accounts.' (*The Economist*, 1 June 2002, p. 12)

There are some signs that this is already happening. In Brazil, in late 2002, Congress finally passed a law forcing clubs to reorganise themselves as companies and to publish properly audited accounts. The insistence on external auditing was also part of an agreement that President Duhalde of Argentina reached with his country's cash-strapped teams in the same year. There is also change coming from within clubs themselves. Macri at Boca Juniors claims that he is insisting on cost control and realistic salaries, 'even if my players call me a mean bastard' (*The Economist*, 1 June 2002, p. 7). Racing Club of Buenos Aires won the national championship for the first time in 35 years in 2001, after being rescued from bankruptcy by private investors and benefiting from a special change in the law, allowing the football activities of the club to be run for profit rather than as a non-profit social club.

Professional management is even appearing at Flamengo in Brazil. In some ways, Flamengo is a prime example of all that is wrong with Brazilian football. Although it is the best-supported team in the country and claims to have 35 million supporters (more than the entire population of Argentina), the club still does not own its own ground. Players have gone on strike for their wages and the club president was accused of financial crimes by the congressional inquiry into football. But during a visit to the club in 2002, it was revealed that it had recently hired Claudio Zohar, a young businessman, to come up with a rational business strategy. Zohar said: 'Until recently most people who ran football clubs were just fans. However, as far as he was concerned, 'the amateur model of corrupt football management has failed'. For him, 'winning titles is just a weapon to make money' (Zohar 2002). When asked whether anybody else in the club agreed with him on that point, he added — rather sadly — that he had not found one yet. In case his 'profit at all cost' philosophy sound a little bloodless to the average fan, Zohar explained that his goal was to get Flamengo back to the situation where it could hang on to its best players — like Zico, the star of the 1980s, who played for Flamengo for 20 years. That would never happen nowadays, but Zohar reckoned that hanging on to your best players is a crucial part of 'building the brand' (*The Economist*, 1 June 2002, p. 12). As he outlined his strategy, Zohar sounded very much like his counterparts at the big European clubs: the goal must be to turn supporters into customers, to develop new sources of revenue, to create financial stability and predictability. There is certainly a lot to do. Even in 2002, Flamengo did not even have that most basic of football club commercial outlets — a club shop from which to sell replica shirts — although it did do a nifty line in condoms packaged in the team colours. Zohar told me proudly that Flamengo condoms were out-selling those of all other Brazilian teams by 30 per cent.

If men like Zohar secure more influence over Latin American football, things may indeed improve. For the moment, however, it remains the case that the state of football administration in Brazil is almost a textbook case of how *not* to run things. It is a lesson that the emerging football powers, still transfixed by all things Brazilian, would do well to remember.

Acknowledgements

I should like to thank all the people in the football world who helped with research for this article, in particular Alex Bellos in Brazil, Peter Hudson in Argentina and Simon Kuper in Paris.

Notes

1   In the summer of 2006, Italian football was hit by allegations regarding the involvement of leading clubs in the nomination of referees to matches in which they were playing. It is often said that Pierluigi Collina, the leading Italian referee of his generation, was rarely chosen to officiate in matches involving Juventus or the two Milan teams, the most powerful clubs in Italy. In September 2006, *Panorama*, BBC's flagship current affairs programme, alleged that 18 past and present Premier League managers had taken 'bungs' or illicit commissions on transfer deals (*Panorama*, 19 September 2006).

2   Parma was undermined by the financial collapse of Parmalat SA; Lazio by that of Cirio SA, another foodstuffs multinational, which led to the resignation of Sergio Cragnotti who had led the club through its most successful period in the 1990s.

3   For Macri's background, see <www.cema.edu.ar/cgc/download/2004/cvmacri.pdf>, which can be found on the website of his foundation Creer y Crecer. In 2005 he became a congressional deputy representing Buenos Aires. He clearly planned to run for the presidency two years later, if possible. However, by early 2007 the realignment of the anti-Peronist forces seemed to make it more likely that he would campaign to become Mayor of Buenos Aires.

4   Deloitte's annual Rich List is based on a club's turnover, not on its profitability or net assets.

5   For an investor's note on the Boca Juniors scheme, dated 2000 but
    still on the internet, see <www.fondos.com.ar/saber/articulos/
    boca.htm>.

10

La crisis y el fútbol:
Economic Change and Political Continuity in Argentine Football

Liz Crolley and Vic Duke

Introduction

The now customary images of violence in football were splashed across the Argentine media. There were 70 injured, following a match between Boca and Chacarita Juniors at La Bombonera on 31 August 2003. The immediate reaction in the media was not to blame fans for their unsociable behaviour, as their European counterparts probably would have done, but to question the suspicious (lack of) intervention of the police and to fire off accusations of political manoeuvring. Mauricio Macri, the president of Boca Juniors, was quick to hint at the involvement of Chacarita club officials in the perpetration of the violent scenes.[1]

A subsequent inquiry into the violent incidents, headed by Judge Mariano Bergés, raises some key issues facing Argentine football: political corruption and illicit links between football clubs, fans, the state and the Argentine Football Association (AFA). Just a few days after the events at La Bombonera, following a preliminary investigation, the Director del Programa de Seguridad en Espectáculos Futbolísticos (Director of Security for Football), former referee Javier Castrelli, drew comparisons between the violence during the match at La Bombonera and political violence in Catamarca on 2 March 2002, which led to the postponement of (government) elections. He also ensured that the actions of the Federal Police were put firmly under the microscope for their lack of intervention (*La Nación*, 5 September 2003). Judge Mariano Bergés clearly shared his suspicions, for he prohibited the police from attending football matches in Buenos Aires for three weeks while the incident that took place at La Bombonera was investigated (*La Nación*, 9 September 2003). Furthermore, the vice-president of Chacarita Juniors, Armando Capriotti, was incarcerated for his involvement in the events of 31 August. While Capriotti himself significantly claimed he was a 'political prisoner', this was not the only case of alleged links between violent groups and football club officials. As Judge Bergés broadened the scope of his inquiry, others were implicated — *barras bravas* of other clubs, other *dirigentes*, other politicians and other officials.[2] Bergés has a reputation for being determined in his pursuit of truth, and unafraid of the political (or personal) consequences of his investigations.

This case, and other examples presented throughout this chapter, serve to illustrate the extent of the politicisation of football in Argentina. As one commentator described it: 'Bergés plunges his sword deep into the heart of the *barra*, but also into the heart of power.' (*Río Negro*, 18 October 2003)[3] While this does appear to be the case, and some high-profile *dirigentes* and politicians were implicated in the inquiry, it was unlikely that its results would lead to significant changes in the way in which football is run. This chapter aims to comment on the effects of *la crisis* on the structures of Argentine football and offers an analysis of the (changing?) relationships between football and politics in Argentina.

The dire financial situation of football clubs and the national crisis Argentina suffered in the early years of the twenty-first century placed immense strains on relationships that have existed for over a century, and that result from the specific functions that football clubs have historically fulfilled in Argentine society. We argue that, despite attempts to change the structures and organisation of football, the mutual system of support that has been built up among the key players in Argentine football still remains. Indeed, it is precisely because of these long-established relationships that football maintains its position within Argentine society. How long these structures will survive in their current form will depend largely on the outcome of debates regarding the organisation, and ultimately the role of football in Argentine society.

Background

The historical development of complex relationships between football and politics in Argentina has been documented widely (Archetti 1994a; Duke & Crolley 1996a, 2001; Sebreli 1998). We have argued elsewhere that there are four main elements in the organisation of Argentine football, and that it is the relationships between them that determine the role of politics in sport and sport in politics. The state (represented by politicians), the AFA, the football clubs and the fans are the key players (Duke & Crolley 2001, p. 99). Other elements, such as business and the media, are also highly relevant, but they are usually linked to one of the key players in some way. *Dirigentes* (directors) of football clubs double as politicians and/or businessmen in such a way that football and politics are inextricably linked. Football forms part of the political system, and any decisions related to football rapidly become politicised (Romero 1994; Sebreli 1998; Levinsky 2003). Football preceded democratic politics in Argentina. Newly formed political parties used football's infrastructure and neighbourhood-based clubs. This feature of Argentine football represents one of its strengths — the government helps out in times of crisis, and at least turns a blind eye to football's problems, allowing it to carry a level of debt that would not be tolerated in other industries, and even introducing new legislation when things get tough. However, this is also its main weakness. Football suffers from poor management, is wide open to corruption and nepotism, and lacks transparency. There is no incentive to increase the efficiency of this style of management.

While it is not unusual for football in Argentina to get into financial difficulties, in recent years Argentine football has been in one of the deepest crises it has ever suffered. The rationalisation of the Argentine economy that took place in the 1990s did not extend to the football industry, and poor management has long been a feature of Argentine football. Most professional clubs are in debt. So serious was the situation at the end of the Torneo de Apertura in 2001 that the president of San Lorenzo de Almagro put his whole team on the transfer market. By July 2003, the media were reporting that clubs in the Argentine First Division owed over AR$240 million. The reasons for this crisis in Argentine football are many, and it is as yet unclear whether or not the solutions proposed thus far will be allowed to be effective given its current organisational structures.

Challenges for Argentine Football

Economic and Financial Crisis for Football Clubs

The general economic depression in Argentina and the crisis which erupted on 21 December 2001 had an impact on all aspects of Argentine society, including football. A government loan of US$40 billion from the IMF failed to allay fears of economic crisis, and in January 2002 Argentina faced a major default on the country's sovereign debt. A 40 per cent devaluation of the peso ensued and bank deposits were frozen (until November 2002). By May 2002, the official national unemployment rate stood at around 2.8 million workers (21.4 per cent of the labour force) and, according to the Instituto Nacional de Estadísticas y Censos (INDEC), 53 per cent of the population lived in poverty — a rate that was 15 per cent higher than that of October 2001 (www.europaworld.com). The De la Rúa government inevitably collapsed, and Argentina entered a period of political, economic and social turmoil. Despite the backdrop of this clear deterioration in labour market conditions, the dramatic fall in household income and the obvious negative impact on football, clubs should actually have benefited to some extent from the country's crisis. The devaluation of the peso meant that the value of debts fell by almost 75 per cent and clubs' revenues were actually greater than ever before.[4] Clubs 'live' in pesos, in the sense of paying salaries and other costs, but receive US dollars for player transfers and for participation in competitions. Thus the reasons why football clubs remain in so much debt must lie, at least in part, elsewhere.

Organisation of Football Clubs

It is argued here that the existing structures of Argentine football, and the politicised links between football's key players, are at least partly responsible for a lack of commercial acumen and development in football clubs. In Argentina, football clubs are not-for-profit private member associations (*asociaciones civiles sin fines de lucro*). Club members (*socios*) elect officials (*dirigentes*) and a chairperson (*presidente*) through an electoral campaign. This has huge implications when *dirigentes* need the support of their fan-base (via the radical arm of the *barras bravas*) in order to be re-elected, and are prepared to make rash promises and compromise their integrity severely in order to maintain it.[5]

Many club *dirigentes* are also businessmen (and they are almost exclusively male), who run private businesses as well as being involved with the football club on a part-time basis. Despite the possibilities that arose during the 1990s of making money through the televising and merchandising of football, and the development of other new business initiatives, most football clubs have so far failed to capitalise on such opportunities. Argentine football clubs have been poorly managed by non-professional *dirigentes*. Rather than bringing their experience as businessmen to the benefit of the football club, they use the club as a platform for free publicity for their own businesses, and for private financial, political and personal gain.[6] Exposure to the mass media is important, and the links between these people and the media are increasingly relevant. Many of the clubs' *dirigentes* are also fans, sometimes former *violentos* who have bullied their way into the club management structure (Levinsky 2003). The integrated structures of fans, *dirigentes* and politicians contribute to benefit all the main players in Argentine football — though not football as a whole. The maintenance of the status quo in Argentine football is therefore desirable for most of those in control. Bergés' investigation was welcomed by many interested in Argentine football, but surely feared by those involved closely in the running of the game who might have been afraid of losing their positions of power if Bergés was allowed to dig deeply enough.

Corruption, Collusion and Violence

The links between football and the government are so explicit that it is generally recognised that nepotism and corruption are rife, particularly via the AFA, and that the government at best turns a blind eye to football's less orthodox customs.[7] When business methods have been questioned, journalists have complained that they have been 'silenced' (Levinsky 2003; Mora y Araujo 2003). It is a small step from political corruption and collusion to violence in Argentine football. The images of violence associated with the sport at football grounds and depicted constantly in the media have also contributed to the long-term decline of football. While this chapter does not discuss the roots and evolution of violence in Argentine football here (instead, see Scher & Palomino 1988; Archetti & Romero 1994; Duke & Crolley 1996b), the role of football's key players in violence is of relevance to the argument. The links between organised violent groups of fans (*barras bravas*), the club *dirigentes*, the AFA and the state are clear. The integrated structures of football and politics facilitate these relationships.

The Poor Image and Marketability of Argentine Football

From a European perspective, where professional football has travelled further along the route of commercialisation, it is apparent that the weaknesses outlined above (and the poor image of football frequently portrayed in the media) contribute to the lack of marketability of Argentine football. Hence the value of gate receipts, television rights and sponsorship will not be maximised. Clubs do not generate the degree of commercial interest they might have done in a stronger economy, where people have the disposable income to spend on attending football, watching it on television — especially pay TV — or buying football-related merchandise. Torneos y Competencias y Traffic (TyT), holders of the television rights for the Copa Libertadores, re-negotiated their deal with the AFA in 2002. TyT argued for a reduction in the amount they paid for football by 30 per cent and hence for lower participation fees paid out to the 32 teams involved (*Terra*, 22 January 2002).

If football is not viewed as prestigious, it will have a negative impact on the value of its sponsorship contracts.[8] The perceived lack of administrative, financial, commercial and managerial competence in Argentine football also has an adverse effect in this area. According to a study reported in *Gerencia Deportiva*, 45 per cent of sponsors of Argentine football felt poorly treated by the *dirigentes* of the club and commented upon a 'lack of professionalism' within Argentine football clubs (*Deporte y Negocios*, 12 December 2001). The structures of Argentine football have not lent themselves to maximising opportunities within the 'market'. There is little optimisation of exchange of information between football clubs and their *socios* or fans and, with the possible exceptions of Boca Juniors and Racing, there seem to be no plans in place to tap into new revenue streams. Football's historical role in Argentine society does not lend itself to treating the football fan as a consumer, as is increasingly the case in some European countries. So what are the directions in which Argentine football can develop from here?

Possible Solutions to Football's Crisis

The Argentine football industry has inherent structural and organisational weaknesses, and it will prove difficult to make radical changes to this infrastructure. As long as football is perceived as being corrupt, violent (there has also been a recent spate of threats and attempts to kidnap footballers or their families), poorly managed and played in unwelcoming stadiums, it will not fulfil its potential, either as a social function or commercially. The game finds itself at an important juncture. Possible solutions that have been considered have included the relocation of clubs (to inland provinces), state involvement in football, and changing football's legal and organisational infrastructures. Some of these suggestions have been extremely controversial.

Relocation of Clubs and Taking Football to the 'Interior'

Some blame the structural problems of Argentine football on the unequal distribution of football clubs in the top division, concentrated in the metropolis of Buenos Aires. There are historical reasons for this.[9] There has been a call to reduce the concentration of professional football clubs in Buenos Aires. Attempts have been made to accommodate top football clubs in two of the stadiums built outside Buenos Aires for the 1978 World Cup. Indeed, Argentinos Juniors (a relatively small *club chico* with between 8,000 and 10,000 *socios*) did briefly move to one of these grounds, Mendoza, in 1994, but the experiment lasted only six months. Significantly, the media company Torneos y Competencias was involved with the club at the time. The idea of basing a professional football club in another city, Mar del Plata, has long been debated (Macri once tried to move Deportivo Español there), but as yet no club has been persuaded to relocate, despite the incentives of the new stadium and a promising (relatively affluent) potential fan-base hungry to witness professional football live. It is not a coincidence that Mar del Plata has hosted the 'friendly' tournament, the Torneo de Verano, since the 1960s.

Many *dirigentes* and journalists agree that Argentine football needs to open up new markets, and one of the most successful ways of doing this would be to have more clubs from the provinces outside Buenos Aires participating in the top division of the Argentine league. Torneos y Competencias went as far as claiming that the key to increased television revenues from the sale of broadcasting rights would be for each province to be represented by a club in the First Division (Gil 2002). This would create new (locally based) rivalries, increase interest in professional football among a wider market, and distribute teams across the country more equally and in a 'more rational' way. The suggestion that every major city should have a professional football club in the First Division predictably met with opposition from smaller clubs in Division One at the time of the proposal, such as Ferro, Platense and Argentinos Juniors, whose status would be threatened by any attempts to alter the structure of professional football in this way. A compromise was reached, involving the introduction of changes to the organisation of football competitions which would increase the possibility of clubs from outside Buenos Aires progressing to the top division.

According to some, however, these theories — which are based on the assumption of increased interest in Argentine football if football were opened to new markets — ignore the historical significance of football in Argentina, and lack an understanding of the role of football in communities and in the construction of identities.

Ground-sharing and Merging of Clubs in Buenos Aires

A few proposals for ground-sharing and merger have to date led to nothing. The president of Boca Juniors, Mauricio Macri, suggested sharing a ground with the club's arch-rivals, River Plate, in June 2000. Boca wished to increase its current capacity significantly, but was unable to do so because of the ground's location in a densely populated area of Buenos Aires. River turned down the proposal. In Santa Fé, Unión and Colón explored the possibilities of ground-sharing in the 1990s.

The two clubs in La Plata also agreed — in theory — to ground-share. Estudiantes' stadium was old and in desperate need of modernisation. Work began on a new stadium, but stopped around Christmas 1999 and the stadium subsequently took years to build. The polemic continued, however. The future of the multifunctional Estadio Ciudad de La Plata (or the Estadio Unico, as it is commonly known) remains in doubt.[10] Indeed, Estudiantes continued to refuse to host home matches in the new stadium, despite being offered almost twice as many tickets for their fans (*La Nación*, 8 August 2003).

State Involvement in Football

Unsurprisingly, given the relationship between football and politics in Argentina, it has not been unusual for the state to intervene in football over the last century (Duke & Crolley, 1996a).[11] Recently, the state has again become involved in football's affairs in various ways. State money supports the football business, on the pretext that football serves an important social function (Sebreli 1998, p. 212). The state also continues to ignore the AFA's immense debt, a significant proportion of which is owed to the government in unpaid taxes. In January 2002, while the country's economy was at a standstill and riots were still taking place on the streets of Buenos Aires, the then President of Argentina, Eduardo Duhalde, and his Minister for Sport and Tourism, Daniel Scioli, were holding talks with the President of the AFA, Julio Grondona, over the future of football. It is highly significant that in times of crisis, the AFA turns to the government for support. Despite all the problems football clubs have endured in recent years, the value of football as a social, cultural and political tool remains considerable. Hence, amid the riots of *la crisis*, the interim Secretary of the Interior, Miguel Angel Toma, moved heaven and earth to get football started again. Several Argentine journalists have commented upon the role of football as a social drug during desperate political upheavals. There is nothing better than football to distract people and occupy time in a society thrown into confusion. So it is highly likely that the government wanted football matches to take place precisely so that the population might put to one side — for a while, at least — other (graver) preoccupations. However, only the championship-deciding matches

(Vélez-Racing and River-Rosario Central) took place. The rest of the league programme was postponed for around five weeks.

Whatever the reasons for overt political involvement in football on this occasion, it is significant that the AFA sought help and was not turned away. On the contrary, the AFA suggested a number of proposals to the government through which it could help football. In addition, Mauricio Macri and José María Aguilar, the presidents of Boca Juniors and River Plate respectively, proposed a state audit of football clubs so that the state would keep an eye on the financial running of sports institutions.[12] As an early result of crisis talks, the government agreed to look into issues of Value-Added Tax payments, to make a contribution (of around 30 per cent) towards costs of crowd safety and to meet again to discuss the future organisation and management of football clubs. Plans to *sanear* (reorganise and ratio-nalise) Argentine football got underway. New financial regulatory standards were discussed by the AFA. According to the framework for professional standards, 'clubs [would] be expected to adhere to a set of minimum control regulations, infrastructure requirements and homo-geneous legal structures' (*Soccer Investor Report*, 2002, p. 32). The AFA forced clubs to acknowledge the fact that the income generated by the game was insufficient to provide for day-to-day operating costs. However, in view of the high level of debt of the clubs, the AFA recognised that in order to implement their plan (the *Plan de Saneamiento*) clubs needed some financial support. The AFA therefore agreed to cancel 35 per cent of clubs' existing liabilities.[13] State involvement in football has, however, gone much further than this, as will become evident via the Racing case study below.

Ownership and Control of Football

Mauricio Macri blames the structures of football clubs for their current difficulties: 'The not-for-profit structure, with *dirigentes* who lack responsibility, has ruined Argentine football. I am putting forward a clear, concrete proposal: either the *dirigentes* take responsibility for their *patrimonio*, like me, or they hand it over into private hands. Undoubtedly, *gerenciamiento* [management] is a valid alternative.' (quoted in www.canal-trans.com, 11 September 2003). However, since football clubs in Argentina remain non-profit-making private-member organisations (*asociaciones civiles sin fines de lucro*), their legal structures do not allow them to be *sociedades anónimas* (limited companies) — as is the case, for example, in Spain. In order for football clubs to modernise their managerial and administrative structures and begin to develop their commercial activities successfully, they would need to alter their legal structures. In 1993, clubs voted overwhelmingly (33 votes to one) against attempts to change from private member associations to private limited companies. Not surprisingly, given the personal vested interests involved, most *socios, dirigentes* and *presidentes* were against this reform. However, with the success of Racing Club (champions in 2001) — the only club wholly managed by a private company — pressures for radical change to take place again began to mount. Some advocated the running of football more firmly along business lines.

Efforts to modernise standards of management, to run clubs more efficiently and along business lines, and to eradicate violence (and in the process try to depoliticise football boardrooms) cannot be successful unless there are fundamental changes in the way football's key players operate. This is perhaps the most radical development, and it is one which has led to some polemical debate in Argentina. According to some, Argentina is being encouraged to develop a football culture that is singularly un-Argentine (and perhaps more European) in nature. Others argue that the change is one which, if managed carefully, does not *necessarily* involve the loss of identity or massively changing the social status of clubs within their communities.

Proponents of changing the legal structures of Argentine football clubs claim to recognise the economic problems of football, its poor management by part-time *dirigentes*, its lack of transparency in the running of the game, and internal wrangling — sometimes of a violent nature — between political factions. They look to other countries as a model for the Argentine game, and favour the outsourcing into private hands of the running of the club's activities. As football's commercial potential is recognised, clubs need to be able to cope with increased business activity and diversified revenue streams, and some believe that this can be done most effectively in a transparent way, with new structures.

At present, although complete privatisation of a football club is not legal, there are several ways around this that have been explored by football clubs. *Gerenciamiento* involves the club handing over the running of part (or occasionally all) of the club to professional businesspeople from a private company. This is a relatively new phenomenon but, during times of extreme financial difficulties after 2001, more clubs considered their options. ISL (International Sport Leisure) bought the right to manage the merchandising sector of San Lorenzo as far back as 2000 as well as Boca's marketing rights, before ISL itself went bankrupt (Gil 2000). Exxel Group (a lesser-known part of the Murdoch media empire) attempted to manage Quilmes Athletic Club (a *club chico*) in 2000–01. Exxel ran everything, from advertising and the commercial side of the club to the transfer of players.[14] Exxel was, however, strongly criticised for creating distance between the club and its fans. Exxel also discussed the management takeover of Ferrocarril Oeste. This, however, presented problems as the group had already moved into Quilmes.[15] As it was, Exxel itself got into financial difficulties, and the deal with Quilmes lasted less than a year.

The management of Club Atlético Platense (of Nacional B) was taken over early in 2002 by Sports International SA, a company with experience of marketing the Argentine national women's hockey team, Las Leonas, and Las Palmas Rugby team. At the time, fans voiced their views that the club was 'selling its soul'. The deal was to include the payment of debts by Sports International as well as a detailed annual investment plan, also funded by the company. The company would receive all revenues from ticketing, merchandising, broadcasting, advertising and sponsorship. Any profits would be divided between the club and the company (not equally, but weighted in favour of the private company). Huracán also developed a strategic commercial alliance with MWCC, and the sports marketing company Fox Sports took over the marketing, brand development, and sponsorship of the club. It was generally seen as a successful venture. The original deal was for one year (2000–01) with an investment of $350,000 by the US media group. It was renewed for the following season (2001–02) with an increased investment amounting to $120,000. Huracán increased its base of *socios* from 2,300 to 6,700 in 14 months.

Gerenciamiento has been heavily criticised by some: '[It] is a criminal act: it destroys the structure of clubs, encourages tax evasion and is a fertile ground for money-laundering.' (*Prensa Obrera*, 6 December

2000) Those cynical of these new developments in football often claim that the prime reason for the creation of *gerenciamiento* relationships is tax evasion.[16] In fact, the government investigated some of the *gerenciamiento* deals for evidence of fraudulent activity.[17]

Importantly, many also recognise the potentially devastating effects that such changes might have on the structures and social role of football in Argentina. Football has historically had strong roots in its community. The associationist tradition has a long history in Argentina and was an initiative of all social groups: English immigrants, the church, neighbourhood groups, social and sporting clubs and political groups, as well as football clubs. The association fulfilled a role that the state did not: it defended the individual, helped personal development, provided services and institutionalised social networks within a community, helping the individual to integrate into that community. Football shared that 'associationist' mentality (Frydenburg 2001). Recent developments and changes in the ways in which football is experienced lead to a conflict of styles and traditions. Levels of violence have increased and there is an increased state presence. There has been a shift in the experience of football from *espectáculo* to media circus, increasingly distant from the public. A desire to exploit football's commercial potential is taking over from the traditional associationist model. It is not surprising, therefore, that there is a conflict between styles and traditions, or that there is a debate over the future of football.

According to research by Frydenburg (2001), the *asociacionismo* of Argentine football is tainted with *politiquería* (political manoeuvring). He claims that there exist three groups of *dirigente*. A minority group is in favour of football clubs maintaining the 'associationist' tradition that they have had since they were established. A second minority group believes that football clubs should be run as *sociedades anónimas*, thus requiring legal changes to the status of football clubs. A majority adopt the pragmatic approach that there is a need to reorganise and rationalise (*sanear*) football's finances, without removing the foundations which enabled them to be appointed as *dirigentes*. For example, Raúl Gamez, former *presidente* of Vélez Sarsfield, recognises the need for the AFA to change its Article 6 and allow *dirigentes* to be paid for their efforts, but he advocates a continuation of the electoral system whereby fans vote for the management team. He does not agree that clubs should be managed by private companies (cited at www.efde-portes.com, April 2001). So many football clubs still see themselves — and function — as social institutions rather than as businesses, and most have vested interests in maintaining the *status quo*. They still perform a role that is largely ignored by many: they allow (poor) children to play football, and provide grants and scholarships for some to attend academies. They play a part in the social fabric of a community.

As one commentator wrote: 'The relationship between a football club and a private company is simple. The company hands over its money and the club hands over everything: its history, the ground, its *socios*, its name, its colours, decision-making powers, people, feelings and emotions. Activities which do not make money will be lost even if they provide a valuable service to the community.' (Zamora 2003) These commentators prefer to emphasise football's moral and social function in Argentine society. They point to the very culture-specific nature of Argentine football which, they argue, prevents it from following comfortably in the footsteps of other countries. In Argentina, the social function of football clubs is deep-rooted and should not be weakened — hence the tension involved in the modernisation of Argentine football.

Racing Club: State Intervention and *Gerenciamiento* in Action?

Gerenciamiento, then, can take many forms, and the rights to different sectors of the club might be 'sold' into (or rather 'managed by') private hands. The biggest success story to date, however, has been that of Racing Club. Racing Club was declared bankrupt on 14 July 1998. Depending on the sources of information, debts were estimated at anything between $32 million and $65 million, owed to hundreds of creditors. On 18 February 2000, the Court of Appeal (Cámara de Apelaciones) in La Plata questioned the process of bankruptcy that the judge, Enrique Gorostegui, was investigating. Under existing laws, Racing could no longer function as a football club and would have to close. But the state did not allow this to happen.

Racing Club was saved by government intervention in football. A new law — the Ley de Fideicomiso, now known as the Sager Law —

was passed through both Houses of Congress in less than 24 hours on 7 July 2000 specifically for the club. This law allowed bankrupt clubs to stay open and remain involved in bankruptcy proceedings if they had enough equity to pay back their debts. Clubs such as Racing would be run by a panel of trustees comprising three people appointed by the courts, and the trusteeship would be responsible for moving the club out of the red and for looking after the interests of creditors.

It is surely relevant that Racing has extensive support (average attendances were around 25,000 for the season 1999–2000), with some influential figures in the media and politics such as (famously) the Vice-President and the Governor of Buenos Aires at the time among its fans (*Olé*, 1 July 2000). To save Racing (or *La Academia*, as the club is known) would undoubtedly be a vote-winner. Furthermore, direct action by fans prevented the auction of club assets (they physically occupied the court, and the police did nothing to intervene). It was because of this law that Racing Club could continue to exist as a professional football club and participate in competitions run by the AFA.

A new structure was established involving its *fideicomiso* (trusteeship) and management by a new body, Blanquiceleste SA. This structure was approved on 29 December 2000. Blanquiceleste was to run all aspects of the club's professional and amateur football, to exploit the club's media and image rights, to undertake the commercialisation of the club, and to assume responsibility for stadium management and maintenance, initially for a period of 10 years.[18] The club continued to compete and indeed won the *apertura* championship in 2001.

It has been suggested that *gerenciamiento* can only be successful in a large club like Racing, and that it cannot work in a smaller club (*club chico*). Others, including Fernando Marín, the president of Blanquiceleste, disagree and believe that any well-organised club can be *gerenciado* (*Clarín*, 7 January 2002).

Conclusion

It was not just the national economic crisis that was responsible for the financial and social problems that Argentine football was suffering at the beginning of the twenty-first century. Indeed, as noted earlier, football did not suffer as much as some other sectors in Argentina. Rather, its problems are complex — including a combination of poor management, corruption, violence and a poor image resulting from the particular structural organisation that evolved after the establishment of football in Argentina. So is it likely that the current relationships between the four key players (football authorities, clubs, politics and fans) will be severed? We would argue that it is not. These alliances have already endured the critical political upheavals of twentieth-century Argentina, and transitions between dictatorships and democracy seem merely to deepen the links. Football's place in Argentine history has performed both 'a "top-down" mechanism of political manipulation by cultural, political, and socio-economic elites in the creation of discourses of statehood' and 'a "bottom-up" medium of social transformation' (Bar-On 1997). The result of this is an extremely strong integration of social, political and football structures which will not be broken.

The state has always supported football. While it was during the Peronist period from 1946 to 1955 that state intervention in football reached its peak, it is during periods of democracy that football becomes a vote-winner. The electoral system, and the consequent organisation of fan groups (the *barras bravas*), ensures the perpetuation of the political interest and importance of football. As capitalist values transfer themselves increasingly to the football arena, the input of businesspeople — and in particular the media — into football grows in significance. Hence it is essential that the 'key players' in the football world have links with diverse industries.

It is ironic that, while many clubs have discussed at least some element of *gerenciamiento*, and effectively closer links with the private sector, the state has continued to consider greater involvement and intervention in football. This inevitably reflects the dichotomy between the roles that football is perceived to perform in Argentine society. On one hand, football must be seen to assume greater responsibility over its financial affairs, both at club and AFA levels — which is difficult (if not impossible) given the electoral system that operates in clubs and the subsequent links between the key players in the game. On the other hand, the state continues to intervene. It will not allow (at least 'big') football clubs to go under (hence the Sager Law), and has so far demonstrated considerable lenience in dealing with football-related violence and debt. On the surface, in an unstable economic environment, Argentine football faces a continuing financial, and perhaps even social, crisis. Beneath the surface lie deeper historically rooted and culture-specific reasons why this crisis will not easily be resolved.

Acknowledgements

The authors would like to thank the following for their contributions to the research for this paper: Pablo Alabarces, Pablo de Biase, Miguel and Andreas Cruzalegui, Sergio Levinsky, Marcela Mora y Araujo, María Graciela Rodríguez, Eric Weil and the late-lamented archive of *El Gráfico*

.

Notes

1   Macri suggested that there were political reasons for the violence, and that his counterpart at Chacarita, Luis Barrionuevo — who was a candidate running for (political) election against Macri — might want Boca to appear unruly. If Macri was incapable of running a football club, surely he could not be entrusted to take responsibility for anything larger (*La Nación*, 1 September 2003).
2   Twenty members of the River *barras* were arrested in the Monumental on 23 October 2003 (*La Nación*, 24 October 2003).
3   All translations are by the authors.
4   Until recently, attendances at football matches were declining steadily, leading to a decrease in gate receipts of 25 per cent between 1996 and 2001 (*Soccer Investor* 2002) and contributing to football's poor economic situation. During the economic depression, many people simply did not have the levels of disposable income necessary to spend on leisure activities such as football, and there was a knock-on effect in the devaluation of broadcasting rights and decline in the value of sponsorship.
5   As mentioned earlier, Judge Mariano Bergés' investigation into the violence of 31 August 2003 revealed illicit links between the Chacarita Juniors board and the club's *barras bravas*.
6   The prime example of Mauricio Macri, *presidente* of Boca, publicly stating that his long-term career goals lie in the political arena, is not the only example. Indeed, many *dirigentes* double as members of Congress.

7   When San Lorenzo, whose *presidente* was Fernando Miele, almost went into liquidation, some suggested that it was Miele's role as Secretary General of AFA which contributed to the fact that the AFA turned a blind eye to the financial plight of San Lorenzo, reluctant to delve into the affairs of the former *presidente*. AFA *presidente* Julio Grondona himself, along with Macri and Miele, has been the subject of investigation for fraudulent activities: see <http://soccernet.com/global/news/2002/1010/20021010argfifafraud.html>, citing a Reuters report.

8   In July 2003, the AFA held deals with Coca-Cola (US$2 million p.a. until 2010); Mastercard (US$1 million p.a. to 2006); Volkswagen (US$2 million p.a. to 2007, plus $500,000 for every tournament in which the Argentine national team wins): *Soccer Business Online*, 23 July 2003.

9   See Bayer (1990) or Duke & Crolley (1996a) for further details of the spread and development of football in Argentina.

10   It was unclear how the stadium's maintenance would be funded. The idea was that whoever played at home would foot the bill for staffing the ticket office and for stadium security, for example. While the stadium has been used for amateur games and rugby matches, Estudiantes and Gimnasia (especially the latter) remain to be convinced of the benefits of using the facilities of the new stadium, which in their view would be expensive to run (*La Nación*, 30 July 2003). As of mid-2006, both Estudiantes and Gimnasia had had their own grounds closed for safety reasons by the local authority; Estudiantes were playing home matches in Quilmes' stadium in southern Buenos Aires, while Gimnasia were playing, under protest, in the new municipal stadium.

11   State intervention reached a peak during the first Peronist period (1946–55) when sport was a mechanism of national integration via the socialisation of the youth, and sporting success was equated with Peronist success.

12   They also agreed that they would lead clubs by establishing some regulatory criteria regarding the organisational structures and finances of both clubs. They agreed to reduce their costs by capping players' bonuses and wages and by reducing the amount spent on crowd control and safety.

13   A loan was sought, secured against the future revenue from the sale of broadcasting rights, but was unsuccessful.

14   Player transfers were dealt with by a committee of six members, three representatives of Exxel and three of the football club. Exxel held the casting vote in case of a split decision.

15   In many countries, multiple ownership of clubs that might meet in
     competition is not permitted by the football authorities. Mexico is an
     exception.

16   A football club in its capacity as an *Asociación Civil sin Fines de Lucro*
     does not pay taxes, and it should not be 'for profit'. It does not matter
     if one sector of the club is run by a company. The football club is still
     an *asociación civil*, and hence all parts of it continue to be exempt from
     paying tax.

17   For example, that drawn up by Miele, San Lorenzo's *presidente*, came
     under scrutiny (*Página 12*, 26 November 2000).

18   It would do this in exchange for an investment of $15 million per
     annum in the professional squad, $3 million in youth development, $2
     million in stadium redevelopment, plus a gradual cancellation of the
     club's debt. Any monies earned through transfer fees would be divided
     between the company and the club. Racing had nine years in which to
     clear its debts, and needed to clear at least 11 per cent per annum.

11

Brazilian Football:
Technical Success and Economic Failure

Luiz Martins de Melo

Introduction

Since World War II, Brazilian football has been the most technically successful sport of its kind in the world. Despite this
tremendous achievement, in financial terms Brazilian football
has spent beyond its means, suffered from severe under-funding and
experienced substantial losses. This chapter argues that economic
conditions in Brazil (such as inequalities in levels of income and 20
years of low economic growth in the 1980s and 1990s) are such that
football cannot look to its internal market to find extra revenues in
the short term. These characteristics, together with others specific to
the management of Brazilian football, have made Brazilian football
hostage to television broadcasting. However, there are ways in which
this situation might begin to be overcome.

Football is the most popular sporting activity in the world. It is an
increasingly 'globalised' sport. The main characteristics of this
process of globalisation include the transformation of the sport into
a phenomenon of mass consumption, with dynamics that reach
different consumer markets; sport as a dynamic component of the
entertainment industry; and an enormous growth in the value of the
image rights of show business and sporting idols.

In order to exploit the capital investment that football in Brazil
needs (to keep its heroes and idols, and to maintain the interest of
the media), the sport requires professionally run organisations to set
up competitions and tournaments as well as to manage the 'spectacle'. Only in this way will the stars and the capital invested attain
social and economic value.

Faced with this overall process of globalisation — which changed the economic premises on which Brazil's football industry was managed — Brazilian football underwent a traumatic period of transition in the late 1990s and early years of the new century. Even after winning five World Cups, and despite the fact that Brazilian football is widely considered to be technically the best in the world, the sport's institutions did not manage to solve several basic structural issues, and failed to establish a management model that was appropriate to deal with the enormous and constantly renewed talent of its players.

This incompatibility between modern football business management and the continuous emergence of new players who become future idols, particularly in European clubs, has been the main source of the structural weakness of Brazilian football. Due to the severity of the economic, managerial, financial and market conditions that they face, football clubs are forced to sell the players that they train for low prices in order to pay their debts, thus decreasing the attractiveness of club matches and driving the public away from the stadiums. This in turn makes clubs in Brazil hostage to television revenues.

Other factors also contribute significantly to the devaluation of the football 'spectacle': urban violence together with organised, aggressive chanting and other bad behaviour; the poor conditions of football stadiums; and a highly critical sports media. Usually the Brazilian media are correct in their assessments, but the habit of consistently pointing out the flaws without suggesting solutions may result in throwing the baby out with the bath water.

This chapter cannot address all the issues mentioned above. In the first section, the economic characteristics of the major European football-playing countries will be compared with key features of the Brazilian economy, to illustrate the extent to which purchasing power differs between consumers in Western Europe and Brazil. The next section presents a comparative analysis of the potential to generate football revenues in Brazil and in European countries. The final section proposes some conclusions that might provide a possible basis for a reform process in the economics of Brazilian football.

A Comparative Macroeconomic Analysis

There is huge disparity between the wealth of European countries and Brazil's relative poverty. Table 11.1 presents some basic information to illustrate the main features of this disparity.

Table 11.1: Comparative Size of Respective Economies, 2002

Country	Population (millions)	Surface area (in 1,000 km^2)	Gross national income ($ billion)	Gross national income per capita ($)
Germany	82	357	1,939.6	23,560
UK	59	243	1,476.8	24,340
France	59	552	1,380.7	22,730
Italy	58	301	1,123.8	24,530
Spain	41	506	588.0	19,860
Brazil	172	8,547	528.9	3,070

Source: World Bank 2003.

It is evident from the figures in this table that Brazil faces great difficulties in generating income that will support an adequate level of the consumer expenditure required to sustain a high-cost economic activity such as football. Additionally, the costs of organising a national league championship in a country as physically large as Brazil are much higher than in any European country, simply because of the internal transport costs involved.

Table 11.2 shows some macroeconomic ratios extracted from Table 11.1, which portray more clearly the vast differences in income and the challenges involved in achieving a healthy Brazilian football economy.

Table 11.2: Macroeconomic Ratios

Country	Population	Surface area	Gross national income	Gross national income per capita
Germany/Brazil	0.48	0.04	3.67	7.67
UK/Brazil	0.34	0.03	2.79	7.93
France/Brazil	0.34	0.06	2.61	7.40
Italy/Brazil	0.34	0.04	2.12	7.99
Spain/Brazil	0.23	0.06	1.11	6.47

Source: Derived from Table 1.

Table 11.2 shows an inverse relationship between population, surface area, and the income indicators. Brazil has more than two or three times the population and over 20 times the surface area of the European countries in the sample. Yet, when analysing economic indicators, the economic frailty of Brazil becomes evident. In terms of gross national income, it barely approaches Spain. In terms of per capita income, the best indicator of a population's purchasing power, the ratio is almost seven times in favour of the European countries that host the 'Big Five' leagues.

The economic challenges faced by Brazil increased during the 1980s and 1990s. The 1980s were characterised by high inflation, generating a stagnation of the Brazilian economy. The 1990s, despite the reduction in inflation that followed the introduction of the Plano Real in July 1994, did not manage to encourage any significant economic growth. Successive crises in the balance of trade that followed this stabilisation of prices led to a more pronounced reduction of gross income per capita in dollar terms: the Brazilian currency, the *real*, was substantially devalued following the government's decision to float it in 1999. This made it even more difficult for football clubs to generate the internal funds necessary to keep key Brazilian players in the country, and it became one of the main reasons for the subsequent mass exodus of promising young footballers to foreign countries, especially to Europe.

The stabilisation of the currency encouraged foreign investment in football, as it did in other sectors of the economy. Some of the main international investors in the sports industry arrived in Brazil in the late 1990s, after Brazil had won its fourth World Cup in 1994 and prices began to stabilise under the Plano Real.[1] There were expectations that such investors would trigger an effective process of change that would modernise and professionalise football, but such expectations soon evaporated. Instead, they aligned themselves with the former team directors, who represented the old amateur order, and almost completely lost the means to manage their investments strategically. They did not opt for the battlefield. They waived their international strategic advantage by assuming that their financial power would be enough to discipline members of the former order, under-estimating the power of local directors and their political allies. The result of this defeat was a significant decay in the financial situation of Brazilian clubs, which became even more dependent on television revenues.

Comparative Analysis of Football Economies

Overall Attendances and Income

A comparative analysis of data concerning Brazilian and European football presents us with a scenario that is even more unbalanced than the macroeconomic one. Table 11.3 indicates revenue levels from major European leagues and from the Brazilian football championship. The numbers in this table practically speak for themselves. What immediately attracts attention is the huge disparity in revenues between European leagues and the Brazilian championship, as well as in the average revenues earned by each team. Furthermore, Brazilian football has a larger number of participants in the national championship, reflecting regional influences in a country of continental dimensions, as already noted earlier.

Table 11.3: Total Revenues in the Top Division of European Leagues and the Brazilian National Championship, 2000–01

Country	Total revenues* (US$ million)	Number of teams	Average revenue of team (US$ million)
Italy	672.0	18	37.3
Spain	608.0	20	30.4
Germany	576.0	18	32.0
England	1,552.0	18	86.2
France	368.0	18	20.4
Brazil	150.0	24	6.3

Source: Deloitte & Touche (2002) and TopSports (2003).

* Excluding transactions involving player transfers.

Table 11.4: Average Attendances, Average Ticket Prices and Ticket Income per Game in 2002

Country	Average attendance at national leagues	Average ticket price (US$)	Average ticket revenues per game (US$)
England	31,000	30.9	957,900
Italy	30,000	27.7	831,000
Spain	28,000	20.8	582,400
Brazil	10,000	3.0	30,000

Source: Deloitte & Touche (2002) and TopSports (2003).

Table 11.4 seeks to present a more detailed vision of this revenue gap between Brazil and Europe. The figures on average attendance and average ticket revenues for each game highlight the vast differences in the revenue-generating power of different stadiums. If the main attraction of a football match (or show) is the star athlete, the place where such stars perform will become the focus for the event. When this does not occur, despite strong television coverage, revenues plummet and the clubs — as well as the organisers of the show — become weak.

Table 11.4 shows that, in order for a Brazilian team to earn an amount equivalent to that earned by European teams, the Brazilian team would have to play 32 matches for every game played in England, almost 28 times for every one in Italy, and around 19 times for every one in Spain.

Table 11.5: Key Ratios Comparing Other Countries with Brazil, 2002

Country	Average attendance at national leagues	Total revenues	Average ticket price (US$)
Italy/Brazil	3.0	4.5	9.2
Spain/Brazil	2.8	4.1	6.9
Germany/Brazil	n/a	3.8	n/a
England/Brazil	3.1	10.3	10.3
France/Brazil	n/a	2.5	n/a

Source: Calculated from Figures in Table 4.

Table 11.5 presents ratios for average attendances, total revenues and average ticket prices. There is a clear imbalance between average ticket prices, total revenues and the macroeconomic indicators of per capita income shown in Table 11.2. While the latter shows a per capita income ratio between Western European countries and Brazil that goes no higher than 8:1, for ticket prices the ratio reaches 10:1, in the case of England, and 9:1 in the case of Italy, suggesting that there is a potential margin for raising the average ticket price in Brazil. The question then becomes whether or not conditions are favourable. Would upper-income people still be attracted to the stadium despite the decaying infrastructure and the emergence of urban and fan violence, as well as excessive exposure of football on television?

Key Revenue Streams

The economic frailty that characterises Brazilian clubs and tournaments leads to an even greater imbalance between the wealth of European clubs and the poverty of those in Brazil. Brazil's richer clubs are poorer than the vast majority of second division clubs in the leading European footballing countries. Figure 11.1 illustrates this. In 2002, the world's richest clubs were 20 times richer than Brazilian ones, a ratio far exceeding the usual macroeconomic inequality indices. This means that inequality in the football industry is much higher than inequalities between countries on a macroeconomic level.

Table 11.6 shows the revenue breakdown for football clubs in 2002–03, by source. It makes it clear that the revenue composition of Brazilian clubs is heavily based upon the sale of television rights. Revenues from the commercial exploitation of sport facilities, sponsorship and from marketing club brands are the lowest among all countries, which illustrates how little control Brazilian clubs have over their own business. It also shows two additional and important factors. First, very few clubs own their stadiums and, when they do, they are poorly maintained. The only exception is the Atlético Paranaense stadium, Arena da Baixada, in Curitíba. The second factor, already mentioned, is the increasing violence inside and outside stadiums, a strong inhibitor of attendance. The low percentage of marketing revenues is related to the income gap between Brazil and Europe, together with the relative lack of effective protection for brands and intellectual property, which leads to a high level of piracy in the marketing of sports goods. A sports product carrying the club's legal trademark can cost up to ten times that of the equivalent unlicensed product. Given the population's average income, most fans have no choice.

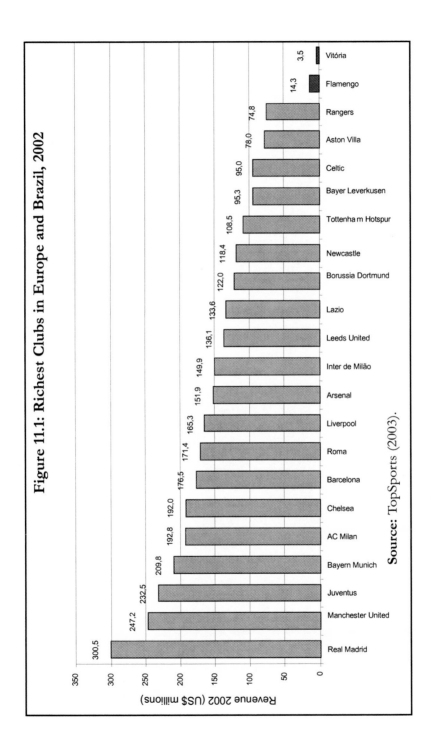

Figure 11.1: Richest Clubs in Europe and Brazil, 2002

Source: TopSports (2003).

Table 11.6: Revenue Breakdown, Europe and Brazil in 2002–03

Country	Revenues from stadium (%)	Broadcasting rights (%)	Sponsorship and merchandising (%)
England	28	42	30
Italy	16	53	31
Spain	36	18	37
Germany	17	40	43
France	15	52	33
Brazil	10	65	25

Source: Deloitte & Touche (2002) and TopSports (2003).

In order to have an idea of the amount of money that circulates in the European football industry, the sale of television broadcasting rights for the five major championships alone totalled US$2.1 billion in 2002 (Deloitte & Touche 2002). By 2005, the total income of the clubs in the five major leagues in Western Europe amounted to US$7.8 billion, of which broadcasting contracts accounted for $3.4 billion and commercial income, including sponsorship, US$2.7 billion (Deloitte 2006).[2] In Brazil, due to economic stagnation, sports marketing decreased from 4.5 per cent of the total advertising market in 1998 to 2.5 per cent in 2002 (TopSports 2002). Football then received close to US$50 million from a total of US$75 million.

Club Expenditures and Player Salaries

Table 11.7 shows salary distribution in Brazilian football. The data indicate a vast disparity between the salaries paid in Europe and in Brazil. This is why Brazilian clubs usually do not succeed in keeping their players. When the clubs try to pay salaries closer to European levels — as they did after Brazil won the 1994 World Cup — they could do so only while the exchange rate remained at parity with the

US dollar. That eventually led the clubs into an even worse economic situation than the fragile one that they were already experiencing. The operation of the Plano Real also led the entire country through a series of balance of payments crises which contributed even further to the erosion of the population's income.

Once the devaluation of the *real* occurred in early 1999, the situation became untenable and the exodus of players abroad increased. Between 1999 and 2003, more than 3,500 Brazilian players were transferred abroad, impoverishing the 'spectacle' of national football even more without actually solving the financial problems of the clubs. On the contrary, the problem became exacerbated.[3]

Table 11.7: Salary Distribution in Brazilian Football, 2002

Ratio between the actual salary and the legal minimum salary	Number of players	Percentage of players
< 1.0	8,638	52.9
1.0–1.9	4,987	30.5
2.0–4.9	1,289	7.9
5.0–9.9	436	2.7
10.0–19.9	293	1.8
> 20.0	701	4.3
Total	**16,344**	**100.0**

Note: The minimum monthly salary at the time was R$240, equivalent to US$80.
Source: Data taken from the Brazilian Football Confederation.

The Management of Clubs

In order to be able to assess the lack of professional management in Brazilian football, a very simple example may be taken directly from the numbers presented earlier in this chapter. Table 11.8 shows a simulation of the Brazilian clubs' unexplored potential revenues, comparing Flamengo — the most popular team in Brazil — with Manchester United, the most popular in England.

The percentage of Brazil's total population which supports Flamengo is 15.5 per cent, and Manchester United fans constitute 4.2 per cent of the English population. If we adopt as a parameter for potential revenues the per capita income of each country, Flamengo would have a level of attainable revenue generation one and a half times greater than Manchester United. However, the English club earns more than 15 times the Brazilian club's income.[4]

Table 11.8: Brazil: The Unexplored Potential of Football Revenues

	Flamengo	Manchester United
Fans in domestic market (millions)	25.0	2.5
Fans (percentage of population)	15.5%	4.2%
Potential for revenue - generation	US$81 billion	US$54 billion

Source: TopSports (2003), newspapers and interviews.

The Modernisation of Brazilian Football

In the 1990s, an effort was made to solve Brazilian football's structural deficiencies by altering the law. From the early 1990s, several sports-related laws were passed in Congress, intending to modernise sport — particularly football. These included the Zico Law (Law 8672, dated 1993), the Pelé Law (Law 9615, dated 1998) and the

Maguito Vilella Law (Law 9981, dated 2000), which modified the Pelé Law — for the worse. More recently, the new Brazilian administration that took office in 2003 approved Provisional Measure no. 79 (the Football Law) and the *Football Fans Act*, intending to force the clubs and their managers to abandon the old practices that have tainted national football during the last decades. In general, the new law made it mandatory for clubs to transform their football departments into legally constituted companies, publishing audited accounts. The law also provided for the end of immunity for ineffective managers, making them liable both in civil and criminal courts for acts undertaken during their term of office. Clubs that did not abide by the law would not receive government support, and their managers would be held liable through their own personal assets in case of maladministration or misuse of resources. However, unless changes take place within the management of football clubs, such new legal requirements will make clubs even more dependent on television revenues.

The modernisation of Brazilian sports laws is essential for the future implementation of professionalism. However, several other conditions still need to be fulfilled, making the approval of the new laws merely one step in the right direction, rather than the only tool required for the redemption of Brazilian football. In short, several improvements need to be made if Brazilian football is to attain a more advanced level of economic and managerial efficiency.

In the first place, the clubs need an increased guarantee of their rights over the income resulting from player transfers. In addition, flexible laws on investor participation in the management of football clubs should be introduced, to encourage new capital investment in football, in order to facilitate the modernisation of stadiums and new models of management. Furthermore, there should be greater control over the transfer of young players abroad. The highest cost paid by Brazil for its lack of organisation in football is not being able to keep its best players within the country. Brazil has the best players in the world, but instead of maximising revenues the country sells its players too early and too cheaply, therefore destroying all possibility of increasing revenues through high-quality sporting events. The economic disparity between Europe and Brazil will continue to ensure that Brazil's best players are exported for many years. On the other hand, if the professional framework of Brazilian football improves, it may become possible to close better deals than at present.

Conclusion

The current situation of Brazilian football clearly highlights the need to transform its management and organisation into more professional, effective and efficient activities. Modern sporting events require stadiums and sports arenas capable of receiving the public with safety and comfort. This includes appropriate kick-off times, organised arrangements for the sale of tickets, adequate parking facilities and good transportation systems, and a well-planned calendar of fixtures. Modern sports stadiums are practically non-existent in the country, making it necessary to increase investment in this area, in order to build new multi-use stadiums and arenas and redevelop existing ones. This would certainly improve Brazil's football revenues.

During the 1930s, the solution for the crisis that then existed in Brazilian football was to grant players professional status. At the dawn of the twenty-first century, the tendency seems to focus on the professionalisation of managers and the adoption of a business management model that preserves the history of clubs but at the same time facilitates their modernisation. Nevertheless, in order to succeed, the change must be accompanied by a reorganisation of the current power structure, granting the big clubs more autonomy to organise tournaments and exploit the huge popularity achieved throughout their history, and at the same time decreasing their dependence on television income for survival.

The globalisation of sport resulting from the opening of the European market to international players, together with the economic disparity between Brazil and Europe — the world's major football market — makes it difficult to reproduce the same model that transformed football into a money-making machine in Western Europe. The salaries paid to major international players make it practically impossible for them to live in a country with an economy such as that of Brazil, since there are no revenues that could support a club at the same level of expenditure as those in Europe.

This analysis suggests, however, that the irreversible introduction of more modern management strategies might provide the solution for the problems of Brazilian football. The transition will be painful for many, and will meet with significant resistance from the groups now in power. A partnership between football and the government, or even state intervention, would be essential to speed up the transition process.

Brazil should follow the same model that was applied in England when the *Football Spectators Act* was passed in 1989. This act is a spectator's code of rights, providing for the modernisation of English clubs' stadiums, leading to the creation of the Premier League and the reformulation of the relationship between football and the English media.

The *Football Spectators Act* in England forced partnerships between clubs, federations and local authorities in order to offer fans high-quality facilities in the stadiums, with excellent standards of safety, hygiene, transportation, catering, and so on. Then a movement emerged in favour of redeveloping English stadiums with government support, through special credit lines to the clubs. This enabled the modernisation of most large stadiums in England, turning them into income-generators as their utilisation rate increased.

This should also be the direction followed in Brazil: the building of new stadiums and the redevelopment of existing ones, if possible, with a subsequent increase in ticket sales and revenues and a decrease in a dependence on television revenues. Without this change, Brazil will continue to be a football country, but without a football 'spectacle'.

Notes

1   Hicks Muse invested in Corinthians, the second most popular team in Brazil. ISL invested in Flamengo, Brazil's most popular club. The Bank of America invested in Vasco da Gama. These are the most notorious examples. All investors left the market a few years later, suffering severe losses, and did not leave behind any apparent signs of modernisation in Brazilian football.

2   Since then, the English Premier League and the French Ligue have both negotiated significantly higher broadcasting deals. In Europe, clubs and leagues are actively exploring the value that they can derive from new technologies.

3   See the website of the Confederação Brasileira de Futebol, <www.cbf.com.br>.

4   It has been particularly difficult to assess the exact income of Brazilian clubs due to the lack of reliable financial statements and accounting. In order to estimate Flamengo's revenues in 2003, several informal sources were used, and these arrived at a consensual amount of US$14 million.

12

Brazilian Football:
The Missed Opportunity of 1997–2000

Elena Landau

As the Brazilian captain, Cafu, hoisted the 2002 World Cup to the delight of supporters in the Yokohama Stadium and the delirium of 180 million people back home, many investors around the world must have been wondering what on earth was going on. The millions of dollars they had ploughed into Brazilian football had simply vanished without trace, with no return, no apparent improvement in infrastructure and no explanation. There were the usual mutterings about Third World corruption and incompetence and yet, here before their very eyes, was concrete evidence that the world's supreme football power was in triumphantly good health.[1] So what had really happened?

Foreign Investment in Brazilian Football

The immediate pre-millennium years (1997–99) saw a worldwide boom in investment in entertainment. Entertainment in Brazil means sport, and sport means football. Therefore football in Brazil, in the eyes of a significant portion of the international financial community, means money — and easy money at that. If only that were true!

Investors worldwide earmarked several hundred million dollars for investment in Brazilian football between 1997 and 1999 via a mixed bag of projects (purchase of equity, brand licensing, club management), aimed not only at providing a quick and substantial return, but also (so it was believed) at transforming the basic infrastructure of football (see Table 12.1). There were high hopes in South America that an influx of First World business and financial management would bring the Brazilian game up to its rightful place nationally as well as internationally.

Football in Brazil, despite being the unofficial religion of millions, was (and, generally speaking, still is) a poorly managed affair. Recognised principles of corporate governance were either ignored or simply not understood, and political and private interests predominated, with the result that a considerable proportion of the revenues was diverted to such ends, facilitated by non-professional management and a staggering lack of transparency in accounting procedures (no proper accounting or records open for public inspection).

What is perhaps even more surprising is the fact that, given the circumstances (which were really no secret), the investors basically chose to hand over the money to the clubs without question. The evaluations made by investors were too optimistic, generating figures based on a discounted cash flow set at unrealistic levels. They failed to consider a very basic fact: Brazil is a First World football nation with an emerging economy. They were dealing with a very different economic and business reality. In fact, one fundamental truth stood out clearly for all to see: Brazilian football was in desperate need of an administrative overhaul.

The investors, it seemed, were either unaware of this or thought they could make money anyway. Due diligence procedures were inadequately undertaken. There was such a rush to capture the big names like Flamengo (the most heavily supported team in Rio de Janeiro and the country as a whole) and Corinthians (the São Paulo club with the biggest fan-base) that nobody thought to examine the true financial situation of the clubs and no effective mechanisms of accountability were established.[2] There were no performance criteria to speak of, and — astonishingly — there were no controls on the disbursements effected by the clubs receiving the money, with the inevitable result that it vanished without trace. ISL put US$80 million into Flamengo, which was spent in one year, with no financial records to show how.[3] The Bank of America (Nations Bank) put US$100 million into Vasco da Gama and bought the brand for 99 years. A few months later, they gave it up, leaving behind both the brand and the money (totally unaccounted for).

Table 12.1: Foreign Investment in Brazilian Football, 1997–99

Date of agreement	Club	Partners	Type of contract	Term	Initial investment	Total intended investment	Sale of players	Investment in stadium	Division of profits
Nov 1997	Bahia	Banco Opportunity	Ownership	Indefinite	US$12m	Indefinite	Divided equally		67% Opportunity; 33% Bahia
March 1998	Vasco da Gama	Nations Bank (Bank of America)	Exploitation of brand under licence	99 years	US$30m	US$150m plus annual costs of football	60% Nations Bank; 40% Vasco	US$30m to expand capacity to 55,000	60% Nations Bank; 40% Vasco
April 1999	Corinthians	Hicks Muse	Exploitation of brand under licence	10 years	US$55m	US$50m per year	85% Hicks Muse; 15% Corinthians	US$100m for 60,000 capacity stadium	85% Hicks Muse; 15% Corinthians
Nov 1999	Flamengo	ISL	Exploitation of brand under licence	15 years	US$80m	US$50m per year	75% ISL; 25% Flamengo	US$100m	55% ISL; 45% Flamengo

Source: Derived from *Lance*, and published in Aidar & Leoncini (2000), p. 91.

We can only speculate on why the investors failed to take the necessary measures. There was certainly euphoria in the air. The market, it seemed, had hit upon a modern El Dorado, and in the rush for gold the sensible good practices developed in times of greater austerity were disregarded. Naturally, there were also darker rumours of corruption. In fact, both Chambers of Congress conducted inquiries into professional football in 2001–02. Some of the leading figures in the sport became the subject of scrutiny, and the results were handed out to the public prosecutor to proceed with investigations.[4]

Matters were not helped by an extraordinary change in the law pushed through Congress just as investment was reaching its peak. The 'old guard' dominating the game (which included members of Congress) saw, it seems, an opportunity to kill the goose and keep the golden egg. The new law imposed severe restrictions on club ownership. Not only could investors not own two clubs in the same division, they could not now even own a single share in a second club in the same division. The second restriction was that professional executives could not be appointed to the board. Investors were therefore obliged to appoint someone already within the club structure — so that, for example, all merchandising and television deals were made by those known to the powers that be, and beyond the reach of external 'interference'. Only after a parliamentary inquiry was set up to find out what went wrong was it possible to implement wide-ranging reforms which then began to bear fruit. Whatever the causes, the results are clear. The money invested was 'wasted' in less than two years, meaning that there was no investment in infrastructure (stadiums and training facilities), and no changes were made to the structure of the television monopoly in which even the major clubs found themselves in a very weak bargaining position.

The Legacy: Continuing Problems of Brazilian Football

Thus, with investors frightened off, the economy sluggish and the old guard still in charge (though considerably weakened following the parliamentary inquiry), the problems remained. The costs that clubs faced far outweighed the revenues (a common problem throughout the world, but particularly acute in Brazil). There continued to be a strong dependence on one source of income (tele-vision). The major television companies, while sympathetic to the cause and open to dialogue (especially in the case of TV Globo, by far the largest network), were well aware that their major source of income was the perennially popular soap operas which dominate peak-time viewing. Football matches in Brazil are transmitted late in the evening, impacting negatively on attendance and audience figures, while pay TV and pay-per-view services are financially beyond the reach of the average spectator. Football merchandising, a major source of income for clubs in Western Europe, offers low returns in Brazil: this is, after all, a poor country (with pockets of wealth), and even those who could afford to fork out a small fortune for an official team shirt (at a cost of approximately 40 per cent of the monthly minimum wage) normally prefer to buy the ubiquitous counterfeits.

Then there was the calendar problem. Unlike Europe, there was no official football season, no fixed dates for the matches, and even the rules which determined how the championship was won could change every year. Economically speaking, it was disastrous. Such a situation meant that the clubs could not sell season tickets, which in turn meant that banks had no security on which to lend money in the long run.

A further problem in Brazil is that there are too many competi-tions. This dilutes interest. Sometimes — especially in cities like Rio de Janeiro and São Paulo — two clubs will play each other so many times in the season in so-called major competitions that the public either don't know or don't care very much about the outcome. It is a bit like having a Cup Final between Manchester United and Liverpool six times in one year.

Television scheduling requirements, as noted above, mean that midweek matches are usually scheduled for 10.00 p.m., with the result that attendance at the stadiums is very low. Even at weekends, stadiums are rarely even half-full. They are not, it must be said, especially comfortable or welcoming environments, and are still seen by many as unsafe, despite the recent crackdown on supporters' violence.[5]

The clubs themselves are poorly represented by the CBF (the Brazilian Football Confederation), which seems bent on pursuing its own interests regardless of whether they coincide with those of the league teams. Although new legislation is in place, partially aimed at attracting new investment but without strong federation backing, real change at a structural level is likely to be attained in the long rather than the short term.

So there are more than enough reasons to apply hard-earned pounds, euros and dollars elsewhere. However, for anyone who still wants to do business in Brazil, the potential is still very much there. Stadium attendance is low, but with the necessary improvements they could quite realistically be drawing in more spectators soon, particularly now that the reforms on safety are kicking in with a vengeance. The television companies are lending a sympathetic ear, and there is real hope for change there too. The first company to market and sell club merchandise at a realistic price is likely to attract both considerable market attention and revenue.

The government of President Lula is acutely aware of the seriousness of the situation and the need for investment. The official inquiry into the 'missed opportunity' was extensive, thorough and surprisingly effective. The old guard emerged both bloodied and humbled. Urgent reforms to tackle violence on and off the pitch have been very successful. There is a strong likelihood of the government refinancing the debts owed by many clubs so that they can, in effect, start afresh.[6]

Reform at Two Clubs

A clear example of the way the wind is blowing is my own club, Botafogo, one of the traditional 'Big Four' in the city of Rio de Janeiro.[7] Crippled by an unpayable debt, poor management, low attendance at matches and general low morale, it seemed that the club was doomed. Then a newly elected popular president decided that enough was enough. The 'old guard' was ousted. Unable, in times of economic difficulty, to attract a major sponsor, the club established its own logo, 'Botafogo no Coração' (Botafogo from the Heart), which struck an immediate chord with supporters and led to a huge increase in sales of merchandise. Club matches were transferred from the Maracanã National Stadium to the local ground: smaller, simpler and cheaper, but resulting in a £30,000 to £35,000 profit per game (as opposed to a substantial loss per game at Maracanã). Due to the restrictions on club ownership/management (described above), three executives were hired and a separate management company established, dedicated exclusively to transforming the club at all levels (from the grass roots upwards), based on transparent, efficient and professional practice. Nine months after the regime change, in 2003, Botafogo was promoted back to the First Division of the National Championship.

A second example of reform is that of Atlético Paranaense, founded in 1924 and one of the major clubs in Curitiba, the biggest city in the state of Paraná.[8] In the mid-1990s, the club was heavily indebted, playing in the second division of the Brazilian championship at an obsolete ground, and lacking training facilities of any quality. In 1995, a new management team took over with the intention of reviving the club via a 10-year strategic plan. The initial objectives were local — to regain football dominance in the state of Paraná and a place in the first division of the Brazilian championship — but were accompanied by a marketing and investment strategy which focused on developing the club's brand around the construction of a new stadium. Additional resources were to be invested in training facilities. The footballing outcome was a succession of victories in the state championship (five over the next decade), and the capture of the Brazilian First Division crown in 2001. In 2005, the team reached the final of the Copa Libertadores. This translated into financial well-being, both through the transfer of players whom the club had trained — including the sale of the Brazilian international Kléberson to Manchester United for US$ 11 million in 2003 — and much-improved attendances as fans were attracted to a new stadium and a successful team.

Conclusion

Isolated reforms conducted by clubs such as Botafogo and Atlético Paranaense will not by themselves be sufficient to change the environment for foreign investors interested in Brazilian football. What is required is for the CBF to introduce some macro changes and enforce them. Without this happening, the fear is that the positive examples coming from these clubs such as these will not hold for long. However, were the CBF, in cooperation with the government, to take effective action to institute the basis for sound management in Brazilian football clubs, the situation would be different.

In such an event, the opportunities for investors in Brazilian football would be as wide and diverse as the country itself. The opportunities for rich pickings would still be there. At the exchange rates prevailing in the early 2000s, British and Euro-zone investors could get a great deal for their money — particularly bearing in mind that salaries and the cost of services at all levels in Brazil are much lower. Good professional guidance would be essential, of course, and such investments would not be for the weak-hearted. Provided investors realised that they would need to bring all their business experience and financial know-how to bear on a still-developing market, there should be no repetition of past mistakes.

Still in doubt? Then consider this. Brazil is a nation with a population of 180 million. Football is our culture, our soul, our life. Think of Brazil and you think of football — the whole world does. Many countries love the sport; we live it. It bridges the huge social divide in our country; it gives us hope in times of crisis; it unites us, it moves us, it drives to excel. And excel we do. We produce world-class players like no other nation. We strive with all our energy to succeed. And you still think you can't make money out of that?

Acknowledgement

This paper is based on the author's experience of participation in the negotiations that led to foreign investment in Brazilian clubs in the late 1990s. Some additional material has been included by the editors.

Notes

1   This paper was written before the 2006 World Cup. Despite the poor performance of Brazil, there was no doubt that the Brazilian team was the best group of players. However, only two of the squad of 23 played for Brazilian clubs, in contrast to 13 in the 2002 World Cup-winning squad, which suggests that, although Brazil has talented footballers coming to the market every year, it is still incapable of keeping its players at home due to the state of the football business within Brazil — in particular, the desperate financial straits in which most clubs find themselves.

2   On the fan-base of the major clubs in Rio de Janeiro and São Paulo, see Soong (2003).

3   The parent of ISL, International Sports Media and Marketing (ISMM), went bankrupt in May 2001, partly as a result of its losses in Brazilian football but also due to over-investment in professional tennis and miscalculation of the value of the media rights for international football (*Financial Times*, 12 April 2001 and 28 May 2001). By then, foreign investors' interest in Brazilian football had faded (*Financial Times*, 3 January 2001).

4   For a foreign journalist's view of the inquiries, see Bellos (2002, Ch. 14). For the view of the man who led the Chamber of Deputies' inquiry, see Rebelo & Torres (2001).

5   Law 10.671/2003 aimed to control violence and improve stadium facilities in Brazil in order to increase attendance. It is known as the Supporters' Code.

6   In September 2006, a new sports lottery, Timemania, was approved by the government. Under this scheme, just over 20 per cent of the proceeds of the lottery, which would be operated by the national treasury, would be used to pay the clubs' debts to the state, estimated at over US$500 million. Excess revenue would be used to fund youth development programmes: *Soccer Investor Daily*, 7 September 2006.

7   The other members of the 'Big Four' in Rio de Janeiro are Flamengo, Fluminense and Vasco da Gama.

8   This paragraph is based on the presentation given at the London conference by Alexandre Rocha Loures, the International Business Manager of Atlético Paranaense.

13

Monkeys and Mosquitoes:
Research into the Fans of Brazilian Club *Internacional*

Antonio Aidar and Rogan Taylor

Introduction

> The value of sport relies on the strength and the spread of
> its customers ... this relatively captive market is the key that
> locks in television ... What drives value in the sports busi-
> ness [is] ... the power of fans — 'fan equity' — and the
> power of television, and the power of players. (Salomon
> Brothers 1997, pp. 3–4)

The financial value of a football club bears a direct relationship
to the number of supporters it has, the strength (intensity) and
length of their bond with the club, and their geographical range
(local, national and international) (Salomon Brothers 1997, p. 7). This
value is sometimes called 'fan equity'. Acquiring it takes time. Building
a stadium involves up to two or three years; buying a whole team can
be done in a week. To change the number and quality of a club's
supporters, however, takes at least one generation — and only then if
everything is done to encourage the process. Once established, fan
loyalty for a single club has (in the past) been almost unshakeable.

The research reported here was commissioned by a leading
Brazilian football club, Sport Club Internacional of Porto Alegre in
the southern state of Rio Grande do Sul, to provide the club's
management with guidelines to increase and strengthen its fan base.
Through quantitative research (questionnaires) and focus groups, the
research explored issues related to identification of the fans, the
'branding' of the club and fidelity. The analysis of the data subsequently informed the advice that was provided for Internacional to

help increase its fan equity. However, it also provides an example of how academic research can discover issues about fan identity and behaviour that can contribute to a broader understanding of both football fandom and the football business in Latin America. To the best of our knowledge, this was the first professional market research to discover the characteristics of a club's fans that has been carried out in Brazil, although fan surveys have become established in football markets such as England since the mid-1990s.

Methodology

The research methods were based upon those often used by commercial interests to identify or profile their customers. This includes collecting basic data (for example, age, gender, address, etc.), together with other details such as occupation, consumer habits, length of support for the club, and emotional involvement with the club.

The data collection methods used in this project included both quantitative and qualitative techniques; the former helped to select and recruit the members of the focus groups that were used to develop themes arising from the initial survey. Questionnaires were distributed to supporters of Internacional who attended matches during the months of September and October 2001 held at Beira-Rio (the home stadium of Internacional). They were also available at the Internacional club stores, on the club website, and delivered direct to club members' homes (as a requisite for the club's new membership card). A total of 3,047 questionnaires were returned and included in the database. Ninety per cent of the completed questionnaires were collected at the games. The data therefore largely reflect the opinions of *active* Inter fans (those who actually attend games). Of these returns, 757 were members of the club and 2,290 were other fans.

Computer analysis of the returns made it possible to identify Internacional's members and to develop a general profile of supporters (members and non-members) so that an appropriate sample could be selected to participate in the focus groups. It was regarded as essential to include substantial focus group work because the relationship between supporters and football is emotional and requires semi-structured dialogues in small groups to explore issues in depth.

The General Profile of Internacional's Active Fans

Some general characteristics about Inter supporters could be gathered immediately from computer analysis of the returned questionnaires. First, 90 per cent of the fans questioned were male, 10 per cent female. In the subsequent analysis, at the club's request, male and female fans were profiled separately in order to identify any differences between them, although in the event there were few. Second, roughly three-quarters of male fans (76 per cent) were under 40, with 22 per cent of the total aged 20 or under. However, that still left a significant proportion (24 per cent) who were 41 or more. Third, 47 per cent of the male supporters questioned were in full-time employment, with another 22 per cent describing themselves as students and 17 per cent as self-employed. Fourth, the majority of fans were single (52 per cent); married men made up 42 per cent of the total, leaving a small residue who were divorced, widowed, etc. Fifth, almost 20 per cent of the fans had been supporting the club for 20 years or more, although around half (48 per cent) described themselves as having supported the club for less than five years.

Analysis of the female fans (11 per cent of the total questioned) showed similar patterns. 49 per cent fell into the 21–40 age bracket, 23 per cent were less than 20, and the remainder were older than 40. As with the men, there was a substantial body of students among the female fans (30 per cent of the total). Those in work made up 53 per cent (33 per cent described themselves as being in full-time employment), but in the case of females the proportion who fell into the residual 'other' category was larger — at 17 per cent — than for the men. In terms of marital status, 54 per cent of the female fans were single and 34 per cent married. 39 per cent of the female fans were parents. The length of time they had been supporting the club was similar to that of the male fans, although a smaller proportion of the female fans (38 per cent compared with 48 per cent for the men) described themselves as supporting the club for less than five years.

These results provided the club with a basic demographic profile of its fans which in many respects was not surprising: across the world, football is viewed by marketers as appealing primarily to young, single males across social classes. Nonetheless, the results do show that a significant minority of Internacional's *active* fans are long-time supporters who have watched the club regularly for over 20 years. A further set of questions identified some of the main features of regular supporters that the club needed for planning purposes, and the figures that follow refer to those who attended more than 20 games in a season.

First, for planning purposes, the club needed to know about the forms of transportation that the fans used to get to the stadium. It was found that just over half (52 per cent) used a car, but a substantial minority (40 per cent) relied on bus transport; the remainder walked. This result had implications both for the club's provision of parking facilities and for public transport on match days.

Second, for marketing purposes, it was desirable to know the extent to which supporters attended games with friends or relations or on their own. Figure 13.1 shows the split. Perhaps the most surprising aspect is the number of regular supporters who attend the game on their own — a higher percentage than for more casual fans.

Figure 13.1: FC Internacional — Who Attends the Game with Regular Supporters?

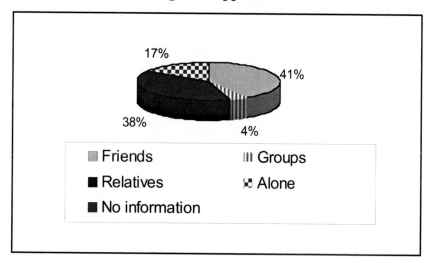

Third, the club needed to know more about the occupational status (and by implication the income) of its most regular supporters. This is shown in Figure 13.2. The most important finding was that over half (55 per cent) of the supporters who attended 20 or more games did not work full-time, but fell into one of the following categories: retired, students, people who hold a part-time job, and those who are unemployed. Internacional obviously needs to be aware of this significant group of 'unwaged' or 'part-waged' regular fans.

Figure 13.2: Occupational Status of Most Regular Supporters

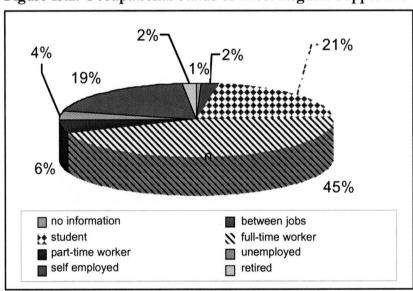

Finally, the club needed to know more about the residence of its most regular fans. While it could obtain information about the residence of its members from its own database, it had no information about the supporters who were not members of the club. The important point here was that while over three-quarters of its regular fans came from Porto Alegre itself, there were significant minorities from Canoas and Viamão, about 10 and 20 kilometres away respectively.

Figure 13.3: Place of Residence of Regular Supporters

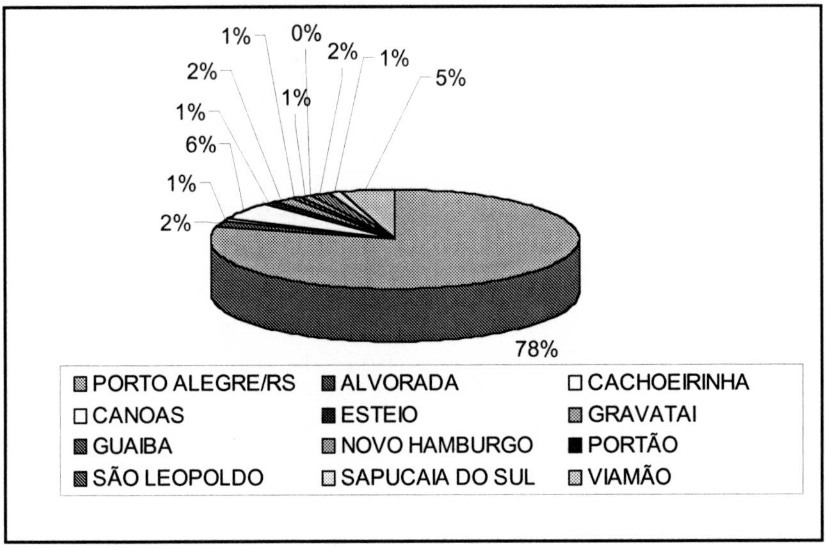

1%
0%
2%
1%
2%
5%
1%
1%
6%
1%
2%
78%
PORTO ALEGRE/RS
ALVORADA
CACHOEIRINHA
CANOAS
ESTEIO
GRAVATAI
GUAIBA
NOVO HAMBURGO
PORTÃO
SÃO LEOPOLDO
SAPUCAIA DO SUL
VIAMÃO

Figure 13.4: The Porto Alegre Region

Portão
Novo Hamburgo
São Leopoldo
Sapucaia
Esteio
Canoas
Gravataí
Cachoeirinha
Alvorada
Porto Alegre
SC Internacional
Estádio Beira-Rio
Viamão
Guaiba
Lagoa dos Patos
0
10
20
kilometres

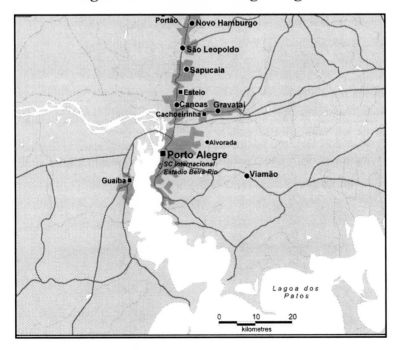

The Focus Groups

Computer analysis of the questionnaires thus provided some preliminary conclusions about the profile and characteristics of Internacional supporters, and identified some important themes. These characteristics were used to guide the formation of the focus groups that would discuss issues that both the club's managers and the researchers considered necessary for the development of a marketing plan and other strategies. For example, if the club directors wished to know more about the supporters who attended more than twenty games a year, and their perceptions of the 'package' offered by the club, then the focus group had to be structured appropriately: part-members and part-non-members; males and females; people equally distributed by age, income levels, and so on. The focus groups would also allow a deeper understanding of the supporters' perceptions of their club, and what it meant to them to be a fan of Internacional as opposed to the other clubs in the region.

The priority list of sub-groups for the club administrators, who were financing the research, was as follows:

1. Supporters from Porto Alegre who attended fewer than five games a year;

2. Members who had children and grandchildren;

3. Members from Porto Alegre who attended fewer than five games a year;

4. Members from Porto Alegre who attended more than 20 games a year;

5. Supporters from Porto Alegre who attended more than 20 games a year;

6. Members between 10 and 13 years of age;

7. Supporters between 10 and 13 years of age;

8. Supporters between 15 and 29 years of age;

9. Members between 18 and 25 years of age.

The research team decided that eight focus groups (with eight to ten people in each) could include all the sub-groups required. Each focus group would have a central issue or question around which the discussions would take place.

The central topics of the eight focus groups are listed below.

1.   Championships and games.

2.   Why fewer than five games?

3.   Why not bring the children?

4.   How do you manage more than twenty games?

5.   What are the problems for a fan living outside Porto Alegre?

6.   Female fans and their issues.

7.   Bringing in the youngsters.

8.   How the fans view the media.

In addition to the specific issue on which each focus group concentrated, there were some basic questions addressed to all. These included:

- Stadium and security issues (including policing, the club shop, food and beverages, etc.);

- Spending patterns on club products;

- Club–fan relations (match games and when the fan buys club products, for example);

- Away match travel (whether it was easy or difficult to attend games out of Porto Alegre and why);

- Ticket purchase methods (internet, in advance, on a walk-up basis, etc.).

Perceptions of Internacional and their Rivals

In the interest of exploring the images and feelings that fans have about their club, and to gain a better understanding of the fans' own perceptions about Inter's 'brand image', selected focus groups were also asked to suggest words and animals which seemed to them representative of either Internacional or the club's greatest rivals, Grêmio.

Members of two focus groups were given one piece of paper and asked to write one word that would mean 'Internacional' for them. The most popular results were:

- love (*amor*);
- passion (*paixão*);
- energy (*energia*);
- fulfilment (*realização*);
- joy (*alegria*);
- life (*vida*);
- family (*família*).

The other six focus groups looked at a collection of words that might describe Inter. People were asked to select the most significant word from this list:

- winner (*vencedor*);
- suffering (*sofredor*);
- 'Club Empresa' (the main sponsor of the Club);
- heroic (*heróico*);
- brave (*raça*);
- historic (*histórico*);
- *popular* ('of the people').

The two most significant words were historic (*histórico*) and *popular* (of the people). Interestingly, female fans added the word 'brave' (*raça*).

Six of the focus groups were also asked to write down one animal which they associated strongly with Inter. These are the results in descending order of popularity, with some of the reasons that were given for the choice:

1. monkey (*macaco*);
2. lion (*leão*), for its strength;
3. falcon (*falcão*), for its capacity to observe the prey;
4. cat (*gato*), for its intelligence and smartness;
5. tiger;
6. buffalo, for its strength and ferocity;
7. gorilla;
8. bull;

9.   snake;

10.   sloth (*bicho-preguiça*), symbolising the club's current situation at the time of the research;

11.   squirrel (*esquilo*), for its intelligence;

12.   horse (*cavalo*), for its beauty.

The significance of 'monkey' for Inter fans has its origins in an intended insult. It was Grêmio fans who first chanted 'Monkeys' at Inter fans. In southern Brazil, the word has the connotation of someone who is 'poor' and 'underclass'. However, the Inter fans adopted it to spite the Grêmio fans and proclaim their identification with the 'club of the poor'.

Members of the focus groups were also asked to think of animals that symbolised their main Porto Alegre rivals, Grêmio. The following results emerged from the data:

1.   deer (*veado*), for its association with homosexuality (there is an organised group of gay fans at Grêmio);

2.   hyena (*hiena*), for its 'sarcastic' laugh and its low status as a 'scavenger';

3.   snake, because it is dangerous;

4.   pig: 'Grêmio has to stay in the mud';

5.   frog, because it is nasty;

6.   cat, treacherous;

7.   rat, disgusting;

8.   fish, essential but vulnerable;

9.   rabbit;

10.   hawk (*gavião*);

11.   skunk (*gambá*), for its smell;

12.   cockroach (*barata*);

13.   ant (*formiga*), because they are easy to kill;

14.   mosquito, because they are insignificant but a nuisance.

The Concept of Being a Colorado and its Relation to the 'Brand Image' of Internacional as 'The Club of the People'

The importance of being a *Colorado* was very frequently mentioned amongst all focus groups as something of considerable significance for Internacional fans. The concept of *Colorado* is a subtle blend of ideas associated with the colour red, as symbolic of the club (it is the colour of Inter's shirt) and of 'the people' who support the club, and of the ties of blood that they feel bind them to Internacional. Inter's fans think of themselves as *Colorados*, and emphasise their bond with the club in terms of the club motto, 'Club of the People'. Being an Inter fan *is* being a *Colorado*; being a *Colorado is* being a fan of the 'Club of the People'. These two concepts appear to be intertwined.

If all people have a flag, a cause, a territory and a spirit, then 'Inter people' possess all of these elements in a well-defined way. For Inter's fans, being part of the '*Colorado* people' confers a powerful sense of collective identity — of never being alone. In the early 1960s, the fans of Liverpool FC in England began to sing: 'You'll Never Walk Alone', expressing a similar sense of unity; the song has since become an almost global 'football anthem'.

The emotional bonds between Inter's fans and the club are some-times expressed by the untranslatable '*bairrismo gaúcho*'. The words carry reference to an historic sense of independence amongst the people of the Rio Grande do Sul, the so-called '*gaúcho* state'. The state is located on the southern borders of Brazil and has, in the past, tried to separate itself off from the rest of Brazil (it is not unlike being a Catalan or a Basque in Spain).[1] Being part of the '*Colorado* people' also indicates a distinct territory. This 'territory' exists not only in reality but also in the imagination. The Inter fan may live far from Porto Alegre, far from the team — even outside Brazil — but he or she remains forever a member of the '*Colorado* people'. This is a special bond, an existential reference, an expression of the uniqueness of Inter's fans.

A people without a land is a people without a home. The Inter fans' sense of the importance of 'territory' explains, subjectively, their enormous bond with the Beira-Rio stadium, which was inaugu-rated in 1969 after a considerable collaborative effort amongst supporters.[2] The importance that the *gaúcho* people give to their roots is doubly emphasised: Beira-Rio is both a real, geographic location and a mystical 'homeland', the spiritual 'rendezvous' of this People. A crowd becomes a 'People' when its members have a shared history. This helps to explain the fans' yearning for great victories, their preference for championships, their desperation about the possibility of relegation. The sense of being '*Colorado* People' grows stronger through knowledge of the club's history of victories and through success over rivals; defeat weakens it.

The Inter 'Brand'

The sum of these cross-weaving themes about the identity, territory and 'soul' of the *Colorado* people and their club is the 'brand' of Internacional. The word 'brand', commonly used in the commercial world to indicate the unique qualities or character of a particular product or service, has also entered the football industry in the past decade. Great clubs *are* great brands, operating locally, nationally and, increasingly for some such as Real Madrid, Barcelona or Liverpool, internationally. But these brands are not like those associated with businesses selling consumable goods like McDonald's or Coca-Cola.

The brand values that football clubs possess are qualitatively different from ordinary commercial brands. They are much closer to the original meaning of the word 'brand'. At root, the word is about *burning a sign* of ownership or particularity. Branded cattle carry the mark of their brand burned on their flesh for life. Football fans are 'branded' by their clubs in not dissimilar ways. The 'brand' itself is the special image imposed or impressed. A club's brand is the 'special something' that sums up the character of the relationship: it too is burnt on the hearts of its fans — in Brazil, usually for life.

Developing the brand of Internacional is consequently a complex process that has to be matched to its target audience. Marketing the club to its own local fans is a sensitive operation (as Manchester United has experienced in England). The club's management has to be acutely conscious of the *way* in which the relationship is articulated by the fans themselves (as in the focus groups). Marketing Internacional to sponsors is, of course, an entirely different kind of operation in which the brand is presented as an essential part of the *value* of the club to its commercial partners. It is a large part of what the club has to offer, but it has to be 'sold' to sponsors; it doesn't have to be 'sold' to fans. They have bought into it already and, like football fans worldwide, they are unlikely to change their allegiance.

It is, however, one thing to have a strong brand and to claim world-wide support in the millions, as clubs like Real Madrid and Manchester United do. It is another thing to monetise it, in the sense of entering into the virtuous circle of turning armchair fans into committed fans, who then contribute to the club's success both through their financial and their vocal support. This is a problem that faces clubs at all levels, and in all parts of the world. Converting occasional fans into regular fans, and regulars into 'members', is in a sense a *process of education*. The club must lead the lesser committed fans towards greater commitment by initiating them into the values at the heart of the club. If Inter is the 'Club of the People', it has a special responsibility. It must be *amongst the people* in its community programmes — its relationships with local schools and hospitals, for example. The players must also be on board. They must be 'branded' by the club too, and used as ambassadors to deliver 'the people' to the people.

The Recommendations Made to the Club

This project was an effective exercise in profiling the fans of Inter and gaining significant information about their opinions and their sense of the club's 'brand'. As a consequence, a number of recommendations were made to the club's management. These could be grouped into the following categories: the demography of Inter's support; the branding of Inter; the club's relationship with its fans; and the stadium and match-day operations.

The Demography of Internacional's Fans

The general profile of Inter's fans revealed an optimistically young audience, with three out of four fans under the age of 40. However, this might mean that there were significant numbers of older fans who were no longer coming to matches. Should these older fans be targeted? And what about those residents of Porto Alegre who showed little interest in Internacional? The data from the questionnaires (with the zip codes of addresses) could be used to plot where Inter's fans actually live in Porto Alegre. In this way, the club would be able to identify the districts where Inter's fans are concentrated. This would help in targeting those districts with few Inter fans.

Clearly there were also too few females attending matches, at only 10 per cent of the active support for Internacional. We recommended that the club should aim to raise this to 15–20 per cent of the total over the next five years. The management would need to consider which strategies it should adopt to achieve these targets. The comments from focus groups seemed to indicate that the possibility of violence at the match was one clear deterrent that might prevent many women and girls from attending matches. These issues would therefore need to be addressed with local police, local government agencies and other relevant bodies.

The Branding of Inter

As far as key brand images are concerned, Inter's fans see the club as principally 'historic' and as a 'Club of the People'. These qualities are therefore an important part of the brand image of Internacional. The fans clearly like the image of the 'monkey' (and they enjoy turning this insult from Grêmio into a positive sign of their love for the club). The whole question of identity is of considerable importance to Inter's fans. They feel as if they are the 'real' fans (compared with Grêmio). They also recognise considerable social value in their relationship with Inter. We suspected that few clubs in Brazil would have such deep roots in the social matrix.

One further suggestion was that Inter should consider adopting the 'Monkey' as its new mascot. This resonates with widespread opinion amongst all the focus groups.

The Club's Relationship with its Fans

Discussions in the focus groups led to a number of recommendations regarding Inter's relationship with its fans and the community.

- Inter should think about ways in which 'core fans' could be rewarded. Some fans suggested the provision of an exclusive social area in the stadium where they could promote the sense of 'community' that they feel. These fans believe that they are the 'heart' of Inter's most dedicated fan group. Inter might directly encourage them to initiate other, less dedicated fans into their group.

- Various focus groups highlighted the need for effective social programmes to be created by Internacional using its facilities to benefit the community (*Programas de Solidariedade Social*). Fans thought that such programmes would attract more children to the club. There are considerable numbers of poor children in Porto Alegre who would gain much from access to some of the club's facilities for sport practice, education, and so on.

- Alongside this, it was felt that Inter should raise the profile of its community work in schools. Discussions indicated this would clearly be very popular, especially with 10–13-year-olds. The prospect of players visiting the schools and organised photo opportunities with youngsters would be very popular too.

- Older fans amongst the focus groups were concerned that media relations were poorly conducted at Inter. It was recommended that the club should consider the appointment of a media liaison officer whose role would be to deliver the club's version of events more effectively than at present. Inter must build more effective communication channels with its fans. Several focus group members declared that the communication between the executive management of the club and the fans was not adequate. Frequently, news stories were 'mismanaged' by the papers. Sometimes fans could not understand actions taken by the management of the club, and such actions were never explained to them.

- The possibility of an 'ombudsfan' might be considered. This could be a voluntary post with responsibility for liaising with the club board to resolve issues and complaints brought by fans.

The Stadium and Match-day Operations

Three general issues were clearly raised in almost all the focus groups. First, the timing of matches was important in attracting active support for the club, and this was revealed particularly in the results from the focus group that concentrated on championships and games. Some fans had small differences relating to the timing of matches at the weekends, with a small majority preferring Saturday matches rather than the team playing on Sundays. However, the timing of matches in order to maximise active support and income (remembering that most of Brazilian clubs' income comes via the sale of broadcasting rights) is one of the most important issues for football in Brazil generally. Second, in the specific case of Internacional, the purchase of tickets was not as easy a task as it should be. A third general complaint, related to the timing of matches, was that leaving the stadium after the games — mainly at night — was tough. For example, some bus lines stopped running before the game was over.

Some other more specific recommendations also came from the focus groups, in particular:

- It would be a good idea to have a 'family area', a special place inside the stadium for the children. The family area could include children alone, children in school parties, and children with their parents/friends. Youngsters should not be forced into these areas, but adults would only be allowed in the family area if they were with children.

- There was a widespread view throughout the focus groups that the threat of violence was clearly an impediment to attracting more fans. The club must consider ways of tackling this issue, perhaps bringing fans and police together to develop more effective protective strategies.

- Very poor toilet facilities for females and males was also recognised by every focus group as an impediment to growing and widening attendance at matches. The club should ensure that these vital facilities are radically improved.

- Food outlets should be improved, especially regarding quality and price. All focus groups agreed that current provision was poor.

- Stadium facilities in general were perceived to need upgrading, despite the pride that Internacional fans had in the Beira-Rio arena. Any plans for a new stadium would need careful consideration, and extensive communication with supporters.

Conclusion

It is no coincidence that Internacional won the Copa Libertadores de América in 2006, for the first time in its history. The work done between 1999 and 2001 by the club's president, Fernando Miranda (at the same time as this research was carried out), placed the financial situation of the club in good order. He concentrated on cost-cutting and rationalisation, and he sold home-produced players like Fabio Rochemback (who was transferred to Barcelona in 2001 at the age of 19) and Lucio (who made his debut for the Brazilian national team in 2000, was transferred to Bayer Leverkusen the following year, and is one of the few players to come out of the 2006 World Cup disaster with an enhanced reputation). This attention to solid financial structures and further investments in youth development also had a beneficial effect. To name just two players who have been selected for the national squad, Nilmar (who moved to Lyon) and Daniel Carvalho (who went to CSKA Moscow) were developed during this period and subsequently sold on by the new club directors. Several improvements on the technical side were taken and made irreversible.

In 2001, Fernando Miranda did not run for re-election. Despite his own attempts to 'rationalise' Inter through serious work, he remained unhappy with the way Brazilian football was being managed generally. The winning candidate in the elections found a club in a reasonably healthy financial situation (much better than when Fernando Miranda took power), and with several improvements on the technical side, including a very sound basis of organisation. The new directors thus benefited from their inheritance. However, one of Fernando Miranda's key colleagues, João Paulo Medina, the Technical Director (or Director of Football) who had helped bring forward so many good players), left Inter when Miranda departed. Medina insisted at the time (2001) that the work he had done would take four to five years to mature. After Inter's victory in the Copa Libertadores, one of the largest newspapers in Porto Alegre interviewed Medina, calling him a prophet. It was, as far as we know, the only act of recognition of a job done very well.

The new directors did not follow the suggestions and recommendations of our research. This reluctance to embrace change is, unfortunately, not uncommon in Brazilian football, due to the general lack of professional management, and the overwhelming influence of the 'big personalities' who dominate so many clubs.

Despite being the most successful football nation in the world on the international stage, domestic football in Brazil still has a long way to go. It seems almost incredible that the annual operational revenue of the 'big' teams (three or four clubs at most) is no more than US$30 million each, in a country with 185 million people who are known to be 'crazy' for football. These clubs turn over less than many in the second level of English football. The value of 'fan equity', therefore, has yet to be properly explored or exploited in a way that would benefit fans and clubs alike.

Acknowledgements

This research was conducted in Brazil during 2000–01. The research team included Clarissa Bueno de Almeida, Renato Giosa Miralla (Research Assistants) and Dr Moisés Rodrigues da Silva Jr (Researcher and Focus Group Coordinator). The project was coordinated by Antonio Aidar and Rogan Taylor. This research would not have been possible without the enthusiastic assistance of Mauricio Andrade, and also Marvio Pereira Leoncini, Juliana Vasques, Alan Zekcer, Ricardo Fasti and Nadia Maria Schuch Freire.

Notes

1   A parallel pride in regional identity can be found amongst fans of FC Barcelona and Athletic Bilbao.
2   For more on the construction of the Beira-Rio stadium and the popular effort involved, see the club's website, <www.internacional.com.br>.

Appendix 1: Sport Club Internacional Questionnaire (for members of the club)

Associate registration number:_____

Name_____

Birthday: / /   . (month/day/year)

Gender: Male ( ) Female ( )

Address (including Zip Code):

_____

_____

Telephone numbers:

Home_____

Work_____

If necessary, cross another alternative

Family Situation

Single ( )   Married ( )   Father/Mother ( )

Grandfather/Grandmother ( )

Employment status

Not working ( )   Student ( )

Work full-time ( )   Work in one shift ( )

Unemployed ( )   Work in the informal market ( )

What period can you be found at your home?

Until 12.00 ( )   From 12.00 to 14.00 ( )

From 14.00 to 19.00 ( )   From 19.00 to 21.00 ( )

When did you become an INTER member?

Before five years old ( )   From five to 10 years old ( )

From 11 to 15 years old ( ) From 16 to 20 years old ( )

After 20 years old ( )

Would you:

Answer a more detailed questionnaire? Yes ( )   No ( )

Be part of a focus group about INTER and its supporters?

Yes ( ) No ( )

(for supporters that go to the stadium to watch games)

Name_____

Birthday: / / . (month/day/year)

Gender: Male ( ) Female ( )

Address (including Zip Code):

_____

_____

Telephone numbers:

Home_____

Work_____

If necessary, cross another alternative

Family situation

Single ( ) Married ( ) Father/Mother ( )

Grandfather/Grandmother ( )

Employment status

Not working ( ) Student ( )

work full-time ( ) Work in one shift ( )

unemployed ( ) work in the informal market ( )

What period can you be found at your home?

Until 12.00 ( ) From 12.00 to 14.00 ( )

From 14.00 to 19.00 ( ) From 19.00 to 21.00 ( )

How many games do you usually watch over one year?

Less than 5 ( ) five to 10 ( ) 11 to 15 ( )

16 to 20 ( ) Over 20 games ( )

Would you:

Answer a more detailed questionnaire? Yes ( ) No ( )

Be part of a focus group about INTER and its supporters?

Yes ( ) No ( )

14

Building the Women's United Soccer Association: A Successful League of Their Own?

Katharine W. Jones

Introduction

The demise of the Women's United Soccer Association (WUSA) in September 2003 hardly left a gaping hole in the US sports scene. In fact, few people noticed that it had gone. That, of course, is part of the problem. Many Americans complain that 'soccer' is too boring, too low-scoring, and that there are insufficient bathroom, advertising or food breaks.

This chapter analyses the WUSA experience. What was it? Why did it fail? And how likely is it to be resurrected? The research is based on participant observation at WUSA games on the East Coast over the three seasons between 2001 and 2003, and on interviews with playing, coaching and backroom staff at one WUSA club in the summer of 2003. Several fans who had attended games in other parts of the country were also interviewed.[1]

What is/was the WUSA?

The Women's United Soccer Association, one of the first professional women's soccer leagues in the world, was founded in 2001 (Liebeskind 2001). It grew out of the success of the US women's soccer team, particularly its win over China in the 1999 World Cup finals. At that final, 90,000 jubilant fans (and 40 million more television viewers in the United States) witnessed Brandi Chastain score the winning penalty, sink to her knees and rip off her shirt in delight (Ballard 2001; *The Economist*, 21 April 2001; Stossel 2003). The nation appeared to be hooked on women's soccer. Chastain made the cover

of *Sports Illustrated* and the team was named the magazine's
Sportswomen of the Year (O'Connor 2003); appearances on David
Letterman's late-night talk show led to some christening the squad
'soccer mamas' (Longman 1999); the team was invited to the White
House, sent to watch the space shuttle launch, and given its own ticker-
tape parade in Disneyland (Wells 2003b). John Hendricks, founder of
the Discovery Channel, admitted he was 'intoxicated' by their display,
and the idea for a women's league was born (Longman 2003a, p. 2).

The time seemed ripe. Finally, perhaps, the United States could
show the world that it was a nation of soccer watchers as well as
players.[2] The league combined pop-feminist rhetoric of the Spice Girls
with the all-American love of unbridled athleticism. The term 'soccer
mom', originally a description of those suburban moms who ferried
their children to and from soccer practice (Peskowitz 2005), could take
on a whole new meaning. Now 'moms' and daughters could watch top-
class female athletes together and celebrate girl power, USA-style.

The league consisted of eight teams (from Philadelphia, New York,
Boston, Atlanta, San Diego, San Jose, Washington DC and Cary, North
Carolina), each of which was allotted members of the US national team
(*The Economist*, 21 April 2001). These players were also given an equity
stake in the league, and higher salaries than the other players (*Pittsburgh
Post-Gazette*, 15 June 2003).[3] The league also recruited 30 top players
from around the world, and other US players were brought in from the
amateur women's leagues (*PR News*, 7 May 2001).

The WUSA league was jointly owned by John Hendricks (of the
Discovery Channel), Amos Hostetter (formerly of Continental
Cablevision) and cable companies such as Cox Communications,
Comcast Corporation and Time Warner Cable (Gunther 2001;
Liebeskind 2001). The WUSA's organising principle was, like Major
League Soccer (MLS) in the United States, the single-entity business
structure. This meant that the league itself owned the teams, but
that the owners each operated one or more teams, owned shares in
the league, and were responsible for local television rights. The aim
was to avoid 'conflict between big and small markets, centraliz[e]
control over licensing and sponsorships, and promot[e] economies
of scale' (Gunther 2001). Unfortunately, as it turned out, this also

meant that the teams were economically linked, so that the failure of one or a few of them could (and indeed did) jeopardise the continued existence of the entire league.

At first all seemed rosy. For advertisers and sponsors alike, the concept of wholesome women providing good, clean family entertainment was too good an opportunity to pass up. In an era when sports stars often appear to be arrogant, spoilt and over-paid, here were young women who played for the love of the game, and who actually embraced the idea of being role models for the girls who adored them. The league recruited some of the best female soccer stars from around the world — Kelly Smith from England, Katia and Sissi from Brazil, Sun Wen from China — and 'discovered' others, such as Marinette Pichon from France.

The inaugural game between Mia Hamm's Washington Freedom and Brandi Chastain's San Jose Cyber Rays drew a crowd of 34,148 at Washington's RFK Stadium (Dell'Appa 2003). The stadiums chosen for the league were mostly mid-sized, and some were on college campuses — which often meant an alcohol ban at games (Whiteside 2001). Parents would be able to take their children for a fun afternoon in the sun, with no fear of bad language, aggressive fans or petulant players. The sponsors were happy. The advertisers were eager. The target audience was enthusiastic. The United States was ready for professional women's soccer.

Making It American?

One of the challenges the WUSA faced from the outset was the need to make soccer more appealing to Americans. There have been numerous previous attempts to interest Americans in soccer, from hosting the FIFA World Cup in 1994 to starting the North American Soccer League (NASL) and the US Football League, but most have failed. By 2001 the men's league, Major League Soccer (MLS), had lost at least $250 million since 1996, and the disjuncture between the number of people in the United States who play soccer and the lack of a viewing audience at stadiums and on television had become very frustrating (Gunther 2001). According to *New York Times* writer Jere Longman's 13-year-old daughter, soccer was 'interesting to play, but boring to watch' (Longman 2003b). Adult commentators complain that soccer has not caught on because it is a low-scoring game (Robson 2002); there are no natural commercial breaks for advertisers; and it does not translate well to television because 'the close-up shots that lend drama to other competition[s] don't work' (Tierney 2003, p. 2).

In order to try to overcome these preconceptions, the WUSA developed ways to 'Americanise' the game, to encourage fans and the media to take soccer seriously as an American sport. One WUSA team's public relations manager explained in an interview that:

> [It's] a positive to make it like other [American] sports, because you don't want to alienate the American fans, make them feel like they're in another country watching a game. You want to make them feel like they're home ... and comfortable ... It's not the pitch; it's the field. It's not nil–nil; it's zero–zero. [You don't want to give them the] sense that they don't know what's going on. Soccer ... has enough to overcome. You don't want to over-come wording [too] ... Look at this *English* sport, with *pitches* and *nil–nils* and (disdainfully) *who cares?* Give me the facts. It's a field, it's a ball, it's one–nothing ... And just make it as American as possible (Interview, May 2003).

Fun, Families, and Food: What Went Wrong?

Another early decision was to appeal to families. The league hoped that its audience would consist of young soccer players and their parents, particularly girls and their moms; they therefore determined to make the experience as entertaining as possible for this audience (Chapin 2000). As the coach explained: 'The reality of sports in America in [the twenty-first century] is ... the whole package. It's not any longer about just going to a ball game with your dad and sitting there and watching the ball game. It's all interactive activities and audience participation.' (Interview, May 2003) Back-room staff did not see other sporting events as their main competitors, but rather child-orientated restaurants, video and arcade games, amusement parks, the movies, or even a day at the beach.

Tony DiCicco, the former coach of the 1999 US women's team who later became WUSA League Commissioner, was inspired by the festive family atmosphere he saw at the beach volleyball tournament at the Sydney Olympics in 2000 (Jones 2002). Hence the league spent money on sound systems and video boards 'designed to hold the fans' attention from start to finish' (Tommelleo 2001).

Indeed, the atmosphere could have been described as carnivalesque (in Rabelaisian terms) if it had not been so manufactured (Bakhtin 1984). There were 'funzones' for children to play in at one side of the pitch, complete with bouncy castles and kicking contests; competitions for soccer balls, t-shirts, towels and other merchandise; half-time entertainment consisting of local girl scouts or female youth soccer teams parading on the pitch; loudspeaker entreaties for one stand to cheer louder than another; give-away nodding-head ('bobblehead') dolls of the players; free autograph books at the gates; 'girl power' music, and catch-phrases from recent movies for fans to chant along to (like 'yeah baby' from *Austin Powers*); interviews with players' families and entreaties to 'de-fend' or graphics depicting a 'great save!' on the big screen; a mascot doing back-flips when her team scored; and a 'pizza dude' advertising the food stands at the edge of the pitch (which seemed to attract more attention from the children than the soccer).

When the administrative staff were asked about the rationale behind this atmosphere, they explained that it simply reflected the nature of modern American sports. No longer is 'the game ... it', as the general manager said: '[This is] what the kids are used to over here.' His sales manager agreed, citing the 'short attention span' of the average American child. The public relations manager was more explicit:

> To the average fan ... zero–zero [means] we didn't see any goals ... Well ... if you have the in-game promotions going on and 'Ho, look at that! That's pretty funny going on up there!' and you hear some music ... in the background and it generates that exciting atmosphere, [then] I think ... for the entire fan-base ... it's a better experience. If there was nothing going on, it would be *bor-ING!* ... But if there's something going on, something for you to tap your feet to, or laugh at, chances are you're going to come back. (Interview, May 2003).

Even Tony DiCicco is quoted as saying: 'We knew our demographic wasn't going to be able to sit and just watch soccer games for two

hours.' (Tommelleo 2001). One of the international players interviewed agreed, pointing out that: 'I don't think they know [whether]
the game can stand alone.' She recounted how shocked her family
had been that the game they had attended had been punctuated by
music and announcements. She had explained to them: 'I just think
that that's their culture — you know, keep the fans involved as much
as possible ... The fans [just] need to be entertained. They don't
know how not to be' (Interview, June 2003).

The general manager of the team had a novel interpretation of
this 'need to be entertained'. He explained that it corresponded to
the 'adult funzones' at most other US sports venues. For example,
the NFL (the National Football League, the gridiron football league)
provides pre-game and half-time entertainment, sells beer and
encourages tailgating (i.e. partying in the parking lot). 'It's not like
we've got some idea that is brand new ... I mean, you go to a minor
league hockey game, and that's all there is. And some would say those
games were boring too.' (Interview, May 2003).

From a European or South American perspective, the atmosphere at WUSA games was somewhat forced and stilted. Any chance
that fans might develop the transgressive, irreverent, grass-roots,
carnivalesque culture common to the game elsewhere in the world
(with chanting, singing, in-jokes, fanzines, protests, the spontaneous
adaptation of absurd costumes or props, and so on) (Bakhtin 1984;
Fiske 1993; Giulianotti 1995, 1999b; Hoy 1994) was effectively
stifled by the WUSA's heavy-handed 'top-down' approach in which
every possible space or silence was filled with officially sanctioned
noise and spectacle. Those few attempts to cater to an adult audience, such as the Atlanta Beat's creation of an adult 'Kickback Zone'
where beer was sold for two dollars for ten minutes after each
Atlanta goal, appeared clumsy and patronising (Parker 2003). In
creating 'spaces' in which fans could have officially sanctioned 'fun',
the WUSA was guilty of excessive micro-management. The *'jouissance*
of ... singing, joking, swearing, wearing of stylized attire and
costumes, engaging in elaborate social interplay, enjoying sexual
activity etc.' that authors like Giulianotti (1995: 194) see as the
essence of football elsewhere was simply not present. This was at
least partly because the WUSA followed the US model of using non-

organic clubs to start leagues from scratch (as opposed to teams originating in workplaces, colleges and sporting clubs, as occurs elsewhere in the world). This has been termed 'GM [genetically modified] football' by British soccer writer Steven Wells (Wells 2003a). As the head coach of Washington Freedom complained: 'Our soccer community [doesn't] value the importance of learning from a high level and supporting a club. We've got kids playing soccer in our market who probably don't know who the Freedom are' (quoted in O'Connor 2003).

By focusing almost exclusively on families, the WUSA made the serious mistake of alienating 'soccer purists'. As the Sales Manager admitted: 'Adults want … us to focus more on the game … They didn't like the interruptions … every five minutes … They think it's distracting.' (Interview, May 2003) His response was that most fans were there with their children, and so they were simply giving the majority of fans what they wanted. However, childless adult fans complained that the atmosphere was infantilising, and that they felt its child-centredness had the potential to debase the sport, as well as the women playing it. One US player seemed to agree, although she phrased her response very diplomatically: 'I do not like it so much … when the music is playing intermittently throughout the game. I've been to some stadiums where … a shot is taken and they'll play music really loud. I think that kind of takes away from it. It's like … it makes it a joke in a way." However, she hurriedly added: 'But I tune a lot of that stuff out' (Interview, June 2003). In essence, the WUSA architects and marketers lacked faith in both the game itself and the ability of an audience in the United States to concentrate for 45 minutes at a time. They also failed to recognise the possible existence of a childless adult fan base. However, personal observation at games on the East Coast suggests that many childless adults were present at the games. Although the league's own statistics suggest that their largest fan base was young girls (*Pittsburgh Post-Gazette*, 15 June 2003), other commentators have suggested that these were not the only group with which the league should have been concerned. James Chung, President of Reach Advisors, an independent Boston-based research and consulting firm which specialises in family issues, conducted focus groups with WUSA fans. He claims that the league made some adults feel 'aggressively unwanted'. Adult women without children sensed an undercurrent of homophobia in the relentless promotion of the 'squeaky clean family image' of the league. Also, by mistakenly assuming that only 'moms' would make decisions about whether to watch soccer, the league left 'soccer dads' — men who passionately wanted their daughters to enjoy sports — out in the cold. One father even said he was made to feel like a 'paedophile in the crowd' (Chung, personal communication, July 2003).

There *were* men and boys at the games I attended, and many of them seemed to be taking the sport seriously. I saw adolescent boys desperate for free WUSA t-shirts, 30-something men watching the action on the pitch intently, and small groups of men in the season ticket holders' stand wearing soccer shirts from around the world, trying to start anti-referee chants. The players interviewed mentioned their initial surprise that boys attended their soccer camps and wanted their autographs, but the people in administrative positions seemed to believe that boys would rapidly tire of watching women playing soccer, and that men would only come to games if pushed to do so by their wives and daughters.

A further mistake was the fact that the league only seemed interested in 'tweens' — girls aged between eight and 12. Chung's focus groups suggested that these girls enjoyed going to the games, but once they became teenagers, they started to feel that it was 'uncool' to remain fans. He claimed that the league made the elementary error of positioning itself for the age group it wished to attract, rather than the age its target group aspired to be. Girls of 14 and 15 who were soccer-mad took their WUSA posters off their bedroom walls because they associated the league with 'kiddie' culture. If they wanted to watch soccer, they did so by themselves in front of the television, rather than going to the games with their team-mates or friends (Chung, personal communication, July 2003). In interviews, back-room employees expressed surprise and disappointment that high school soccer teams did not seem as interested in the games as they had predicted. Yet, when asked about future promotions, staff mentioned that forthcoming games would be geared to the themes of girl-scout night, sleepover night and beach night — all activities that the teenage market would probably spurn.

Commitment and Mismanagement

The focus on a family-friendly atmosphere appears to have back-fired, and might have played a role in the league's demise. Few, however, apportion any blame to the players — who were widely regarded as 'the most refreshingly wholesome personalities to ever participate in professional sport' (Taylor 2003). They did much to try to make the league a success.

In a rather surreal touch, one US pundit pointed to the increased number of goals per game in the first two seasons — from an average of 2.80 to 3.32 — as evidence that play was improving (Newberry 2002). However, the quality of play *did* improve over the three years; commentators agreed that the players were 'strong, aggressive, compet-itive and skilful ... exemplify[ing] the ideals of hard work, team play and self-sacrifice' (Stossel 2003). Players also took pay cuts (25 per cent in the case of the founding players) and agreed to cut rosters when the stability of the league started to look vulnerable (Fisher 2003a; Furlong 2003; McHugh 2003). They cheerfully offered soccer clinics, did community outreach, media and charity work, and signed autographs for an hour after every game, rain or shine, win or lose, before meeting with fans in a local restaurant for a post-game party. Many did this on a $30,000 salary, making cutbacks by living on macaroni and cheese, sharing laundry loads to save water, or living hundreds of miles away from husbands or partners and children (Davis 2002; Issenberg, 2003).

This commitment to women's soccer in general, and the WUSA in particular, only makes the financial mismanagement all the more tragic. For that is what ultimately led to the suspension of the league on 15 September 2003. The league had started well. Its initial busi-ness plan anticipated attendances of 6,500 fans per game, and this assumption was later revised upwards when attendances were higher than expected (Chapin 2000; Lisovicz 2001). At the end of the first season, there were even hints that two more teams might be added to the league (Whiteside 2001).

However, the management made serious mistakes that led to the demise of the WUSA. One set of problems related to financial management. By the end of the first season it was evident that the league had run through its five-year operating budget (Davis 2002; Fisher 2003a; Robson 2002). As one official commented: 'We were all around spending wildly without a gatekeeper.' (Lynn Morgan, cited by Parker 2003) This caused cost-cutting measures to be instituted, including replacing the CEO, reducing the marketing budget and moving the head offices from New York City to Atlanta (Snowden 2001).

A second set of issues relates to attendances. These dropped from an average of around 8,000 in the first season to 7,000 in the second season and then to 6,650 in 2003 (Parker 2003). Initially attendances had been artificially inflated by 'double-headers' with MLS (Major League Soccer) games, and by the turnout of 34,148 for the inaugural game at RFK stadium in April 2001 (Whiteside 2001; Reynolds 2002). Yet most of the stadiums used were relatively small — one that was used in the first season only held 6,400 spectators — and as initial attendances were higher than expected, this seems an unfair complaint — especially as the WNBA (Women's National Basketball Association) and MLS both experienced similar drops in attendances after the first burst of excitement had worn off (Whiteside 2001; Newberry 2002). However, chance factors may also have exacerbated the attendance decline. Mia Hamm's injury in 2002 might have been a factor in a 51 per cent decline in attendances for the Washington Freedom, although ultimately the Freedom's attendance record was to prove one of the best in the league (Fisher 2002). The following summer, extremely bad weather on the East Coast did not help attendances, although officials at one East Coast club pointed out to me when interviewed that, even in the torrential rain, they would get at least 5,000 soaked fans sitting on the bleachers (Fisher 2003b).

Third, the management of the broadcasting contracts for WUSA also raises questions. Television ratings were lower than expected. The cable networks TNT and CNN/Sports Illustrated only showed eight games in the first season to an average of 360,000 homes — a far cry from the 40 million who had tuned in to watch the 1999 Women's World Cup Final (Snowden 2001). However, the league's subsequent decision to move from TNT and CNN/SI to PAX, a TV channel few had heard of, was viewed as mystifying by many observers (Howard 2002). Although PAX was a 'family channel' with a reach of 84 million and a target audience of 25–55-year-old women, it was not renowned for its sports features (*Business Wire*, 18 December 2001; Reynolds 2002). PAX then showed games on Saturdays between 4.00 and 6.00

p.m., at exactly the same time as ESPN2 was showing the MLS games, and at the same time as many children would be out playing soccer (Howard 2002; Ballard 2001). Ratings by the third year had dropped from 360,000 households to a dismal 100,000 households (Howard 2003). ESPN, the premier sports channel in the United States, claimed that the WUSA had walked away from making a deal with it when the going got tough, as did a women's lifestyle channel that would have shown the games at the potentially more sensible time of 5.00 to 7.00 p.m. on Sundays (Howard 2002, 2003).

Further problems related to marketing and sponsorship. The austerity measures put in place in 2002 by the new CEO had two effects: they frightened investors away from a league that was obviously in financial trouble; and they reduced the marketing budget, making it harder for the league to sell itself adequately (Fisher 2003b). The league did not even use its owners' cable TV channels to advertise its games (Howard 2003). Sponsorship packages were combined with a media buy-in, making the cost of sponsoring the league at least one million dollars — something to which brand managers would not usually agree (Taylor 2003). Although the business structure was changed to a modified franchise model that gave individual teams more control at the local level, this seemed to worry investors and sponsors further, as a similar move in the WNBA had meant that two teams folded (Fisher 2003b; Parker 2003). By September 2003, it was clear that only two of the eight sponsors that were necessary to keep the league afloat would commit to spending $2.5 million in 2004 (Howard 2003).

Overall, the quality of WUSA's management appears to have been poor throughout its history. According to some insiders, the lack of soccer knowledge and business knowledge combined to make the WUSA a 'woefully run league'. Examples of mismanagement include not returning phone calls and failing to put together an adequate business plan (Howard 2003). Moreover, the WUSA's relationship with the MLS — a vital ally in its attempt to interest the US public in soccer — was at best defensive, and at worst hostile (Snowden 2001). One WUSA player is reported to have warned the MLS not to ride on its coat-tails, and some suggest that the MLS drew up its own plans for a women's soccer league (Howard 2003; Snowden 2001). The poor relationship may have proved fatal when help was needed.

In the end, WUSA was unable to persuade the US Soccer Federation to give it financial assistance on at least two separate occasions, and ultimately the publicly traded companies that owned the league could not sustain the losses, estimated at between $16 and $20 million annually (Berkowitz 2003; Howard 2002, 2003).

In fairness to the WUSA, its employees did make efforts to improve the situation. By August 2002, budget cuts had provided a 30 per cent drop in expenses and the association had managed a 40 per cent increase in revenues, including sponsorship deals with McDonalds, Coca-Cola and Maytag to add to its already impressive list of blue-chip sponsors. Tony DiCicco was put in charge of 'Youth Energizes Stadiums' to try to encourage youth soccer organisations to become more involved with the WUSA (Straus 2002). However, in the case of the New York Power, the local soccer organisations on Long Island actually refused to distribute marketing materials for the WUSA, suggesting that grass-roots outreach was not always as successful as the league had hoped (Reynolds 2002).

The Future?

On 22 September 2003, a committee was set up under the guidance of John Langel, a lawyer for both the players' association and the women's national team, to explore the options for resurrecting the WUSA (Reynolds 2003). It attracted interest from old and new investors and sponsors (Vega 2003). Julie Foudy, captain of the US women's soccer team and chair of the committee, explained that: 'People are saying, "What's the deficit? $16 million? That's it?" We should have done something!' (Howard 2003) In 2003, one report claimed that eight to ten major corporations showed serious interest in investing, and between 20 and 30 companies had inquired about sponsorship (Peterson 2003).

In June 2004, the league put together two 'soccer festivals' in California and Minnesota. These featured 'double-header' games between reconstituted teams, coaching clinics, space for player–fan interaction, and separate meetings with investors. Some 7,123 fans gathered to watch the Philadelphia Charge beat the San Jose CyberRays (a crowd many lower division men's clubs in Europe would envy)

(*Associated Press*, 27 June 2004a; Mahoney 2004). Meanwhile, the 2004 US women's national team games were billed as part of a 'fan celebration tour', designed to re-stimulate interest in the players and say goodbye to veteran players Mia Hamm, Julie Foudy and Joy Fawcett, all of whom retired in November 2004 (www.WUSA.com).

Various proposals for the resurrection of the league are currently under consideration; what seems certain, though, is that the eventual business plan will be much more modest than in 2001, and that the form any new league takes will be dependent on the amount of money raised (McHugh 2004). In July 2004, former US women's coach and commissioner of the WUSA, Tony DiCicco, met with a select group of owners, potential sponsors and outside consultants to put together a business plan. He explained that investors in the new WUSA would be asked for less money this time around: 'There would be less expenditures, less revenue and a more realistic budget.' (*Associated Press*, 22 July 2004b) The revamped WUSA would use a more traditional franchise model in the hope that this would ensure each team's financial independence (McHugh 2004).

In December 2004, the Women's Soccer Initiative, Inc. (WSII) was announced, with Tonya Antonucci, a former soccer player and sports business specialist, chosen as CEO to supervise the re-launch efforts (www.WUSA.com). Although the WUSA website includes the names of five sponsors (McDonalds, Adidas, Coca-Cola, Deutsche Bank and Under Armour), it does not appear to have been updated since December 2004. There is, however, a 'Keep the WUSA Dream Alive' campaign on the website. This is a response to what DiCicco described as 'an incredible outpouring of support' from fans, which included emails, phone calls, cheques, cash and offers to hold fundraisers (*Associated Press*, 16 February 2004c). Fans who pledged $235 were promised season tickets when the league eventually re-started (www.WUSA.com).

In 2005, only five domestic international games were played by the US national women's team (compared with 43 during the three-year period 2002–04) and women's soccer consequently received much less media attention (Zeigler 2006). However, women's soccer continues to flourish at other levels in the form of amateur leagues like the W League and the Women's Premier Soccer League (www.womensoccer.com). Tonya Antonucci, CEO of WSII, has been 'intentionally flying under the radar' as she works on putting together a new league (Carlisle 2005). Insiders are talking about sharing sponsorships and 'soccer-specific stadiums' with the men's soccer league (MLS) (Carlisle 2005; James 2006; Porteus 2006; Zeigler 2006). In a July 2006 interview with Reuters, Julie Foudy said that she did not envisage a WMLS (James 2006), implying that the new women's soccer league would not be financially dependent on the men's league (as the WNBA basketball league is on the NBA).

There have been rumours on the internet that a new league will be up and running by 2007 (Mike 2005) or 2008 (Porteus 2006, www.wikipedia.com). Meanwhile, as this chapter was going to press, the Women's National Professional Soccer League announced that it would launch on October 1, 2006 (www.wnpsl.com). CEO and founder of the WNPSL Ron Clark was fielding phone calls from interested parties, including former employees of the WUSA (Interview, 22 September 2006). In contrast to the dead WUSA website and lack of specific information about a re-launch timetable, the WNPSL is sending out franchise packets, ready to replace the WUSA — or compete with it, if it ever comes back.

Conclusion

The WUSA is not the only women's professional league to have struggled in the United States. The WNBA (Women's National Basketball Association) suffers declining attendances and low television ratings and is kept afloat by money from the NBA (Blackistone 2003; Fisher 2003c).). At least three other women's sports leagues — in basketball, softball and bowling — have shut down since 1996 (Blackistone 2003; Fisher 2003c; Romano 2003). Market research indicates that both women and men are more interested in men's than women's sport (*The Hamilton Spectator*, 5 December 2002). However, the WUSA did spark women's interest in soccer: according to the league, 70 per cent of its fans were female, and young girls appreciated the female role models the league provided (*Pittsburgh Post-Gazette*, 15 June 2003). As one 12-year-old girl complained: 'Boys don't want to watch girls. Why should we have to watch boys?' (Jensen 2003)

Women's sports in the United States suffer from a vicious circle: sponsorship is dependent on television ratings (or the promise of future ratings), but there are so many men's sports on television that there is little room left for women (Bradley 2003: Blackistone 2003).

However, Americans love winners. They loved Brandi and Mia in 1999, and are justifiably proud that the US women have won two World Cups and the 2004 Olympic gold medal (Schultz 2004). The United States is one of the few countries in the world where the women's game is given as much respect as the men's. It remains to be seen whether the women's professional game will be able to make a comeback, and whether the new crop of players will become as famous as the players of 2001–03.

Acknowledgements

This study was supported by a Philadelphia University Research and Development Grant. I would like to thank Steven Wells and Patricia McDaniel for reading and commenting on earlier drafts of this chapter. Thanks also to the participants at the 'Fútbol, Futebol, Soccer? Football in the Americas' conference in London for their helpful suggestions.

Notes

1   To avoid confusion with American (gridiron) football, the accepted American terminology 'soccer' will be used in this paper. The paper relies extensively on press reports of the time; for the most part, these were accessed via Lexis/Nexis.

2   At last count, 19 million children in the United States aged six and older play soccer (Davis 2002; Fisher 2003a).

3   Salaries ranged from $25,000 to $85,000 per year (Weiner 2001).

15

Round Pegs in Square Holes?
The Adaptation of South American Players to the Premiership

Marcela Mora y Araujo

> This book is no use for playing football. It is only useful for knowing that books are no use for playing football. Only players are useful for that ... and sometimes not even them, if the circumstances don't help them. (Panzeri 2000)

Introduction

In this introductory remark to his seminal book about football tactics, first published in 1967, Dante Panzeri addresses the crucial importance of football players. It may seem an obvious statement, but it is true nevertheless. Following the phenomenal success of football as a consumer industry, the growth in broadcasting revenue and the rises in ticket prices that have taken place over the last 10 to 15 years, we are currently facing a scenario in which the top level of elite players have become celebrities of global proportions (Banks 2002). Their wage packets and transfer deals are permanently under scrutiny, their every move and sponsorship deal is subject to intense media exposure. In this context, the notion of professional footballers as workers has almost disappeared. However, their employers are dependent upon them for business survival and success. This chapter addresses the circumstances which surround elite players, particularly South American footballers playing in the United Kingdom, and the way in which they are treated by their employers, the Premier League clubs.

An incident involving Diego Maradona once provided the author with a reminder of how the footballer's role in the football industry can be forgotten. The incident took place at Stamford Bridge, home of Chelsea Football Club. We were to watch a game for which the sports goods company Puma had secured several thousand pounds' worth of corporate tickets. As soon as we entered the luxurious glass reception area to the VIP executive boxes, an usherette informed us that Mr Maradona was in breach of the dress code — a shirt and tie were required, but Maradona was wearing a t-shirt, jeans and trainers. Maradona did not receive the news well; he refused all offers of accommodation from various record companies and other advertisers who had their own private boxes where no formal dress code applied. At one point, he turned to me, furiously and said: 'What nobody here seems to understand is that all this,' and he waved his arm round denoting the luxurious reception and the well-dressed patrons, 'all this is possible thanks to the footballer. The footballer is the most important thing in the football business, and nobody recognises this.' There is some truth in that. Shortly after that incident, Maradona was in a hotel elevator in Spain and got stuck between two floors. He suffered an attack of claustrophobia which made world headlines because he smashed the place, and when he and his business manager Guillermo Coppola returned to Argentina a few days later, the latter was imprisoned for alleged cocaine possession. Maradona's life spiralled into a sordid tale of drug abuse involving hookers and corrupt judges. Countless column inches around the world ensued, analysing what had happened and what had gone wrong. Jorge Valdano is said to have commented at the time: 'Poor Diego. For so many years we have told him repeatedly you're a god, you're a leader, you're the best. And it seems we forgot to tell him the most important thing: "You're a man."'[1]

This anecdotal evidence serves to highlight the issues which arise in this chapter: the notion of footballers as the principal attraction of football, the athletes we pay to see and care to support, but also the notion that these footballers are people. They may earn a lot of money and enjoy the lifestyle and fame of rock stars, but when it comes to moving countries, settling into new communities and adapting to new cultures, they face the same problems as other migrant workers. To return to Panzeri's comment, the footballers are the ones who make the show of football the most popular game in the world, and if the circumstances are not appropriate, then their performance can and does suffer.

This chapter focuses on these circumstances in the hope of developing a better understanding of the factors that influence performance on the pitch — especially in England, and particularly with regard to South American players. Argentina and Brazil have traditionally been great exporters of footballers, and this trend does not look as though it is going to shift. In Europe, the main importers of players have always been Spain and Italy, where South American players enjoyed untarnished success throughout most of the last century. In England, in contrast, this has not been the case. In recent years, England has become more of a buyer, following the Bosman Ruling and the economic prosperity of the Premiership. However, whereas in Spain and Italy South American players have consistently ranked among the most successful players (as top goal-scorers, footballers of the year, and so on), in England even some of the most expensive internationals, such as Juan Sebastián Verón, have struggled to find a place in the starting line-up at their clubs.[2]

The reasons for this fall broadly into two categories: football-related factors and non-football-related factors. Each of these categories will be discussed briefly in the hope of establishing a broader field of inquiry in which to assess the performance of elite South American players in the Premiership. The evidence is drawn from extensive interviews with elite footballers, managers, agents and businessmen for newspaper articles over the past 12 years, and it suggests that the plight of the footballer away from home is far from easy. Does England present a harder environment for adaptation than other European countries?

In order to attempt to answer these questions, the first issue to be analysed will be the contrast between England and South America in styles and tactics — both on the pitch and in terms of training and dressing room preparation. It is possible that these differences prove difficult for foreign players to overcome. Second, the focus will turn to the cultural, linguistic and lifestyle differences which may affect a player's life outside his work. It is highly likely that the two factors are interrelated; the distinction into two categories is a convenient tool for organising the information rather than a claim that they should be considered as totally separate and independent. The conclusion will suggest that it is not an impossibility for South American footballers to succeed in the Premiership. Rather, footballers should be regarded as workers in a very particular industry. If the industry attempts to provide the circumstances for such players to adapt more easily, the players will perform better. This is possible, but it may prove to be a challenge for many English clubs.

The Contrast between England and Southern Europe

It is difficult to obtain exact figures for the number of professional South American players who play outside their home country, but a rough estimate by a journalist in Argentina in 2003 reckoned that around 700 first division players were currently working abroad (private communication). Figures for Brazil and Uruguay are likely to be similar. Most of these players will have migrated to other Latin American countries, with Mexico currently topping the list, but Spain is currently the most popular European destination. Indeed, Southern Europe has long been attractive territory for Latin American footballers. *The Economist* reported some 10 years ago that, out of 70 foreign footballers playing regularly in Italy's Serie A, 26 were South American. Tony Mason notes that between January 1980 and December 1993, out of a total of 2,509 players who left Argentina, 75 went to Asia, 537 to Europe and 1,863 to other Latin American countries, adding: 'Of these 90 per cent were attackers or creative midfield players, and these included the leading goal-scorer in every season.' (Mason 1995, p. 137)

This serves to illustrate how very proficient, in terms of football success, South American players tend to be in Italy and Spain. An EFE news wire from 1994 stated that: 'Out of 170 goals scored in Italy's *Serie A* [that season] 67 were the work of foreign players. Two Argentines topped the list: Batistuta with nine and Balbo with seven. At least five other South Americans were among the top ten.' Whereas some time ago it was unfathomable to 'imagine Italy without Batistuta', more recently players such as Hernán Crespo and Marcelo Salas have also ranked among the top scorers in the Italian league.

In Spain also, the title of *Pichichi* — which is awarded to the top goal-scorer in La Liga — has frequently been won by Latin American players. Alfredo Di Stéfano succeeded in winning it five times. Hugo Sánchez, who is still the highest goal-scorer in the Spanish league with 234 goals, was also *Pichichi* five times. Argentina's Mario Kempes won the *Pichichi* title twice. Iván Zamorano of Chile claimed the accolade in the 1994–95 season, following the Brazilians Bebeto and Romario, who had won it in the 1992–93 and 1993–94 seasons respectively.

A significant point is that, in the Spanish and Italian leagues, South American players have neither been a novelty, nor have they found it hard to adapt to their new environment. On the contrary, the contribution that players (and coaches) such as Di Stéfano and Helenio Herrera made earlier this century to the football of Spain and Italy respectively can be considered intertwined with the identity of the football of such countries.

In England, by contrast, South American players have been scarce and none has achieved anything like the success that their fellow countrymen have enjoyed on the continent. Although not the first Latin Americans in English football, Osvaldo Ardiles and Ricardo Villa have perhaps been the only ones to have made a name for themselves in English football, and the latter primarily because of one goal scored at the FA Cup Final in 1981. Other than this one moment of brilliance, Villa rarely even started most games. Ardiles is the only one who settled down beyond his playing years and went up the career ladder to enter management, but even his experience was not entirely happy. The Brazilian midfielder Juninho is perhaps a recent exception. He became a favourite at Middlesbrough in the mid-1990s. Nonetheless, the presence of South Americans in English football has not been anything like as noticeable as in the rest of Europe.

One obvious reason for this is, of course, the facility for South Americans to obtain Spanish and Italian passports as opposed to British ones. When Alfredo Di Stéfano first went to Spain, he was still an Argentine national, but following a ban on foreign players in both Spain and Italy, several players (including Di Stéfano) adopted the nationality of the country where they were playing, and then played for their new national sides. In Italy this phenomenon was known as *oriundi*, and it had the (perhaps) unexpected side-effect of players being recruited for military service. The ban had been imposed with the hope that local talent would be nurtured, but it did not work. Eventually a quota system for foreign players was introduced. In the Spanish League, no more than three foreign players could be fielded at any one time, for example. The number of foreigners that a team could field in European competitions was also limited by UEFA in the early 1990s.

The Bosman Ruling opened the gateway for South American players in Europe by applying European employment law to football and other sports. This meant that footballers from other European nations could no longer be considered 'foreign' in countries belonging to the European Union (thus outlawing the quotas that UEFA had imposed in its own competitions), and provided for freedom of movement for footballers — just as for any other worker — within the EU (Dabscheck 2004). In England, particularly, this led to an increase in South American imports, since footballers who would never have qualified for British nationality might qualify for an Italian or Spanish passport through their parents or grandparents, and thus be considered EU citizens. However, the United Kingdom retained work permit regulations for footballers who did not have an EU passport, even though the number of 'foreign' footballers in a team was no longer limited. These regulations included a demand that the footballer for whom the club was applying for a permit should have represented their country in at least three-quarters of the competitive internationals that it had played in the previous year.

Despite these restrictions, the Premiership has now become a very attractive option for South American players, and if we factor in the depression of the global transfer market in general since 2001 and the devaluation of South American currencies such as the Brazilian *real* or the Argentine *peso*, the English pound can go a long way for a South American club which sells a player. Some players such as Facundo Sava from Fulham or Luciano Figueroa (bought by Birmingham in the summer of 2003) rarely, if ever, started a game or even made it to the substitutes' bench. However, their seven-figure transfers, regarded as loose change in the Premiership, might allow their clubs of origin to survive for years.[3]

This sale of players to Europe is the lifeline of many Latin American clubs, which are often bankrupt. It is neither a new phenomenon, nor one which is likely to stop. Indeed, whereas in the

1978 World Cup Mario Kempes was the only member of the squad playing outside Argentina (in Valencia, Spain), by 2002 only one member of the national squad still played in Argentina, with all other members based abroad (the only Argentine-based player was Claudio Hussain). This suggests that in Argentina and Brazil, at least, the tendency is now for top talent to move to markets where wages are higher and the competition stronger.[4]

Football-related Factors

We are all familiar with the cliché that the English game is faster than Latin American football, consists of more long balls, and is characterised by power and speed. The South American player, whether an Argentine dribbler or a 'beautiful' Brazilian, is prone to have a more lingering relationship with the ball, and is able to perform more delicate skills with it.

Clichés are clichés because they are true. The notion of the South American child who plays football in the vacant lots of a city and finds a vehicle for self-expression with the ball underlies much of what we have come to regard as the typical South American style. Poverty and good weather have conspired to create the circumstances in which boys from a very young age relate to the ball in a wholly different way. In the first instance, the ball is the collective toy which every boy craves. The aim is to get hold of it and, once in possession, enjoy it as much as possible. Juan Sasturaín, the Argentine novelist and football writer, comments that even the name 'football' is wrong, because it isn't a game you play with your feet: it's a game you don't play with your hands. Thus the South American player, from his very origins, develops a feel for the ball whereby he can roll it upwards with his foot, flick it to his head, catch it with one shoulder, bounce it on his knee, and continue thus for an indefinite amount of time. It may be pushing the cliché too far, but it can be suggested that boy and ball enter a dance — a tango, a lambada — and that this desire to possess the ball and then enjoy it fully before passing it on remains into professionalism.

European football finds this style of playing with the ball a distraction which slows down the pace of an otherwise fast game.

In 2004 it was reported that Barcelona fans were complaining about Juan Román Riquelme, when he was with the club, on the grounds that he was too slow. An Argentine fan leapt to his defence: 'But he's had the ball for over five minutes!' Similarly, a range of tricks and specific skills which have actual names in Spanish seemingly have no translation into English. While the figurative term 'showboating' can be used to describe every one of these different actions in order to resolve this problem of translation, this illustrates perfectly the cultural contempt in one place for what is considered the mark of a superior player in the other.

The case of Juan Pablo Angel is revealing. Born in Colombia, his move to Aston Villa came from River Plate in Buenos Aires, and for this reason he can be considered an Argentine export (most South American players in Europe, regardless of country of origin, are transferred from Argentine or Brazilian clubs to which they have moved from their original youth teams). Angel arrived in Birmingham hailed as one of the top scorers in the Argentine league. He found it hard to settle, unable to find his level on the pitch, and he left critics wondering whether the purchase had been worth it. Although much of his turbulent adaptation period can be explained by what was going on in his life off the pitch (about which more later), perhaps the most telling explanation came from Boca Juniors' president, Mauricio Macri, who said in an interview: 'What do you expect? Here he's in the middle of those incredibly fast long balls flying in the air above his head and the guy comes from playing with Aimar and Saviola ...', and as he uttered these last words Macri wriggled his middle fingers in a physical illustration of the kind of detailed skill characteristic of these players.

The stylistic differences between England and Latin America — not just in the game itself but also in the approach to the game — spill over into the dressing room and training etiquette. Many South American players comment on the lack of encouragement from team-mates and the unforgiving nature of the team. They feel that individuality is frowned upon. With time, many have come to understand that what they at first saw as lack of encouragement is actually encouragement of a different sort. But the social and cultural subtleties are at odds with the Latin temperament, which is generally more literal and direct. Cristián Bassedas apparently lamented the lack of 'Vamos, Carajo!' from his peers at Newcastle United. This expression, difficult though it is to translate, essentially means 'C'mon!' with a mild swear word thrown in. It is very frequently employed in football and politics, denoting a belief that victory is achievable if everyone rolls up their sleeves.

The display of control over the ball which the South American player attempts when he gains possession is precisely what the local fans covet: delicate touches, back flicks, and so on make the terraces rise in admiration. The European game is less interested in the spectacle and more concerned with speed and potency. Individual displays of ability are of less interest to the fan than efficiency and effectiveness, and they are more likely to be regarded as selfish and fancy. This is true for Italy and Spain as well as England, but the cultural and linguistic barriers, among other extenuating factors, make the adaptation easier in the Southern European countries. It is these factors that now provide the focus of attention.

Non-football-related Factors

Once the playing is over, there is a whole range of other issues which the migrant worker, regardless of the industry in which the work is conducted, must address. In the first instance, language is the most daunting. Spanish (for the Portuguese-speaking Brazilians) and Italian are both easier to master, and certainly easier to understand upon first arrival. English is completely different from the South American footballer's native language, and the feeling of alienation for the newcomer can be overwhelmingly negative. In an interview shortly after he signed for Chelsea, Hernán Crespo commented: 'I can't work out how to connect my computer, and I don't even know who to call about it and how to ask for what.' This sense of being at a total loss is so at odds with how we have come to regard elite footballers that they are probably the least likely people to be offered help or assistance when they most need it.

One high-earning South American international asked a close friend: 'Have you any idea how horrible it is to sit in the changing rooms not saying anything?' Anyone who has ever been to a country where they do not speak the language will know the feeling, but because we do not think of elite athletes as 'normal' people, or we have increasingly come to think of them as surrounded by staff and assistants who take care of their every need, it comes as a surprise to everybody to know quite how vulnerable they can feel.

The language factor aside, Italian and Spanish cultures are more open, more welcoming and warmer than the English. For Argentines, even the food is similar. This may seem trivial, but the importance of dietary influence — particularly for the athlete — cannot be under-estimated. The weather also plays an important role — perhaps the darkness even more than the cold. Rome is colder, Claudio Canniggia's wife told me once over the phone from Glasgow in mid-January, but Italy and Spain have light even throughout the winter. The dark, short days — even without the rain — can make England more inhospitable for players who grew up practising their skills 'after five pm, when the sun's not so strong'.

The weather is more than just a talking point. On the pitch, the wet grass invites the faster game more characteristic of the Premiership. José Pekerman, who managed Argentina's national youth squads to several world titles before taking responsibility for the national team in the 2006 World Cup, once said to me only half-jokingly that he thought the differences in style between Argentine and English football were due to the weather. The wet grass means it is practically impossible to dribble and fiddle with the ball in the way that the dry earth of the *potrero* allows. And Nolberto Solano, the Peruvian imported by Newcastle United from Boca Juniors, also told me that he believed the dampness of the ground contributed noticeably to the speed of the ball and the need to keep it in the air as much as possible.

The weather, the food and the language are all part of the blurry concept of 'culture'. Cold climates drive people to earlier bedtimes, and also make alcohol a more acceptable part of social intercourse. After a year in Manchester, Diego Forlán commented that he rarely returned home before 2.00 a.m. when he lived in Buenos Aires. Yet his most likely activity until that time was probably drinking coffee or Coca-Cola and chatting with friends, or simply playing cards. English footballers who stay out until the early hours during the week would invariably be tarnished as 'stop-outs'. English pub culture is about drinking as much as possible in a short space of time. Endless pints of warm beer rarely appeal to South Americans, and the sheer volume of alcohol that is considered normal among British players often shocks and further alienates Latins who are used to spending the whole night sharing a *mate* and playing cards.[5]

These conditions often mean that the players become more prone to mixing with their compatriots, if they have any nearby, or to bringing over friends, relatives and agents (the latter often a mixture of the two former) to stay as often and for as long as possible. In this way, a vicious cycle begins. The player compensates for the difficulties in adapting by surrounding himself with a familiar entourage. This in turn means he is less likely to make an effort to adapt to the local customs. Wives become crucial as the essential link with the community around them. Some may speak a little English. They meet other mothers at schools and deal with local people on a regular basis when running the domestic side of their lives. However, other wives feel just as isolated as their husbands; they do not have a working command of the English language, and complain and transmit their unhappiness to their partners. 'We are nomads,' the former wife of Pedro Verde said to me once, referring to the way that daily life is planned around the career moves of the husband.

Increasingly, the way in which the transfer market operates and the pressures for everyone in the football business to maximise profits means that players might not know at midnight whether they will be moving country at 9.00 a.m. the following day. Yet each international transfer entails a man and often a whole family uprooting at short notice.[6] In most industries, workers who move between such radically different places would take months to prepare for such a move and, in the case of those who work for large multinational companies, be thoroughly helped and advised.

Once again, the case of Juan Pablo Angel serves to illustrate a point. When he first arrived at Aston Villa, it was obvious that he was not finding his form on the pitch. We all knew that his football performances were not living up to expectations. However, much less reported — indeed, not reported at all until much later — were the strenuous personal difficulties he was undergoing during this period. Shortly after arriving in Birmingham, Angel's wife was taken seriously ill and had to undergo surgery and remain as an in-patient in an intensive care unit. They had a newborn son, who was cared for by Angel. At night, he would sleep in an armchair by his wife's hospital bed, cradling the baby in his arms. He knew nobody in Birmingham, and had not yet managed to establish any new friendships to support or assist him in any way. When his wife recovered, and after he had met some Spanish speakers who lived locally, his performance on the pitch began to improve. In the early stages of his time at Villa, indeed, Angel's *de facto* personal assistant and interpreter was a Birmingham-born Latin American Studies graduate with whom he had become acquainted by chance meeting while staying at the hotel the club had arranged for him. This is neither surprising nor unusual. In the context of the cultural isolation in which these players function upon first arriving in England, they come to rely almost exclusively on chance encounters with people with whom they share a common background — however tenuous. Friendships are thus forged, no doubt some long-lasting and valuable, but nevertheless unlikely under any other circumstances. One footballer and his wife even asked an English-speaking friend to accompany them during delivery of their baby, so concerned were they that the language barrier would make giving birth an intolerably difficult process.

The Role of the Club

Army personnel are moved around on a scale similar to footballers. However, they are housed in barracks or camps where all the facilities are provided, and the Army at least assists them with most needs — even if they do not cater for them fully. Multinational organisations also often shift their staff around. Even the middle-ranking managers of a company (or the employees of a diplomatic service or international organisation at a similar level) would have more infrastructure available to them to ease the transition into a new environment and culture, let alone those on the salary levels of Premiership footballers, which range from perhaps a quarter of a million to several million pounds a year. Certainly they would have a secretary or personal assistant, they would be provided with mobile phones, they would probably have a company car or driver, and they would doubtless get assistance with health-care plans and schooling information. Most Premier League clubs provided none of this for their players, even in 2005. Some assisted with language teaching early on, but in the majority of cases even the issue of arranging or paying for the lessons has been left in the hands of the players themselves.

Increasingly, modern approaches to football management acknowledge the importance of non-football factors on the pitch. Middlesbrough employed a Brazilian woman full-time to aid its Brazilian players with things they might need, to send flowers to the wives, and so on. Sir Alex Ferguson is said to initially have hired Carlos Queiroz because he would be able to communicate with the foreign players. Manchester United also offered the translator whom they occasionally used for press conferences and tours a post as the club's official language teacher.

Clearly, the need for the social and cultural isolation to be overcome is shifting from being some 'namby pamby' side-issue that clubs can ignore to gradually being accepted as an important part of ensuring that what is normally a substantial investment becomes a success. Without wanting to sound as though South Americans would flourish in the Premiership if only their wives got sent some flowers, it is clear that if footballers were regarded more widely as highly skilled, and in some cases irreplaceable, workers then their performances would improve. They would be highly trained, extremely well-paid workers, but nonetheless workers who, if they were carrying out their activity in practically any other industry, would be privy to a level of aid and assistance to which they simply do not have access in football. Footballers' status as 'stars' or celebrities probably works against them in this instance, but that does not diminish the need for the clubs to take on the responsibility as employers and ensure that the cultural transition is given as much importance as the footballing one — and both should be credited with being harder than we like to think.

Issues such as what players like to drink and how they like to spend their leisure time go right to the heart of team bonding. In most countries, players gather the night before every game, spending the night in what is known in Spanish America as *la concentración* (the 'concentration'). England is one of the few countries where this does not happen frequently. Players enjoy the freedom of simply arriving at the stadium two hours before a home game, and for the older players and those with families this is a welcome change from spending two to three nights a week sharing rooms under curfew like schoolboys. However, it does mean less opportunity for team bonding, and makes developing relationships beyond football difficult. Hernán Crespo again provides us with another example to illustrate this point. He mentioned in an interview that one of the things he was finding particularly hard at Chelsea was the inability to chat with team-mates in the dressing room: 'I need to joke around, to ask about their lives … I like to know if they have kids, if they've studied … the last thing you're likely to talk about is football.' Clearly, players work better together the better they know each other.

Conclusion

Cultural differences, language difficulties and differences in style of play all conspire to make it hard for South Americans who arrive in the English game to adapt. This paper has outlined some general traits, but it must also be pointed out that, in the real world, modern football is departing slightly from the clichés. Specifically, the South American leagues are becoming increasingly fast and competitive, while England is seeing an emergence of skilful players who could match the *potrero* talents. In England, more and more clubs are seeking to administer and manage themselves as businesses. Those which are listed on the stock market have a duty to their shareholders to maximise profits and returns on investment. Meanwhile, in South America, club football faces financial turmoil, and efforts to modernise the way football is managed increasingly point to emulating the first world as the best option. This reinforces the need to sell players. There is no indication that the export of talent from South America to Europe will diminish, and while the Premiership continues to be the richest league in Europe it will remain among the most tempting — if not *the* most tempting — of markets. The football and non-football differences between South America and England make the task of adaptation all the more difficult for the individuals who have to 'endure' it. It is not impossible, though. It is difficult: a radical shift in attitude (from players and clubs, and so on) is needed before we will be able to see the emergence of a Batistuta in the Premiership. However, English football can be enriched tremendously by the growing presence of South American talent, and the South American players can get a lot out of the experience as well.

Until recently, we have tended to consider factors affecting players' well-being, their personal circumstances, the life they lead 'outside' football, as the domain of gossip or irrelevant secondary issues. Only tactics and technical talk were regarded as the valid domain for pursuing footballing excellence. A truly modern football industry should increasingly understand that the importance of such apparently 'secondary' matters is directly relevant to what happens on the pitch, and that it is in the interests of the business, the industry and the spectacle itself to ensure that these issues are taken more seriously, and that better formal structures are set in place in order to provide these highly paid workers with a more suitable environment in which to nurture their professional capabilities. We are probably still a long way from having psychological support in the way of counselling, but increasingly managers seek players who are both talented athletes and have the spirit to adapt to the local environment.

In short, only footballers are useful for playing football — and sometimes not even then if the circumstances do not facilitate it. However, much can be done to ensure that the circumstances are as helpful as possible, and English football has a long way to go in that respect.

Acknowledgements

I am indebted to a number of people for their advice when preparing this chapter: Sheryl Campbell, Lola Carrasco, Liz Crolley, Klaus Gallo, Patrick Harverson, Hernán Crespo, Nolberto Solano, Facundo Sava, Jorge Valdano, Juan Sebastián Verón. And to all professional footballers everywhere: the life and soul of the industry.

Notes

1   This quotation has been repeated frequently. For one instance, see Martin Amis's review of Maradona's autobiography, *El Diego*, in *The Guardian*, 31 October 2004.

2   Transferred from Lazio in Italy, Juan Sebastián Verón started 24 out of 38 league matches in his first season, 2001–02. The following season he started 21. Transferred to Chelsea, he started five matches in his first season, 2003–04, but was loaned to Inter Milan the following season, following three unsuccessful campaigns in England.

3   Sava was transferred from Gimnasia y Esgrima of La Plata, Figueroa from Rosario Central.

4   In the 2006 World Cup, three of the Argentine squad, including two of the goalkeepers, still played in Argentina. The comparable figure for Brazil was two, again including a goalkeeper. In contrast, only three of the Mexican squad played outside the country. For the lists of players and the clubs with whom they were registered, see <http://worldsoccer.about.com/b/a/257622.htm>. A development reflecting this tendency is that international friendly matches involving South American sides now often take place in Europe in order to reduce the demands on players to travel — for example, the Brazil v Argentina friendly at the new Emirates stadium in London in September 2006.

5   *Mate* is a form of tea, a hot beverage common in the Rover Plate countries, which is normally drunk from a gourd passed around among friends: to share a *mate* symbolises acceptance and friendship.

6   The global adoption of two transfer 'windows' a year following the introduction of new international transfer regulations by FIFA in 2001 has made last-minute dealing even more frenetic. A good example is the sudden transfer of the Argentines Carlos Tévez and Javier Mascherano from Corinthians in São Paulo to West Ham United in London on the last day of the transfer window in August 2006. The Brazilian player, Julio Baptista, arrived at Arsenal from Real Madrid the same day.

Bibliography

Abrams, N.D. (1995) 'Inhibited but not "Crowded Out": the Strange Fate of Soccer in the United States,' *International Journal of the History of Sport*, vol. 12, no. 3, pp. 1–16.

Aidar, A.C.K. and Pereira Leoncini, M. (2000) 'As leis econômicas e o futebol: a estrutura do novo negócio,' in A.C.K. Aidar, M. Pereira Leoncini and J.J. de Oliveira, *A nova gestão do futebol* (São Paulo: FGV), pp. 77–96.

Aidar, A.C.K., Leoncini, M.P. and de Oliveira, J.J. (2000) *A nova gestão do futebol* (São Paulo: Fundacão Getúlio Vargas).

Alabarces, P. (2002) *Fútbol y patria. El fútbol y las narrativas de la nación en la Argentina* (Buenos Aires: Prometeo, Libros de Confrontación).

Alabarces, P. (2004) 'Entre la banalidad y la crítica: perspectivas de las ciencias sociales sobre el deporte en América Latina,' *Memoria y civilización*, no. 7, pp. 39–77.

Alabarces, P. (ed.) (2000) *Peligro de gol: estudios sobre deporte y sociedad en América Latina* (Buenos Aires: CLACSO).

Alabarces, P. (ed.) (2003) *Futbologías: fútbol, identidad y violencia en América Latina* (Buenos Aires: CLACSO).

Alabarces, P., Coelho, R. and Sanguinetti, J. (2001) 'Treacheries and Traditions in Argentinian Football Styles,' in G. Armstrong and R. Giulianotti (eds.), *Fear and Loathing in World Football* (Oxford: Berg).

Alabarces, P. et al. (2005) *Hinchadas* (Buenos Aires: Prometeo Libros).

Alabarces, P., Coelho, R., et al. (2000) '"Aguante" y represión: fútbol, violencia y política en la Argentina,' in P. Alabarces (ed.), *Peligro de gol: estudios sobre deporte y sociedad en América Latina* (Buenos Aires: CLACSO-ASDI).

Álvarez, G. (2001) *La difusión del fútbol en Lima* (Lima: Universidad Nacional de San Marcos, Tesis de Licenciatura).

Anderson, B. (1983) *Imagined Communities: Reflections on the Origin and Spread of Nationalism* (London: Verso).

Andrews, D.L. et al. (1997) 'Soccer's Racial Frontier: Sport and the Suburbanization of Contemporary America,' in G. Armstrong and R. Giulianotti (eds.), *Entering the Field: New Perspectives on World Football* (Oxford: Berg), pp. 261–82.

Appadurai, A. (1996) *Modernity at Large: Cultural Dimensions of Globalization* (Minneapolis: University of Minnesota Press).

Arbena, J.L. (1990) 'Generals and *Goles*: Assessing the Connection between the Military and Soccer in Argentina,' *International Journal of the History of Sport*, vol. 7, no. 1, pp. 120–30.

Archetti, E. (1992) 'Argentine Football: A Ritual of Violence?' *International Journal of the History of Sport*, vol. 9, no. 2, pp. 209–35.

Archetti, E. (1994a) 'Masculinity and Football: The Formation of National Identity in Argentina,' in R. Giulianotti and J. Williams (eds.), *Game Without Frontiers: Football, Identity and Modernity* (Aldershot: Arena).

Archetti, E. (1994b) 'The Moralities of Argentine Football,' paper presented at the Third European Association of Social Anthropologists Conference, Oslo.

Archetti, E. (1994c) 'Argentina and the World Cup: In Search of National Identity,' in J. Sugden and E. Tomlinson (eds.), *Hosts and Champions: Soccer Cultures, National Identities and the USA World Cup* (Aldershot: Arena).

Archetti, E. (1995a) 'Estilo y virtudes masculinas en *El Gráfico*: la creación del imaginario del fútbol argentino,' *Desarrollo Económico*, vol. 35, no. 139, pp. 419–41.

Archetti, E. (1995b) 'In Search of National Identity: Argentinian Football and Europe,' *International Journal of the History of Sport*, vol. 12, no. 2, pp. 201–19.

Archetti, E. (1997) '"And Give Joy to my Heart": Ideology and Emotions in the Argentinian Cult of Maradona,' in G. Armstrong and R. Giulianotti (eds.), *Entering the Field: New Perspectives on World Football* (Oxford: Berg), pp. 31–52.

Archetti, E. (1998a) 'The Meaning of Sport in Anthropology: A View from Latin America', *European Review of Latin American and Caribbean Studies*, no. 65, pp. 91–103.

Archetti, E.P. (1998b) 'The *Potrero* and the *Pibe*: Territory and Belonging in the Mythical Account of Argentinian Football,' in N. Lovell (ed.), *Locality and Belonging* (London: Routledge).

Archetti, E.P. (1999) *Masculinities: Football, Polo, and the Tango in Argentina* (Oxford: Berg).

Archetti, E.P. (2003) 'Playing Football and Dancing Tango: Embodying Argentina in Movement, Style and Identity,' in N. Dyck and E.P. Archetti (eds.), *Sport, Dance and Embodied Identities* (Oxford: Berg).

Archetti, E. and Romero, A. (1994) 'Death and Violence in Argentinian Football,' in R. Giulianotti and J. Williams (eds.), *Game Without Frontiers: Football, Identity and Modernity* (Aldershot: Arena).

Arguedas, J.M. (1998 [1958]) *Los ríos profundos* (Madrid: Cátedra).

Associated Press (2004a) 'WUSA Begins Ticket Drive to Fund Planned Return,' 16 February.

Associated Press (2004b) 'Spirit 2, Courage 1; Charge 2, CyberRays 0,' 27 June.

Associated Press (2004c) 'More Modest Business Plan Could Relaunch WUSA: Potential Investors Hope to Revive Women's Pro Soccer by 2006,' 22 July.

Auyero, J. (2006) 'The Political Makings of the 2001 Lootings in Argentina,' *Journal of Latin American Studies*, vol. 38, no. 2, pp. 241–65.

Bakhtin, M. (1984) *Rabelais and His World* (Bloomington, IN: Indiana University Press).

Bale, J. and Maguire, J. (eds.) (1994) *The Global Sports Arena: Athletic Talent Migration in an Interdependent World* (London: Cass).

Ballard, C. (2001) 'Kick Wanted,' *Sports Illustrated,* no. 94, p. 20 (14 May).

Banks, S. (2002) *Going Down: Football in Crisis* (Edinburgh: Mainstream).

Bar-On, T. (1997) 'The Ambiguities of Football, Politics, Culture and Social Transformation in Latin America,' *Sociological Research Online*, vol. 2, no. 4, <www.socresonline.org.uk/2/4/2.html>.

Bayer, O. (1990) *Fútbol argentino* (Buenos Aires: Editorial Sudamericana).

Beck, U. (2000) *What is Globalisation?* (Cambridge: Polity).

Bedoya, R. (1997) *Un cine reencontrado: diccionario ilustrado de las películas peruanas* (Lima: Universidad de Lima).

Belli, C.G. (1979) *En alabanza del bolo alimenticio* (Mexico City: Premià).

Bellos, A. (2002) *Futebol: The Brazilian Way of Life* (London: Bloomsbury).

Benavides, M. (2000) *Una pelota de trapo, un corazón blanquiazul* (Lima: Fondo Editorial de la Pontificia Universidad Católica del Perú).

Berkowitz, S. (2003) 'WUSA Asks Federation for Commitment,' *USA Today,* 22 August.

Blackistone, K. (2003) 'Women's Pro League's No Hit in the Marketplace,' *Pittsburgh Post-Gazette,* 18 September.

Bourdieu, P. (1984) *Distinction: A Social Critique of the Judgement of Taste* (London: Routledge).

Bradley, M. (2003) 'Noble Effort, Too Few Buyers,' *Atlanta Journal and Constitution,* 16 September.

Brewster, K. (2005) 'Patriotic Pastimes: The Role of Sport in Post-Revolutionary Mexico,' *International Journal of the History of Sport*, vol. 22, no. 2, pp. 139–57.

Brick, C. (2001) 'Can't Live With Them, Can't Live Without Them,' in G. Armstrong and R. Giulianotti (eds.), *Fear and Loathing in World Football* (Oxford: Berg), pp. 9–21.

Bryce Echenique, A. (1990 [1968]) *Huerto cerrado* (Barcelona: Plaza & Janés).

Bryce Echenique, A. (1993 [1970]) *Un mundo para Julius* (Madrid: Cátedra).

Buarque de Hollanda, B.B. (2003) 'O descobrimento do futebol: modernismo, regionalismo e paixão esportiva em José Lins do Rego,' Programa de Pós-Graduação em História Social da Cultura, Pontifícia Universidade Católica (PUC-RJ).

Burns, J. (1996). *Hand of God: The Life of Diego Maradona* (London: Bloomsbury).

Business Wire (2001) 'WUSA Signs Television Agreement with PAX TV; Paxson Corporation Becomes Official Sponsor; 22 WUSA Games are Scheduled for PAX TV During 2002 Season,' 18 December.

Cain, L.P. and Haddock, D.D (2005) 'Similar Economic Histories, Different Industrial Structures: Transatlantic Contrasts in the Evolution of Professional Sports Leagues,' *Journal of Economic History*, vol. 65, no. 4, pp. 1116–47.

Caldeira, J. (2002) *Ronaldo: glória e drama no futebol globalizado* (São Paulo: Editora 34).

Cardoso, F.H. (1972) 'Dependency and Development in Latin America,' *New Left Review*, no. 84, pp. 83–95.

Carlisle, J. (2005) 'Antonucci Lays the Groundwork,' *ESPN Soccernet*, 20 March, <http://soccernet.espn.go.com/columns/story?id=328319&root=wusa&cc=5901>.

Carranza, M.E. (2005) 'Poster Child or Victim of Imperialist Globalization? Explaining Argentina's December 2001 Political Crisis and Economic Collapse,' *Latin American Perspectives*, vol. 32, no. 6, pp. 65–89.

Cashmore, E.E. (1984) 'Review of Janet Lever, *Soccer Madness,*' *American Journal of Sociology*, vol. 90, no. 3, pp. 683–84.

Casual Auditores Independentes (2006a) *Auditoria e Negócios no Futebol* (São Paulo: Casual Auditores).

Casual Auditores Independentes (2006b) *Results of the Casual List of Brazilian Football Clubs*, <www.footballeconomy.com/stats/casual_brazil_football.pdf>.

Chapin, D. (2000) 'New League, Familiar Faces: WUSA Hope to Capitalize on US Team Members' Popularity,' *San Francisco Chronicle*, 3 December.

Chung, J. (2003) Personal communication, July.

Cicalese, L. Curto, M. and Presman, B. (2002) *Fútbol, identidad nacional y hegemonía en una Argentina global: Mundial Corea-Japón 2002* (Buenos Aires: Mimeo).

Clark, G. and O'Connor, K. (1997) 'The Informational Content of Financial Products and the Spatial Structure of the Global Finance Industry,' in K. Cox (ed.), *Spaces of Globalization: Reasserting the Power of the Local* (London: Guilford).

Collins, S. (2006) 'National Sports and Other Myths: The Failure of US Soccer,' *Soccer and Society*, vol. 7, nos. 2–3, pp. 353–63.

Confederação Brasileira de Futebol website, www.cbf.com.br.

Conn, D. (1997) *The Football Business: Fair Game in the '90s?* (Edinburgh: Mainstream).

Conn, D. (2004) *The Beautiful Game? Searching for the Soul of Football* (London: Yellow Jersey).

Corsino, L. (1984). 'Review of Janet Lever, *Soccer Madness,*' *Sociology and Social Research*, vol. 68, no. 4, pp. 527–28.

Crolley, L. and Duke, V. (2001) '*Fútbol*, Politicians and the People: Populism and Politics in Argentina,' in J.A. Mangan and L. Da Costa (eds.), *Sport in Latin American Society: Past and Present* (London: Frank Cass).

Cueto, M. (1982) *La reforma universitaria de 1919: universidad y estudiantes a comienzos de siglo* (Lima: Pontificia Universidad Católica del Perú, Tesis de Bachiller en Historia).

Da Matta, R. (ed.) (1982) *O universo do futebol: esporte e sociedade brasileiro* (Rio de Janeiro: Pinakotheke).

Dabscheck, B. (2004) 'The Globe at their Feet: FIFA's New Employment Rules I,' *Sport in Society*, vol. 7, no. 1, pp. 69–94.

Davis, K. (2002) 'Not Just for Kicks,' *Kiplinger's Personal Finance,* no. 56, p. 7.

Degregori, C.I. (1994) 'Dimensión cultural de la experiencia migratoria,' *Páginas,* no. 130, pp. 18–29.

Delgado, F. (1999) 'Major League Soccer, Constitution and [the] Latino Audience(s),' *Journal of Sport and Social Issues*, vol. 23, no. 1, pp. 41–54.

Dell'Appa, F. (2003) 'On Soccer: Problems Were Sizable — WUSA's Plans May Have Been Too Big,' *The Boston Globe,* 16 September.

Deloitte & Touche (2002) *Annual Review of Football Finance 2002* (Manchester: Deloitte & Touche).

Deloitte & Touche (2002) *World Football 'Rich List' 2002* (Manchester: Deloitte & Touche).

Deloitte & Touche (2006) *Annual Review of Football Finance 2006: All Eyes on Europe* (Manchester: Deloitte & Touche).

Deloitte & Touche (2006) *Football Money League 2006: Changing of the Guard* (Manchester: Deloitte & Touche), available from <www.deloitte.com/dtt/article/0,1002,sid%253D70402%252 6cid%253D73888,00.html>.

Deustua Carvallo, J., Stein, S. and Stokes, S. (1986) 'Entre el offside y el chimpún: las clases populares limeñas y el fútbol, 1900–1930,' in S. Stein (ed.), *Lima obrera 1900–1930, Vol. 1* (Lima: El Virrey), pp. 119–62.

Diez Canseco, J. (1973 [1934]) *Duque* (Lima: Peisa).

Duke, V. and Crolley, L. (1996a) (1996) *Football, Nationality and the State* (London: Longman).

Duke, V. and Crolley, L. (1996b) 'Football Spectator Behaviour in Argentina: a Case of Separate Evolution,' *Sociological Review*, vol. 44, no. 2, pp. 272–93.

Duke, V. and Crolley, L. (2001) '*Fútbol*, Politicians and the People: Populism and Politics in Argentina', *International Journal of the History of Sport*, vol. 18, no. 3, pp. 93–116.

Escobar, A. (1994) *Encountering Development: the Making and Unmaking of the Third World* (Princeton: Princeton University Press).

Fábregas Puig, A. (2001) *Lo sagrado del Rebaño: el fútbol como integrador de identidades* (Zapopan, Jalisco: El Colegio de Jalisco).

Fisher, E. (2002) 'Many Empty Seats, a \$40 Million Loss and an Unable Mia,' *Washington Times*, 19 July.

Fisher, E. (2003a) 'Still Kicking: MLS, WUSA Upbeat Despite Trouble,' *Washington Times*, 5 April.

Fisher, E. (2003b) 'Waning Interest: Small Crowds, Ratings Leave WUSA Gasping,' *Washington Times*, 19 August.

Fisher, E. (2003c) 'A Bare Market: Women's Pro Sports Find the Going Tough,' *Washington Times*, 17 September.

Fiske, J. (1993) *Power Plays, Power Works* (London and New York: Verso).

Flores Galindo, A. (1994) 'Nuevos caminos de la praxis: los orígenes del movimiento obrero,' in *Alberto Flores Galindo: Obras Completas, Vol. 2* (Lima: SER), pp. 233–50.

Fox, J. (1994) 'The Difficult Transition from Clientelism to Citizenship: Lessons from Mexico,' *World Politics*, vol. 46, no. 2, pp. 151–84.

Frank, A.G. (1971 [1967]) *Capitalism and Underdevelopment in Latin America* (New York: Monthly Review Press).

Frank, A.G. (1969) *Latin America: Underdevelopment or Revolution* (New York: Monthly Review Press).

Freyre, G. (1943) *Sociología* (Rio de Janeiro: José Olimpio).

Freyre, G. (1964) 'O negro no futebol brasileiro,' in M. Filho (ed.) *O negro no futebol brasileiro* (Rio de Janeiro: Civilização Brasileira).

Friedman, J. (1994) *Cultural Identity and Global Process* (London: Sage).

Frydenburg, J. (2001) 'La crisis de la tradición y el modelo asociacionista en los clubes de fútbol argentinos,' *Revista Digital*, vol. 6, no. 29, <www.efdeportes.com>.

Furlong, J. (2003) 'WUSA on Bumpy Financial Ride. Founding Players Take Pay Cuts, Projected Break-Even Season Pushed to 2007,' *The Herald-Sun*, 13 May.

Galeano, E. (1996) *El fútbol a sol y sombra* (Santiago: Pehuén).

García Canclini, N. (1994) *Consumidores y ciudadanos: conflictos multiculturales de la globalización* (México: Grijalbo).

García Canclini, N. (1995) *Hybrid Cultures: Strategies for Entering and Leaving Modernity* (Minneapolis: Minnesota University Press).

Gargurevich, J. (1987) *Prensa, radio y TV: historia crítica* (Lima: Horizonte).

Gebauer, G. (1999) 'Les trois dates de l'équipe d'Allemagne de football,' *Les cahiers de l'INSEP*, no. 25, pp. 101–11.

Gerencia Deportiva (2001) *Estrategias de Sport Management and Marketing como negocios rentables: caso fútbol argentino*, Buenos Aires, www.deporteynegocios/gerencia/seguridad/futbol_argentino.asp

Ghersi, E. (2003) 'Barras bravas, teoría económica, y el fútbol,' *Estudios Públicos*, vol. 90, pp. 29–45.

Gil, G.J. (2000) 'Monopolio televisivo y "gerenciamiento": el fútbol como mercancía,' *Revista Digital*, vol. 5, no. 26, www.efdeportes.com.ar.

Gil, G.J. (2002) 'Las fundaciones emocionales del fútbol argentino,' *Revista Digital*, vol. 7, no. 55, www.efdeportes.com.ar.

Gilbert, A. (1998) *The Latin American City* (London: Latin America Bureau).

Giulianotti, R. (1995) 'Football and the Politics of Carnival: An Ethnographic Study of Scottish Fans in Sweden,' *International Review for the Sociology of Sport* vol. 30, no. 2, pp. 191–224.

Giulianotti, R. (1999a) 'Built by the Two Varelas: The Rise and Fall of Football Culture and National Identity in Uruguay', *Culture, Sport, Society*, vol. 2, no. 3, pp. 134–54.

Giulianotti, R. (1999b) *Football: A Sociology of the Global Game* (Oxford: Polity Press).

Glanville, B. and Weinstein, J. (1958) *World Cup* (London: Robert Hale).

Gleizer, M. (1997) *Identidad, subjetividad y sentido en las sociedades complejas* (México: FLACSO).

Goldblatt, D. (2002) *World Football Yearbook, 2002–03* (London: Dorling and Kindersley).

Goldemberg, I. (1984) *Tiempo al tiempo* (Hanover, NH: Ediciones del Norte).

González Prada, M. (1976 [1894]) *Pájinas libres. Horas de lucha* (Caracas: Biblioteca Ayacucho).

Goos, H. (2006) 'Secrets of Success,' *Der Spiegel*, Special International Edition no. 2, pp. 106–09.

Gordon, C. and Helal, R. (2001) 'The Crisis of Brazilian Football: Perspectives for the Twenty-First Century', *International Journal for the History of Sport*, vol. 18, no. 3, pp. 139–58.

Govea, M. (2002) 'Las empresas juegan con todo al Mundial,' *Clarín Económico*, no. 26, May.

Grenier, Y. (2001) *From Art to Politics: Octavio Paz and the Pursuit of Freedom* (Boston: Rowman and Littlefield).

Guedes, S. (1998) *O Brasil no campo de futebol: estudos antropológicos sobre os significados do futebol brasileiro* (Niterói: Editora da UFF).

Guedes, S. (2000) 'Malandros, Caxias e estrangeiros no futebol: de heróis e anti-heróis,' in L.G. Gomes, L. Barbosa & J.A. Drummond (eds.), *O Brasil não é para principiantes; Carnavais,*

Malandros e Heróis 20 anos depois (Rio de Janeiro: Editora FGV), pp. 125–42.

Gunther, M. (2001) 'Women's Soccer League will have Trouble Scoring,' *Fortune*, 16 April.

Hall, S. (1984) 'Notas sobre la deconstrucción de lo popular,' in R. Samuels (ed.), *Historia popular y teoría socialista* (Barcelona: Crítica).

Halliday, F. (2002), 'The Pertinence of Imperialism,' in M. Rupert and H. Smith (eds.), *Historical Materialism and Globalization* (London: Routledge).

Hamelink, C.J. (1983) *Cultural Autonomy in Global Communications: Planning National Information Policy* (New York: Longman).

Hamilton, A. (2001) *Um jogo inteiramente diferente! Futebol: a maestria brasileira de um legado britânico* (Rio de Janeiro: Gryphus).

Hancock, M. (ed.) (2006) *World Cup 2006* (*Guardian* Newspaper supplement June).

Hannerz, U. (1989) 'Notes on the Global Ecumene,' *Public Culture*, vol. 1, no. 2, pp. 66–75.

Hannerz, U. (1992) *Cultural Complexity: Studies in the Social Organization of Meaning* (New York: Columbia University Press).

Harvard Business School, *Real Madrid Club de Fútbol*, Case Study N9-504-063, 13 May 2004 (Boston: Harvard Business School).

Held, D., McGrew, A., Goldblatt, D. and Perraton, D. (1999) *Global Transformations: Politics, Economics and Culture* (Oxford: Polity Press).

Hobsbawm, E.J. and Ranger, T.O. (eds.) (1983) *The Invention of Tradition* (Cambridge: Cambridge University Press).

Howard, J. (2002) 'PAX Pact Doesn't Meet WUSA's Goals,' *Newsday*, 7 April.

Howard, J. (2003) 'WUSA the Epilogue: Lack of Television Insight is No. 1 Reason League is on the Shelf,' *Newsday*, 12 October.

Hoy, M. (1994) 'Joyful Mayhem: Bakhtin, Football Songs, and the Carnivalesque,' *Text and Performance Quarterly*, no. 14, pp. 289–304.

Humphrey, J. and Tomlinson, A. (1986) 'Reflections on Brazilian Football: A Review and Critique of Janet Lever's *Soccer Madness*,' *Bulletin of Latin American Research*, vol. 5, no. 1, pp. 101–08.

Issenberg, S. (2003) 'Sister, Can You Spare a Dime?' *Philadelphia Magazine,* June.

Jackson, J. (2006) 'Profile: Pini Zahavi — Football's First and Only Super-Agent,' *Observer Sports Monthly*, 26 November.

James, S. (2006) 'U.S. Women's League Can Rise Again, Says Foudy,' *The Guardian,* 26 July.

Jenkins, G. (1998) *The Beautiful Team: In Search of Pelé and the 1970 Brazilians* (London: Simon & Schuster).

Jenkins, R. (1996) *Social Identity* (London: Routledge).

Jensen, M. (2003) 'Young WUSA Fans Get Kick to the Heart,' *Philly.com,* 21 September, <www.philly.com>.

Jones, J. (2002) 'An Uphill Battle,' *Chicago Sun-Times,* 3 June.

Karush, M.B. (2003). 'National Identity in the Sports Pages: Football and the Mass Media in 1920s Buenos Aires,' *The Americas*, vol. 60, no. 1, pp. 11–32.

Kay, C. (1989) *Latin American Theories of Development and Underdevelopment* (London: Routledge).

Kollman, R. (2002) 'El festejo es algo seguro para dos de cada tres,' *Página 12*, 1 June 2002.

Kramer, J. (2006) 'The Grass is Greener at Home,' *Der Spiegel,* Special International Edition no. 2, pp. 56–59.

Kuper, S. (1996) *Football against the Enemy* (London: Phoenix).

Lanfranchi, P. (1994) 'Exporting Football: Notes on the Development of Football in Europe,' in R. Giulianotti and J.

Williams (eds.), *Game Without Frontiers: Football, Identity and Modernity* (Aldershot: Arena).

Lanfranchi, P. and Taylor, M. (2001) *Moving with the Ball: the Migration of Professional Footballers* (Oxford and New York: Berg).

Latouche, S. (1996) *The Westernization of the World: The Significance, Scope, and the Limits of the Drive Towards Global Uniformity* (Cambridge: Polity).

Leite Lopes, J.S. (1997) 'Successes and Contradictions in "Multiracial" Brazilian Football,' in G. Armstrong and R. Giulianotti (eds.), *Entering the Field: New Perspectives on World Football* (Oxford: Berg), pp. 53–86.

Leite Lopes, J.S. (1999a) 'The Brazilian Style of Football and Its Dilemmas,' in G. Armstrong and R. Giulianotti (eds.), *Football Cultures and Identities* (London: Macmillan), pp. 86–98.

Leite Lopes, J.S and Faguer, J-P. (1999b) 'Considerações em torno das transformações do profissionalismo no futebol a partir da observação da copa de 1998,' *Estudos Históricos* no. 23, <www.cpdoc.fgv.br/revista/asp/dsp_edicao.asp?cd_edi=41>.

Lever, J. (1983) *Soccer Madness: Brazil's Passion for the World's Most Popular Sport* (Chicago: University of Chicago Press).

Lever, J. (1988) 'Sport in a Fractured Society: Brazil under Military Rule,' in J.L. Arbena (ed.), *Sport and Society in Latin America: Diffusion, Dependency, and the Rise of Mass Culture* (Westport, CN: Greenwood), pp. 85–96.

Levine, R.M. (1980) 'Sport and Society: The Case of Brazilian Futebol,' *Luso-Brazilian Review*, vol. 17, no. 2, pp. 233–51.

Levinsky, S. (1995) *El negocio del fútbol* (Buenos Aires: Corregidor).

Levinsky, S. (2003) Personal communication, June.

Liebeskind, K. (2001) 'Women's Soccer Takes Shot at Pros,' *Advertising Age*, vol. 72, no. 16, 16 April.

Lisovicz, S. (2001) 'Women's Soccer, CNNfn,' *Transcript of CNN Interview with Barbara Allen on Business Unusual*, 30 August, online at *Lexis-Nexis*.

Lomnitz, L. (1982) 'Horizontal and Vertical Relations and the Social Structure of Urban Mexico,' *Latin American Research Review*, vol. 17, no. 2, pp. 51–74.

Longman, J. (1999) 'Pride in Their Play, and in Their Bodies,' *New York Times*, 8 July.

Longman, J. (2003a) 'Women's Soccer League Folds on Eve of World Cup,' *New York Times Online*, 16 September.

Longman, J. (2003b) 'Backtalk; Miscasting WUSA's Target Audience,' *New York Times*, 28 September.

Lyra Filho, J. (1954) *Taça do Mundo 1954* (Rio de Janeiro: Irmãos Pongetti).

Mahoney, R. (2004) 'Weekend Doubleheader Key to Potential Revival of WUSA,' *USA Today*, 25 June.

Malca, O. (2000 [1993]) *Al final de la calle* (Lima: Libros de Desvío).

Marcuse, H. (1964) *One Dimensional Man: Studies in the Ideology of Advanced Industrial Society* (London: Ark).

Markovits, A.S. (1990) 'The Other "American Exceptionalism": Why is There No Soccer in the United States?,' *International Journal of the History of Sport*, vol. 7, no. 2, pp. 230–64.

Markovits, A.S. and Hellerman, S.L. (2003) 'Women's Soccer in the United States: Yet Another American "Exceptionalism",' *Soccer and Society*, vol. 4, nos. 2–3, pp. 14–29.

Mason, T. (1995) *Passion of the People? Football in South America* (London: Verso).

McHugh, E. (2003) 'WUSA Hopes Less Now will Add Up to More Later,' *Patriot Ledger*, 5 April.

McHugh, E. (2004) 'Campaign to Save Women's Soccer League Under Way,' *Patriot Ledger*, 21 February.

Melo, L.M.O. (2002), 'Esporte como fator dinâmico da indústria do entretenimento,' in Fábio Sá Earp et al. (eds.), *Pão e Circo: fronteiras e perspectivas da economia do entretenimento* (Rio de Janeiro: Palavra e Imagem).

Mike, H. (2005) 'Pro Women's Soccer Looking to Return in 2007,' *My Soccer Blog*. 15 January, <http://mysoccerblog. blogspot.com/2006_01_15_mysoccerblog_archive.html>.

Miller, R. (1993) *Britain and Latin America in the Nineteenth and Twentieth Centuries* (London: Longman).

Millones, L., Panfichi, A. and Vich, V. (2002) *En el corazón del pueblo: pasión y gloria de Alianza Lima 1901–2001* (Lima: Fondo Editorial del Congreso del Perú).

Milza, P. (1990) 'Le football italien: Une histoire à l'échelle du siècle,' *Vingtième Siècle*, no. 26, pp. 49–58.

Mora y Araujo, M. (2003) Personal communication, August.

Moura, G. (1998) *O Rio corre para o Maracanã. Um estudo sobre o futebol e a identidade nacional* (Rio de Janeiro: Editora da Fundação Getulio Vargas).

Muñoz Cabrejo, F. (2001) *Diversiones públicas en Lima 1890–1920: la experiencia de la modernidad* (Lima: Red para el Desarrollo de las Ciencias Sociales en el Perú).

Naciones Unidas — Programa de las Naciones Unidas para el Desarrollo (NU — PNUD) (2002) *Informe sobre el desarrollo humano del Perú* (Lima: PNUD).

Newberry, P. (2002) 'WUSA Deals with Hard Questions After Thrilling Title Game,' *Associated Press*, 25 August.

O'Connor, A. (2003) 'Babe City Loses Its Attraction for American Public,' *The Times*, 17 September.

Obregón, O. (1981) 'El clásico universitario: un teatro de masas de invención chilena,' *Araucaria de Chile*, no. 13, pp. 99–124.

Ollé, C. (1992 [1981]) *Noches de adrenalina* (Lima: Lluvia Editores).

Panfichi, A. (1994) 'Fútbol e identidad: esta urgencia de decir nosotros,' in A. Panfichi (ed.), *Fútbol: identidad, violencia y racionalidad* (Lima: Pontificia Universidad Católica del Perú), pp. 17–30.

Panfichi, A. and Portocarrero, F. (eds.) (1995) *Mundos interiores de Lima 1850–1950* (Lima: Centro de Investigaciones, Universidad del Pacífico).

Panfichi, A. and Thieroldt, J. (2002) 'Barras Bravas: Representation and Crowd Violence in Peruvian Football,' in E. Dunning, P. Murphy, I. Waddington and A. Astrinakis (eds.), *Fighting Fans, Football Hooliganism as a World Phenomenon* (Dublin: UCD Press).

Pansters, W.G. (ed.) (1997) *Citizens of the Pyramid: Essays on Mexican Political Culture* (Amsterdam: Thela).

Panzeri, D. (2000 [1967]) *Fútbol: la dinámica de lo impensado* (Buenos Aires: Paidós).

Papa, A.and Panico, G. (1993) *Storia sociale del calcio in Italia: dai club dei pionieri alla nazione sportiva (1887-1945)* (Bologna: Il Mulino).

Parker, D.S. (1998) *The Idea of the Middle Class: White-Collar Workers and Peruvian Society, 1900–1950* (University Park: Penn State University Press).

Parker, W. (2002) 'WUSA Rides Out Dip; Fan Honeymoon Over, League Stays Course,' *Atlanta Journal and Constitution,* 23 August.

Parker, W. (2003) 'Women's Pro Teams Still Rise to Challenges; Serious Hurdles: Pro Basketball, Soccer Leagues Confront Attendance, Economy Woes,' *Atlanta Journal and Constitution,* 2 August.

Parodi, D. (2002) 'Entre la jarana y el fútbol,' in L. Millones, A. Panfichi and V. Vich (eds.), *En el corazón del pueblo: pasión y gloria de Alianza Lima 1901–2001* (Lima: Fondo Editorial del Congreso del Perú), pp. 53–66.

Perdigão, P. (2001) *Anatomia de uma derrota: 16 de julho de 1950 — Brasil X Uruguai* (Porto Alegre: L&PM).

Pereira, L.A. de M. (2000) *Footballmania: uma história social do futebol no Rio de Janeiro, 1902–1938* (Rio de Janeiro: Nova Fronteira).

Peskowitz, M. (2005) *The Truth Behind the Mommy Wars: Who Decides What Makes a Good Mother?* (Emeryville, CA: Seal Press).

Peterson, L. (2003) 'WUSA's Future Hinges on Meeting; Committee Will Convene after the Women's World Cup Third-Place

Game to Discuss a Plan to Revive the League,' *Los Angeles Times,* 11 October.

Pieterse, N. (1995) 'Globalization as Hybridization,' in M. Featherstone, S. Lash and R. Robertson (eds.), *Global Modernities* (London: Sage).

Pittsburgh Post-Gazette (2003) 'A Hard Sale: Women's Pro Leagues are Struggling to Find Their Way in Troubled Times,' 15 June.

Pollarollo, G. (2000 [1991]) *Entre mujeres solas* (Lima/Bogotá: Peisa/Arango).

Polley, M. (1997) *Moving the Goalposts: A History of Sport and Society Since 1945* (London: Routledge).

Porteus, L. (2006) 'U.S. Women's Pro League Prepares to Blast Back onto Soccer Scene,' *Fox News,* 28 June, <www.foxnews.com/story/0,2933,201438,00.html>.

Portocarrero, G. (1995) 'El fundamento invisible: función y lugar de las ideas racistas en la República Aristocrática,' in A. Panfichi and F. Portocarrero (eds.), *Mundos interiores: Lima 1850–1950* (Lima: Centro de Investigación de la Universidad del Pacífico).

PR News (2001) 'Soccer Stars Embrace PR to Give League Launch a Good Kick,' vol. 57, no. 18, 7 May.

Quijano, A. (1980) *Dominación y cultura* (Lima: Mosca Azul).

Rachum, I. (1978) '*Futebol*: the Growth of a Brazilian National Institution,' *New Scholar,* vol. 7, nos. 1–2, pp. 183–200.

Rebaza Soraluz, L. (2000) *La construcción de un artista peruano contemporáneo: poética e identidad nacional en la obra de José María Arguedas, Emilio Adolfo Westphalen, Javier Solguren, Jorge Eduardo Eielson, Sebastián Salazar Bondy, Fernando de Syszlo y Blanca Varela* (Lima: Pontificia Universidad Católica del Perú).

Rebelo, A. and Torres, S. (2001) *CBF/Nike: as investigações da CPI do Futebol da Câmara dos Diputados desvendam o lado oculto dos grandes negócios da cartolagem e passam a limpo o futebol brasileiro* (São Paulo: Casa Amarela).

Reynolds, M. (2002) 'Cable's League of Its Own, Soccer's WUSA, Struggles,' *Multichannel News,* 26 August.

Reynolds, M. (2003) 'WUSA Experiment Ends,' *Multichannel News,* 22 September.

Robertson, R. (1992) *Globalization; Social Theory and Global Culture* (London: Sage).

Robson, D. (2002) 'Still Waiting for that Winning Kick,' *Business Week,* 21 October.

Rodrigues Filho, M. (1964 [1947]) *O negro no futebol brasileiro,* Preface by Gilberto Freyre (Rio de Janeiro: Civilização Brasileira).

Rodríguez, M.G. (2003) '¿Cómo leer las prácticas populares? Una propuesta teórico-metodológica,' paper presented at the conference 'Actuales desafíos de la investigación en comunicación: Claves para un debate y reflexión transdisciplinaria,' Red Nacional de Investigadores en Comunicación, FDyCS, Universidad Nacional del Comahue, General Roca, 13–15 November.

Rodríguez, M.G. (2005) 'The Place of Women in Argentine Football,' *International Journal of the History of Sport,* vol. 22, no. 3, pp. 231–45.

Röhrig Assunção, M. (2005) *Capoeira: A History of an Afro-Brazilian Martial Art* (London: Routledge)

Romano, J. (2003) 'WUSA's Demise Expected,' *St Petersburg Times,* 18 September.

Romero, A. (1994) *Las barras bravas y la contrasociedad deportiva* (Buenos Aires: Nueva América).

Rosemblatt, K.A. (2000) 'Domesticating Men: State Building and Compromise in Popular Front Chile,' in E. Dore and M. Molyneux (eds.), *Hidden Histories of Gender and State in Latin America* (Durham, NC: Duke University Press).

Ruy, C.O. (2002) *Felipão: a alma do penta* (Porto Alegre: ZH Publicações).

Said, E. (1995) *Orientalism* (Harmondsworth: Penguin).

Salazar, J. (1980) *La ópera de los fantasmas* (Lima: Mosca Azul/Ediciones Treintaitrés).

Salcedo, J.M. (1982) 'Así jugamos porque así somos,' *El Diario Marka*, 20 June.

Salomon Brothers (1997) *UK Football Clubs: Valuable Assets?* (London: Global Equity Research).

Sanborn, C. and Panfichi, A. (1997) 'Fujimori y las raíces del neopulismo,' in F. Tuesta (ed.), *Los Enigmas del Poder: Fujimori 1990–1996* (Lima: Fundación Ebert).

Sánchez León, A. (1980) 'Fútbol: un espejo para mirarnos mejor,' *Quehacer*, no. 7, pp. 119–27.

Sánchez León, A. (1981a) 'Perú. España 82: alegría sin igual y otros pormenores,' *Quehacer*, no. 13, pp. 112–17.

Sánchez León, A. (1981b) 'Fútbol: casi un estilo de ser peruanos,' *Debate*, no. 10, pp. 64–69.

Sandoval-García, C. (2005) 'Football: Forging Nationhood and Masculinities in Costa Rica,' *International Journal of the History of Sport*, vol. 22, no. 2, pp. 212–30.

Santa Cruz, E. (1996) *Origen y futuro de una pasión: fútbol, cultura y modernidad* (Santiago: LOM-ARCIS).

Sarlo, B. (2001) 'La deuda,' in *Tiempo presente: notas sobre el cambio de una cultura* (Buenos Aires: Siglo XXI).

Scher, A. (1996) *La patria deportista* (Buenos Aires: Planeta).

Scher, A. and Palomino, H. (1988) *Fútbol: pasión de multitudes y de elites* (Buenos Aires: CISEA).

Schultz, J. (2004) 'Athens 2004: Soccer's Adorned Fab Five End "Quite a Journey Together",' *Atlanta Journal-Constitution*, 27 August.

Sebreli, J. (1998) *La era del fútbol* (Buenos Aires: Editorial Sudamericana).

Shirts, M. (1988) 'Sócrates, Corinthians, and Questions of Democracy and Citizenship,' in J.L. Arbena (ed.), *Sport and Society in Latin America: Diffusion, Dependency and the Rise of Mass Culture* (Westport, CN: Greenwood), pp. 97–112.

Sklair, L. (1995) *Sociology of the Global System* (2nd edition) (Baltimore: Johns Hopkins University Press).

Smith, A.D. (1991) *National Identity* (London: Penguin).

Smith, A.D. (1999) *Myths and Memories of the Nation* (Oxford: Oxford University Press).

Smith, B.L. (2002) 'The Argentinian Junta and the Press in the Run-up to the 1978 World Cup,' *Soccer and Society*, vol. 3, no. 1, pp. 69–78.

Snowden, R. (2001) 'Jury Still Out on WUSA Future,' *Soccer365.com*, 3 September, <www.soccer365.com/US_home/Features_ Interviews/ page_38_8811.shtml>.

Soccer Investor (2002) *Latin American Football 2002: A Soccer Investor Report* (London: *Soccer Investor*).

Soong, R. (2003) 'Brazilian Football Fans', www.zonalatina.com/ Zldata283.htm.

Stein, S. (ed.) (1986a) *Lima obrera, 1900–1930* (2 vols) (Lima: Ediciones El Virrey).

Stein, S. (1986b) 'Los contornos de la Lima obrera,' in S. Stein (ed.), *Lima obrera 1900–1930, Vol. 1* (Lima: Ediciones El Virrey), pp. 11–28.

Stein, S., Deustua, J. and Stokes, S. (1986) 'Entre el offside y el chimpún: las clases populares limeñas y el fútbol 1900–1930,' in S. Stein (ed.), *Lima obrera, 1900–1930, Vol. 1* (Lima: Ediciones El Virrey), pp. 119–62.

Stokes, S. (1986) 'Etnicidad y clase social: los afro-peruanos de Lima 1900–1930,' in S. Stein (ed.), *Lima Obrera 1900–1930, Vol. 1* (Lima: Ediciones El Virrey), pp. 171–252.

Stossel, S. (2003) 'Save the Women's Soccer Association,' *Boston Globe*, 4 October.

Straus, B. (2002) 'Half-Full or Half-Empty? WUSA Glass a Bit of Both,' *Washington Post,* 23 August.

Sugden, J. and Tomlinson, A. (1998). *FIFA and the Contest for World Football: Who Rules the People's Game?* (Cambridge: Polity).

Svampa, M. (2005) *La sociedad excluyente. La Argentina bajo el signo del neoliberalismo* (Buenos Aires: Taurus).

Talmon, J.L. (1967) *Romanticism and Revolt: Europe 1815–1848* (London: Thames and Hudson).

Taylor, C. (1998) *The Beautiful Game: A Journey through Latin American Football* (London: Phoenix).

Taylor, R. (2003) 'Top of the Mind: Yes, We Can Save Women's Pro Soccer,' *Brandweek,* 29 September.

Tejada, L. (1988) *La cuestión del Pan: el anarco-sindicalismo en el Perú 1880–1919* (Lima: INC-Banco Industrial).

The Economist (2001) 'United States: A League of Their Own,' 21 April.

The Hamilton Spectator (2002) 'Success Depends on Marketing; Women's Sports: Professional Leagues,' 5 December.

Thiesse, A-M. (1999) *La création des identités nationales: Europe, XVIIIe-XXe siècles* (Paris: Seuil).

Thompson, E.P. (1979) *Tradición, revuelta y conciencia de clase* (Barcelona: Crítica).

Thompson, E.P. (1990) *Costumbres en común* (Barcelona: Crítica).

Thorndike, G. (1978) *El revés de morir* (Lima: Mosca Azul).

Tierney, M. (2003) 'Founders Cup: WUSA Faces Challenge,' *Atlanta Journal and Constitution,* 24 August.

Tomlinson, J. (1996) *Globalization and Culture* (Cambridge: Polity).

Tommelleo, D. (2001) 'DiCicco has Women's League on the Move,' *Associated Press,* 1 September.

Topsports, <www.topsports.com.br>.

United Nations (1995) *World Urbanization Prospects: The 1994 Revision* (New York: United Nations).

United Nations, Comisión Económica para América Latina y el Caribe (2001) *Urbanización y evolución de la población urbana en América Latina (1950–1990)* (Santiago: United Nations).

Vargas Llosa, M. (1982 [1967]) *Los cachorros* (Madrid: Cátedra).

Vega, D. (2003) 'WUSA has Second Chance,' *Boston Herald,* 26 October.

Vickery, T. (2003) 'Clubs Give Thugs a Free Rein,' BBC Online, 29 September, http://news.bbc.co.uk/sport1/hi/football/world_football.

Vilhena, L.R. da P. (1997) *Projeto e missão: o movimento folclórico brasileiro* (Rio de Janeiro: Editora da FGV).

Villanueva, L. and Donayre, J. (1987) *Antología de la música peruana: canción criolla, vol. 1* (Lima: Latina SA).

Vogel, A. (1982) 'O momento feliz: reflexões sobre o futebol e o ethos nacional,' in R. Da Matta et al. (eds.), *O universo do futebol: esporte e sociedade brasileira* (Rio de Janeiro: Pinakotheque).

Votre, S. and Mourão, L. (2003). 'Women's Football in Brazil: Progress and Problems,' *Soccer and Society,* vol. 4, nos. 2–3, pp. 254–67.

Wallerstein, I. (1974) *The Modern World System, Vol. 1: Capitalist Agriculture and the Origins of the Modern World Economy in the Sixteenth Century* (London: Academic Press).

Walsh, A. and Giulianotti, R. (2001) 'This Sporting Mammon: A Normative Critique of the Commodification of Sport,' *Journal of the Philosophy of Sport,* no. 28, pp. 53–77.

Walvin, J. (1975) *The People's Game: The Social History of British Football* (London: Allen Lane).

Weiner, R. (2001) 'WUSA: Creating a Legacy: US Women at Fore of Premier Soccer League Ready to Kick Off,' *USA Today,* 13 April.

Wells, S. (2003a) Personal communication, October.

Wells, S. (2003b) 'Americans Fear Brandi Flop,' *The Guardian Unlimited*, 19 September 2003, <www.sport.guardian.co.uk>.

Whiteside, K. (2001) 'WUSA Leader Thrilled About Inaugural Season,' *USA Today*, 16 August.

Wolf, E.R. (1966) 'Kinship, Friendship, and Patron–Client Relations in Complex Societies,' in M. Banton (ed.), *The Social Anthropology of Complex Societies* (London: Tavistock).

Women's United Soccer Association, The Official Website of the WUSA, <www.wusa.com>.

World Bank (2003) *World Development Indicators* (Washington: World Bank).

World Soccer (2006) 'World Cup Central: 2006 World Cup Squads in Full,' <http://worldsoccer.about.com/b/a/257622.htm>.

Zamora, I. (2003) 'La gente quiere saber', <www.ar.geocities.com>.

Zeigler, M. (2006) 'Women's Soccer in the USA: Where Has All the Love Gone?,' *San Diego Union Tribune*. 22 July.

Zohar, C. (2002) Personal communication, March.

INSTITUTE FOR THE STUDY OF THE
AMERICAS

UNIVERSITY OF LONDON · SCHOOL OF ADVANCED STUDY

The Institute for the Study of the Americas (ISA) promotes, coordinates and provides a focus for research and postgraduate teaching on the Americas – Canada, the USA, Latin America and the Caribbean – in the University of London.

The Institute was officially established in August 2004 as a result of a merger between the Institute of Latin American Studies and the Institute of United States Studies, both of which were formed in 1965.

The Institute publishes in the disciplines of history, politics, economics, sociology, anthropology, geography and environment, development, culture and literature, and on the countries and regions of Latin America, the United States, Canada and the Caribbean.

ISA runs an active programme of events – conferences, seminars, lectures and workshops – in order to facilitate national research on the Americas in the humanities and social sciences. It also offers a range of taught master's and research degrees, allowing wide-ranging multi-disciplinary, multi-country study or a focus on disciplines such as politics or globalisation and development for specific countries or regions.

Full details about the Institute's publications, events, postgraduate courses and other activities are available on the web at www.americas.sas.ac.uk.

Institute for the Study of the Americas
School of Advanced Study, University of London
31 Tavistock Square, London WC1H 9HA

Tel 020 7862 8870, Fax 020 7862 8886, Email americas@sas.ac.uk,
Web www.americas.sas.ac.uk

Recent and Forthcoming Titles in the ISA series:

Making Institutions Work in Peru: Democracy, Development and Inequality since 1980
edited by John Crabtree

Right On? Political Change and Continuity in George W. Bush's America
edited by Iwan Morgan and Philip Davies

Francisco de Miranda: Exile and Enlightenment
edited by John Maher

Caciquismo in Twentieth-Century Mexico
edited by Alan Knight and Wil Pansters

Democracy after Pinochet: Politics, Parties and Elections in Chile
by Alan Angell

The Struggle for an Enlightened Republic: Buenos Aires and Rivadavia
by Klaus Gallo

Mexican Soundings: Essays in Honour of David A. Brading
edited by Susan Deans-Smith and Eric Van Young

America's Americans: Population Issues in U.S. Society and Politics
edited by Philip Davies and Iwan Morgan

Bolivia: Revolution and the Power of History in the Present. Essays
James Dunkerley

American Civilization
Charles A. Jones

INDUSTRY GROUP

WANT TO WORK IN THE FOOTBALL INDUSTRY?

University of Liverpool Management School
MBA (Football Industries)

The MBA (Football Industries) is the first postgraduate degree specifically designed for those who want to work in the commercial and business side of football. Established in 1997, the MBA at the University of Liverpool has successfully trained and delivered students from Europe, Africa, Asia and the Americas into the global football business.

Modules include: International Football Industry, Football & the Law, Football & Finance and Football & the Media as well as the core MBA modules.

• PLACEMENT OPPORTUNITIES IN THE INDUSTRY

• A COMPREHENSIVE GUEST SPEAKER PROGRAMME

• 15,000 WORD DISSERTATION SUPERVISED BY ONE OF OUR STAFF

One Year Full-Time or Two Years Part-Time